THEORY AND INTERPRETATION OF NARRATIVE
James Phelan and Peter J. Rabinowitz, Series Editors

NARRATIVE STRUCTURES
and the
LANGUAGE OF THE SELF

Matthew Clark

 THE OHIO STATE UNIVERSITY PRESS • COLUMBUS

Copyright © 2010 by The Ohio State University.
All rights reserved.

Library of Congress Cataloging-in-Publication Data

Clark, Matthew, 1948–
  Narrative structures and the language of the self / Matthew Clark.
    p. cm.—(Theory and interpretation of narrative)
  Includes bibliographical references and index.
  ISBN 978-0-8142-1128-1 (cloth : alk. paper)—ISBN 978-0-8142-9227-3 (cd)
  1. Self in literature. 2. Self (Philosophy) in literature. 3. Subject (Philosophy) in literature. 4. Subjectivity in literature. 5. Narration (Rhetoric) I. Title. II. Series: Theory and interpretation of narrative series.
  PN56.S46C57 2010
  809'.93384—dc22
                    2010023781

This book is available in the following editions:
Cloth (ISBN 978-0-8142-1128-1)
CD-ROM (ISBN 978-0-8142-9227-3)

Cover design by Fulcrum Creatives, LLC
Text design by Juliet Williams
Type set in Adobe Minion Pro

♾ The paper used in this publication meets the minimum requirements of the American National Standard for Information Sciences—Permanence of Paper for Printed Library Materials. ANSI Z39.48–1992.

CONTENTS

Acknowledgments		vii
Introduction	The Self and Narrative	1
PART ONE	**PHILOSOPHICAL FABLES OF THE SELF**	
Chapter 1	The Reflexive Self: Descartes and Ovid	13
Chapter 2	The Furniture of the Self: Montaigne, Highsmith, Dostoevsky	27
Chapter 3	The Dyadic Subject: Hegel, Aristophanes, Hemingway	44
Chapter 4	Doubles and Doubled Doubles: Knowles and Austen	64
Chapter 5	Freudian Thirds: Heinlein, Stevenson, Forster, Wharton	80
PART TWO	**THE CASE OF THE SUBJECT**	
Chapter 6	Introduction to Part Two: Deep Subjectivity	97
Chapter 7	Agents, Patients, and Experiencers: le Carré, Weldon, Kesey, Woolf	115
Chapter 8	Dative Subjects: Stevenson, Fitzgerald, Kesey, Robbe-Grillet	130
Chapter 9	Instrumental Subjects: Knowles, Eliot, Davies	147
Chapter 10	Locative Subjects: Mahfouz, Lem, Forster	161
Conclusion	Narrative and the Self: Hartley, Sartre, Ishiguro	179
Bibliography		193
Index		203

ACKNOWLEDGMENTS

Thanks are due to several people who read all or part of this book and contributed to its creation. Ross Arthur in the kindest way told me that one whole chapter had to be cut. Doug Freake's questions about the self were part of the reason I became interested in the project in the first place. Sol and Bessie Goldberg have been the best of sympathetic critics. Mark Goldberg told me to read Ishiguro. A positive word from Gregory Nagy came at just the right time. James Rives encouraged me when I feared the book would never find a home. Special thanks are due to James Phelan and Peter Rabinowitz, who saw some potential value in an eccentric project and improved it vastly. The editors at The Ohio State University Press, Sandy Crooms and Maggie Diehl, are brilliant and funny and a pleasure to work with. I have always been blessed with wonderful editors, and none has been better than these.

I dedicate this book to Reva Marin, artist and scholar, companion.

INTRODUCTION

The Self and Narrative

I. The Self and the Subject

My grandfather (my father told me) had twenty different business cards, for twenty different businesses, so he could adapt himself (his self) to almost any opportunity he might encounter. Perhaps it was this story which convinced me at an early age that the self is fluid, mutable, multiple.

When my grandfather pulled out one of his business cards, there was most likely a story to go along with it, a story to explain the self he was claiming to be. Literary stories also express versions of the self. This book is an exploration of some of the roles a self can take in literature—some of the modes of subjectivity. The characters brought together in a narrative, I assume, are not random collections but structured sets, and these sets correspond to various manifestations of the self. Much of my argument tries to demonstrate the shape and structure of these narrative sets.

Probably every narrative must have some underlying concept of the self and subjectivity, but these concepts are not always thematized. My project concerns only those narratives in which the question of the self matters—but this is quite a large group; as I have worked through the exploration, I have continually been surprised to discover applications where I did not expect them. Investigation of the self turns out to be a major project of the Western narrative tradition. My hope is that the tools, terms, and techniques I present will illuminate works of this kind. In addition, I hope to show that concepts of the self based on the binary opposition of subject and object are unable to account for the various kinds of subjectivity expressed in narrative. I do not propose a complete theory of the self and subjectivity, and I am not sure that such a complete theory is possible. I will be content if this study can lead to an increased awareness of the complexity of the self and of stories about the self.

Two concepts, then, are basic to the discussion: the *self* and the *subject*. Both are notoriously difficult. The self, as I understand it, is related to a certain feeling of identity; but this formulation is hardly a definition. Every discussion must start somewhere, with some term that is left undefined; I begin this exploration without defining the self, but by the end of the discussion my own sense of the self will be reasonably clear. A few initial comments, however, are in order.

I am sympathetic to the idea that the self has developed through the ordinary process of Darwinian evolution, perhaps as a way of organizing increasingly complex behaviors—but I am not expert in this area, and I would not want to make dogmatic assertions.[1] Furthermore, the self seems to be connected in some way to memory and responsibility. What you remember belongs to your self; the memories of another person are not directly part of your self, though they may become so through learning. On the other hand, there are things you have done and things that have happened to you that you do not remember, and nonetheless these may be part of your self.

You cannot rightly be held directly responsible for the actions of another self. If I rob a bank, you should not be punished. (I pass over the hidden or shared responsibility of such figures as crime bosses and editors.) On the other hand, we do not always consider people responsible for their actions. If you are insane, if you are not yourself, you may be judged not guilty of murder, even if you were the killer.

The word "subject" has a variety of meanings—eighteen, according to the *Oxford English Dictionary*. In this book I am primarily interested in four kinds of subject: the grammatical subject, the logical subject, the psychological subject, and the subject of narrative. None of these is exactly the same as any of the others, and yet our conception of each is to some extent influenced by the others.

The grammatical subject combines several different functions. In the major European languages the subject can be the topic of a statement, it can be the agent of an action, or it can be the noun with which the verb agrees. Different languages have different ways of marking the subject, and some languages may not have subjects at all.

The logical subject is that which has attributes, that about which some-

---

1. For discussion of the neurology of the self in Darwinian terms, see Roldolfo R. Llinás, *I of the Vortex: From Neurons to Self.*

thing can be said. The subject of a logical proposition is most likely also the grammatical subject of a sentence, just as the Cartesian subject, the *I* of "I think, therefore I am," is also a grammatical subject.

The psychological subject is the center of consciousness, the center of voluntary action, and perhaps the center of the unconscious self as well. The Cartesian *I* is a subject not only in logic but also in psychology. This psychological subject is opposed to the object, which is anything presented to the consciousness of the subject.

The subject of narrative is any character who is centrally involved in a story. A story may have one subject or several. These stories may be literary, or they may be the stories you tell yourself about yourself. The narrative subject is likely to be the topic of statements, it is likely to have attributes, and it is likely to be the center of action and experience.

A narrative subject can appear in various roles, such as the role of the agent—the self which acts—or the role of the patient—the self which is acted upon—and so on. Thus a narrative subject, as I understand it, is the role taken on by a self in a story. This definition can be generalized: the subject is the self in a role, and the self becomes a subject when it plays a role. Self here is the more general concept, whereas subjects are more particular. Subject roles can be interpersonal—for instance, one person observing another ("I" and "thee")—but they can also be intrapersonal—the observer and the observed within the divided Cartesian self ("I" and "me"). I would be willing to say that a self is what all subjects have in common, as long as we remember that what all doughnuts have in common is a hole. The reader will notice that Part One of this study tends to speak of the self, particularly in the examination of the various models of the self presented by Descartes, Hegel, Plato, Freud, and Mead, while Part Two tends to speak of various subjectivities as manifestations of the self.

A self in a story may take on different subject roles at different times, and perhaps even different roles at the same time. Thus even if one believes in a unitary self, subjectivity is various. The quality of a role is that role's subjectivity: agent subjectivity, patient subjectivity, and so on. The narrative subject is at the center of my discussion, but clearly the meaning of this subject borrows from the other meanings of the word; and because all four types are linked, whatever we can conclude about this narrative subject will also apply in some measure to the other kinds of subject.

My method throughout is to use brief theoretical accounts as a basis for concrete interpretations of specific narratives. In Part One, "Philosophical Fables of the Self," I examine versions of the self presented by Descartes, Hegel, Freud, and Mead. Chapter 1 deals with Descartes' concept of the single reflexive self. Descartes' concept of the subject turns out to be very much like the subject in Montaigne and other reflexive writers, and these are the topic of chapter 2.

Descartes' self is essentially solitary, even in company, but Hegel's Dialectic of the Master and the Slave introduces an essential second self: in this philosophic fable, self-consciousness can arise only when two consciousnesses confront each other. Aristophanes (as depicted in Plato's *Symposium*) suggests that the relationship between two selves can be erotic rather than hostile. I discuss these fables in chapter 3, and in chapter 4 I use the Hegelian/Aristophanic model to examine narratives in which the self is doubled. When two selves begin to move apart, a space opens for a third character. Chapter 5 adapts a Freudian myth to examine this narrative third, and ends with Mead's model of the social self.

Part Two, "The Case of the Subject," extends the discussion to other roles of the self, to other kinds of subjectivity. In a sense, these roles of the self, these modes of subjectivity, develop Mead's social self through concepts derived from Case Grammar in linguistics: these concepts are explained in chapter 6, which serves as an introduction to Part Two. Chapter 7 deals with the linguistic functions of the agent, patient, and experiencer and applies this model to narratives of agency, patience, and experience. Chapter 8 explores the dative of interest, the subject as witness. Chapters 9 and 10 are concerned with the instrumental subject and the locative subject. The Conclusion draws together the various discussions into a coherent, if incomplete, account of the self and some of the roles of the self in narrative.

The result of the discussion is thus a complex field of subject positions in narrative, including self-reflexive Cartesian subjects; Hegelian double subjects; subjects of the Freudian third; agents, patients, and experiencers; witnesses; instrumental subjects; and locative subjects. Each of these is a way of being a self, and any theory of the self or the subject must include at least these positions—though the possibility of further elaboration is not excluded.

This field of subject positions helps to illuminate a central project of the Western narrative tradition, but it also reflects a reality of our lives. At any moment anyone is likely to be taking on some one (or perhaps more than one) of these positions. If a part of the function of literature is to help us understand ourselves, then an analysis of the self in literature is fundamental.

II. The Subject and Narrative

This study is concerned with the varieties of subjectivity, but it is equally concerned with narrative, since the self becomes a subject only by playing a role in a story. In other words, I am interested in both character and plot and in the interrelationship of the two. I do not agree with Aristotle that action trumps character, or with E. M. Forster that character trumps plot, but rather with Henry James, who asks, "What is character but the determination of incident? What is incident but the illustration of character?"[2]

The study of character and plot goes back at least as far as Aristotle's *Poetics,* but modern narratological approaches begin with Vladimir Propp's seminal study, *The Morphology of the Folktale.* Propp offers a grammar of the Russian folktale, consisting of a sequence of thirty-odd events, such as "One of the Members of a Family Absents Himself from Home," "An Interdiction is Addressed to the Hero," "The Interdiction is Violated," and so on, until the final events, "The Villain is Punished" and "The Hero is Married and Ascends the Throne."[3] Not all of these events have to be present in any one tale, but those that do occur must occur in fixed order, and these thirty-odd events form the entire repertoire of events in the genre.

Propp's grammar has proved too specific to be directly adaptable to other narrative genres, and many of the more recent models of narrative grammar have sacrificed specificity in order to gain generality. Claude Bremond has proposed a system of "elementary sequences" with three obligatory phases: the event that opens the process, the event that realizes the process, and the event that closes the process.[4] In any extended narrative there will be a number of elementary sequences combined in various ways. In Thomas Pavel's modification of Bremond's system, a "move" consists of a "problem," a "solution," and perhaps also an "auxiliary" through which the solution is achieved.[5] More recently, Emma Kafalenos has proposed a system with five key moments and five subsidiary moments. The five key moments are (A), a destabilizing event; (C), a decision by some character or group of characters to alleviate the destabilizing event; (C'), an initial action to alleviate the destabilizing event; (H), a primary action to alleviate the destabilizing event; and (I), the success or failure of the primary action to alleviate the destabilizing event.[6] This system is fundamentally an elaboration of the three elements

---

2. See Aristotle, *Poetics,* VI.9–11; E. M. Forster, *Aspects of the Novel,* chapter III, pp. 44–68; Henry James, "The Art of Fiction," in *Henry James: Selected Literary Criticism,* edited by Morris Shapira, p. 80.
3. See Propp, *Morphology,* chapter III, pp. 25–65.
4. See Bremond, "La logique des possibles narratifs," in *L'analyse structurale du récit,* pp. 7–33.
5. See Pavel, *The Poetics of Plot: The Case of English Renaissance Drama.*
6. See Kafalenos, p. 7. The subsidiary moments are (B), a request that someone alleviate A; (D), the alleviating character is tested; (E), the alleviating character responds to the test; (F),

in Bremond's and Pavel's systems. I will return to Kafalenos's system in a moment.

The second aspect of Propp's system is a set of "spheres of action," that is, roles which are found in the Russian folktales. According to Propp, there are seven spheres of action (though a single sphere of action may be distributed among several characters, and a single character may manifest more than one sphere of action). These spheres of action are 1) the sphere of action of the villain; 2) the sphere of action of the donor; 3) the sphere of action of the helper; 4) the sphere of action of a princess (a sought-for person) and her father; 5) the sphere of action of the dispatcher; 6) the sphere of action of the hero; and 7) the sphere of action of the false hero. A. J. Greimas has proposed a system with six roles, called *actants,* divided into three sets of binary oppositions (again, a role may be divided among more than one character, and a character may manifest more than one role).[7] The first set is the subject (corresponding to Propp's hero) and the object (corresponding to Propp's sought-for person). The second pair is the giver or sender (roughly corresponding to the father of the princess) and the receiver (roughly corresponding to Propp's dispatcher). The third set is the helper (corresponding to Propp's donor and helper) and the opponent (corresponding to Propp's villain and false hero).[8]

Propp's spheres of action and Greimas's actants are in some ways similar to the narrative subjects discussed in this study, but they are also quite fundamentally different.[9] Propp's theory claims to account for all the characters in his genre, the Russian folktales, and Greimas's theory claims to account generally for all of the possible characters in narrative. The system of narrative subjectivity that I present, on the other hand, is designed to account for only those narrative roles that achieve a certain level of narrative significance.[10] On the other hand, my system of narrative subjectivity insists that any of the roles identified can become a center of subjectivity, whereas in the systems proposed by Propp and Greimas, the hero or the subject is clearly at

---

the alleviating character acquires empowerment; and (G), the alleviating character arrives at the place or time to alleviate A. The order of moments in her system is indicated by alphabetical order. I have simplified Kafalenos's wording, but I hope I have retained the essential points of her system.

7. See Greimas, *Structural Semantics,* chapter X, "Reflections on Actantial Models," pp. 197–221; Greimas is committed to the kind of binary model of subject and object that I critique.

8. For a good summary of Propp, Greimas, and other theorists, see Robert Scholes, *Structuralism in Literature,* pp. 104–11; Rimmon-Kenan, *Narrative Fiction: Contemporary Poetics,* pp. 20–22 and 34–35; and David Herman, *Story Logic,* pp. 93–94, 121–27.

9. Kenneth Burke's pentad (act, scene, agent, agency, and purpose) is in some ways closer to my system: see *A Grammar of Motives,* p. xv and passim.

10. The measurement of this significance is a matter of judgment, but for example this system does not account for characters who are merely narrative tools.

the center of the story, and the other roles are secondary. This concentration on the hero or the subject can also be found in the system proposed by Kafalenos, which I have discussed above. Her system is constructed around the character she calls the C-actant, that is, the character who decides to alleviate the destabilizing event. This character will by definition be an agent (though Kafalenos's conception of agency is fairly broad). The central position Kafalenos grants to the C-actant perfectly suits her project, which is narrative causality, but it does not suit my project, which is narrative subjectivity.

In any action there may be a number of participants who take on different roles and different kinds of subjectivity. The number and the nature of the roles in a narrative constitute what I call *narrative geometry* (the term is introduced in chapter 3 and gradually elucidated throughout the book). The grouping of stories with similar narrative geometries produces interesting and sometimes surprising juxtapositions. But each narrative manifests its narrative geometry in its own way. A love triangle, for example, can be seen from the perspective of any of the three principals, or from the perspective of an onlooker (as in F. Scott Fitzgerald's *The Great Gatsby*), or from the perspective of someone used by other characters (as in L. P. Hartley's *The Go-Between*). The story, that is, the bare events, perhaps can be thought of independently of any particular role, but the plot, that is, the events as they are formed into a narrative, will privilege certain roles. Thus plots can be associated with any of the various roles I discuss—a Cartesian plot privileges a Cartesian subject, a Hegelian plot privileges Hegelian subjects, and so on. Most plots are to some extent mixed, but usually one kind of subjectivity dominates.

III. Narrative and Method

Narrative interpretation can be approached from two sides, the side of the storyteller and the side of the reader; these, of course, are reciprocal. On the one side, a storyteller presents an interpretation of some aspect of the world, real or imagined, and narrative as interpretation is a form of thought. In these terms the texts I discuss can be seen as presenting various narrative interpretations of what it is to be a self. On the other side, interpretation is something that readers or critics do to texts as they attempt to understand the interpretation of the world presented by the story.

For my purposes, narrative thought can be seen to present itself simultaneously in three aspects: the formal, the mimetic, and the thematic.[11] The-

---

11. These distinctions can be related to James Phelan's scheme of thematic, synthetic, and

matically, a work of literature may express some general idea or group of ideas; mimetically, it expresses these ideas through particular characters in particular situations; and formally, it communicates through a cultural code of narrative conventions.

On the other side, critical interpretation can also be formal, mimetic, or thematic, or all three at once. Much of the ordinary use of language is primarily thematic; the mimetic and formal aspects are present, but they function in service of the theme and they come to attention only when they are somehow problematic.[12] Artistic language, however, tends to foreground the formal and the mimetic, to varying degrees. Thus an interpretation that is only thematic runs the risk of reducing the total meaning of the story. To paraphrase Robert Frost, narrative is what gets lost in thematic interpretation. If we were interested only in themes, we would not need stories.[13] In these terms the themes I am interested in have to do with the nature of subjectivity; these themes are mimetically expressed through various stories that show various particular kinds of subjectivity; and these stories reflect formal conventions, such as the narrative geometries I describe in this study.[14]

Literary interpretation often occurs at the level of the individual work, but groups of works may also be taken as an interpretive unit. For example, the story of Oedipus concerns a son who kills his father and marries his mother, whereas the story of Hippolytus concerns a (step)mother who falls in love with her (step)son, who is killed by the curse of his father. Orestes kills his mother to avenge her murder of his father, whereas Procne kills her son Itys to take revenge on her faithless husband Tereus. Oinomaos tries to keep his daughter Hippodameia for himself but is killed by his daughter's suitor, Pelops, whereas Smyrna disguised herself in order to sleep with her father, who tried to kill her when he found out the truth. Taken together,

---

mimetic components of fictional characters (see *Reading People, Reading Plots*, pp. 2–3 and passim) and more generally to three levels of linguistic analysis: semantic, grammatical, and pragmatic. These three aspects can also take their place in Roman Jakobson's six-part scheme: emotive, referential, poetic, phatic, metalingual, and conative (see Jakobson, *Language in Literature*, p. 66 and p. 71; and Robert Scholes, *Structuralism in Literature*, pp. 24–26.)

12. I hasten to say that the concepts of "ordinary language" and "artistic language" are convenient fictions.

13. For a critique of thematic interpretation (as well as ironic and historical interpretation), see Richard Levin, *New Readings vs. Old Plays*.

14. In one sense of the word, interpretation is required only when we do not understand; if we understand, we don't need interpretation. The narratives I discuss are generally not obscure, I think; and I do not claim that I have uncovered themes that have never before been seen. But in another sense, interpretation can explain how the meaning of a narrative is achieved; this kind of interpretation may not offer a new thematic interpretation, but it increases and enriches our mimetic and formal understanding and experience of the story.

these stories reveal the ancient Greek fascination with the formal permutations of bad family relationships in a way that no single work could do. Likewise, Jean-Paul Sartre's *Nausea* shows one version of the subject, whereas Robert Louis Stevenson's *The Master of Ballantrae* shows another version, and L. P. Hartley's *The Go-Between* shows still another version. These and all of the other stories discussed here taken together reveal a complex model of the self that cannot be derived from any narrative read on its own.

In the course of my exploration of narrative subjectivity, I have freely plundered some areas in which I am hardly expert—a little philosophy, a little psychoanalysis, and a good deal of linguistics. This plundering gives the project a somewhat digressive character, for which I do not apologize. What seems at first to be a digression will often return as a theme or a way of thinking at various points in the discussion. When I discuss a theory in linguistics or psychology or philosophy, I will almost never be interested in whether or not the theory is true; for example, I discuss Descartes' concept of the subject at some length, not because I think it is true—or false—but because it provides one model of the self, the reflexive self, which is manifested in a set of narratives.

The method I use is heavily influenced by the study of language, but it is not structuralist, at least in the most common understanding of the term. I also do not associate myself with any particular school of post-structuralist thought. Structuralism tended toward binary analyses. I grant binaries where they seem appropriate, but phenomena often demand a richer analysis.[15] In philosophy and also in casual discourse, subjectivity is most often seen as a binary phenomenon, as we see in the frequent dichotomy of subject and object or self and other. I believe that this binary division is inadequate; a more complex and subtle analysis of the self and subjectivity can be found in the narrative categories described here.

Structuralism was largely based on Saussure's theory of the sign and Jakobson's theory of phonology; the method used here is based on a post-Saussurian analysis of syntax and deep-structure semantic roles. Structuralism often claimed that all the structures of a cultural moment in some sense hang together. Social reality, however, seems to me complex and contested, and I do not believe that history always moves through sharp, epistemic ruptures. Structuralism aspired to be a science. Though I admire the achievements of science, I do not believe that science is the highest form of thought, and I do not claim any scientific status for this discussion.

15. The binarism of structuralism, however, has sometimes been exaggerated, since structuralism included such concepts as markedness, neutralization, and mediation, none of which is strictly binary.

My approach to linguistics is amateur and eclectic. I grew up in the great days of Chomsky's revolution, but I have also read the work of many linguists who are not part of his school. My approach is most obviously indebted to Case Grammar and to Charles Fillmore's "The Case for Case" in particular, but I also admire the work of Kenneth Pike, M. A. K. Halliday, Dwight Bolinger, Ronald Longacre, William Labov, and Talmy Givon, among others. Because the study of language is (perhaps) the most advanced of the human sciences, it may sometimes provide models for investigations in other areas. But each area is ultimately unique, and it is a mistake to assume that the structure of language is necessarily the structure of anything else.

Language can certainly be ambiguous, but I do not believe that there is an endless and uncontrollable slippage of the sign. I do believe in authors, and I believe that authors are responsible for what they write, though I also believe that the best evidence for the author's intention is usually to be found in the text. Writers, like other users of language, may not be entirely aware of what they mean. I do not believe that language is isomorphic with the world, but I do believe that a theory of meaning must include a theory of reference, however complicated that may be. Moreover, any fundamental element of language is likely to express something about our way of being in the world. Language reflects society at a relatively superficial level—that is, mostly through vocabulary. The deeper structure of language is compatible with many quite different social structures, including those yet to exist. Some of the forms of subjectivity that I explore in this study seem to correlate with fundamental features of language; I do not claim, however, that the categories of narrative analysis must be the same as the categories of grammatical analysis.

In any case, the categories I suggest are not intended to exhaust the possible forms of subjectivity, though I believe that they apply to a large number of narratives. Additional categories may be suggested by other grammatical forms or by other fields. Once we move beyond the binary opposition of subject and object, subjectivity is potentially without limit, varying with every person in every situation. But we need some categories in order to grasp this profusion; which categories and how many we choose will depend on our needs. The kinds of subjectivity I have described account for a large and interesting group of narratives, and these narratives in turn describe the kinds of subjectivity of greatest interest to writers and readers.

PART ONE

Philosophical Fables of the Self

CHAPTER 1

The Reflexive Self
Descartes and Ovid

In this chapter I introduce the simplest kind of self: the single self reflecting on itself. This is the self as described by Descartes and the self as described in Ovid's story of Narcissus. This form of the self can be examined through a variety of disciplinary perspectives: philosophy, psychology, literature, and linguistics. The solitary self has a kind of double aspect, as both observer of itself and itself observed. The grammatical form of the Cartesian self is the reflexive pronoun. Though the Cartesian self is its own foundation, it is also empty, and so it must be furnished by the world and the discourse in which it exists. This Cartesian self is typically the subject of diaries and memoirs, both fictional and nonfictional, which I discuss in chapter 2.

I.

René Descartes opens his *Discourse on Method* with a little autobiography. "From my childhood," he says, "I lived in a world of books, and since I was taught that by their help I could gain a clear and assured knowledge of everything useful in life, I was eager to learn from them" (3). But his reading left him dissatisfied, as did his time in school. He liked mathematics, because the proofs were certain and self-evident, but he was not impressed by philosophy: "when I noticed how many different opinions learned men may hold on the same subject, despite the fact that no more than one of them can ever be right, I resolved to consider almost as false any opinion which was merely plausible" (6). He therefore decided to give up his formal studies: "I resolved to seek no other knowledge than that which I might find within myself, or perhaps in the great book of nature" (6). He spent some years traveling to learn the customs and minds of people of various types and stations, but the knowledge he found there was no more secure than the knowledge he had found in philosophy. And so, "after spending several years in thus studying the book of nature and acquiring experience, I eventually reached the decision to study my own self, and to employ all my abilities to try to choose the right path" (7).

He was then in Germany, and there he was caught by the onset of winter. "There was no conversation to occupy me, and being untroubled by any cares or passions, I remained all day alone in a warm room. There I had plenty of time to examine my ideas" (7). His conclusion, of course, was that the only thing he could know with immediate certainty was his own existence: "I think therefore I am" (21).[1] Everything else in his system, including the existence of God, the world of nature, and other people, is built on this foundation of knowledge of the self. The self, however, is its own foundation; there is nothing below the self on which it is based.

Descartes presents his philosophic account of the self though the telling of a story; and later we will find that Hegel, Plato, and Freud also give narrative accounts of the self. It should be no surprise, therefore, that other stories—stories which were not intended as philosophic accounts—offer versions of the self, as I will describe throughout this study. But the philosophic accounts of the self aspire to a kind of abstract generality, whereas the literary accounts of the self and its roles insist on the particular circumstances of each story and each self.

Descartes' autobiographical narrative creates a curious doubleness in his subjectivity: on the one hand, there is the *I* that tells the story, the *I* that is René Descartes. Here we meet a person at a particular time and place—in a warm room in Germany—a person with a body and emotions, and a history as well. But in addition to this physical and historical *I*, there is also the *I* of the cogito, "I think, therefore I am": this *I* is merely a thinking substance, with no history and no characteristics. This self would be the same no matter where it is. There is a long and complex road between the thinking substance *I* and the *I* who is René Descartes.

---

1. The *Discourse* was published first in French and only later translated into Latin. The phrase "cogito, ergo sum" comes from the later Latin edition, but the phrase is now often called *the cogito*, and I will adopt this handy title. For my discussion of the Cartesian subject, I have consulted L. J. Beck, *The Metaphysics of Descartes: A Study of the Meditations*; L. Aryeh Kosman, "The Naive Narrator: Meditation in Descartes's Meditations"; Dalia Judovitz, Subjectivity and Representation in Descartes: The Origins *of Modernity*; Hassan Melehy, *Writing Cogito: Montaigne, Descartes, and the Institution of the Modern Subject*; and Hiram Caton, *The Origin of Subjectivity: An Essay on Descartes*.

The division within the Cartesian self has been noted by many philosophers and psychologists. As William James remarked:

> Whatever I may be thinking of, I am always at the same time more or less aware of *myself,* of my *personal existence.* At the same time, it is I who am aware, so that the total self of me, being as it were duplex, partly known and partly knower, partly object and partly subject, must have two aspects discriminated in it, of which for shortness we may call one the *Me* and the other the *I.* I call these "discriminated aspects," and not separate things, because the identity of *I* with *me,* even in the very act of their discrimination, is perhaps the most ineradicable dictum of common sense and must not be undermined by our terminology here at the outset, whatever we may come to think of its validity at our inquiry's end.[2]

We could equally say that the duality of *I* and *me* is an ineradicable experience and must not be undermined by our terminology.

Something like this experience of duality is noted in a literary form by Henry James. Here the heroine of *Washington Square,* Catherine Sloper, is deciding what to do now that her father has forbidden her to marry her impecunious suitor Morris Townsend:

> She had an entirely new feeling, which may be described as a state of expectant suspense about her own actions. She watched herself as she would have watched another person, and wondered what she would do. It was as if this other person, who was both herself and not herself, had suddenly sprung into being, inspiring her with a natural curiosity as to the performance of untested functions.[3]

There is much in common in these accounts of the self presented by René Descartes, William James, and Henry James—an autobiographical philosopher, a philosophical psychologist, and a psychological novelist.

In all of these accounts, the grammatical form of the solitary but self-regarding self is the reflexive pronoun. Although Descartes wrote "I think, therefore I am" ("Je pense, donc je suis"), his statement perhaps can be expanded to something like "I observe myself thinking, and therefore I know that I exist"—or "... therefore I know myself to exist" or "... therefore I know that my self exists." In English we can say "I observe myself," but we can also

---

2. William James, *Psychology, Briefer Course,* p. 176, quoted in Russell Meares, *Intimacy and Alienation,* p. 9.
3. Henry James, *Washington Square,* p. 74.

say "I observe my self," where the reflexive pronoun has split into a possessive pronoun and the rather mysterious noun "self," so the final full form of the cogito could be "I observe my self thinking, therefore I know that my self exists."

Although Descartes' formulation of the cogito ("Je pense, donc je suis") does not use the first-person reflexive pronoun, he often uses the form elsewhere—sixteen times in just the first part of the *Discourse on Method*—and in crucial contexts, such as the passage quoted above from near the end of Part One: "But after I had spent some years studying in the book of the world and trying to acquire some experience, I resolved one day to study within myself too...." ["Mais après que j'eus employé quelques années à étudier ainsi dans le livre du monde et à tâcher d'acquérir quelque expérience, je pris un jour résolution d'étudier aussi en moi-même...."]. Descartes' project is to study within himself in order to find the self—and once he has found himself, on this foundation to construct his knowledge of God and the world. All depends on this initial self-reflection.

The reflexive pronoun is formed variously in various languages.[4] In English it is formed by combining personal pronouns with the word "self." These forms are also used as emphatic pronouns, as in "I will do it myself" or "She herself told him the story." German has a word for "self"—the cognate "Selbst"—which is also used in many combined forms, such as Selbstbehauptung (self-assertion), Selbstbeherrshung (self-control), Selbstbeobachtung (self-observation), Selbtsgespräch (conversation with oneself), and many, many more. This word "Selbst" is not, however, used in the reflexive pronouns, which are simple forms:

myself	mich (in the dative: mir)
yourself (familiar)	dich (in the dative: dir)
yourself (formal)	sich
himself, herself, itself	sich
ourselves	uns
yourselves (familiar)	euch
yourselves (formal)	sich
themselves	sich

So the German for "I shave myself" (a standard grammar-book example) is "Ich rasiere mich." In sentences like this, the reflexive is used because a

---

4. For discussion of reflexive pronouns from a linguistic point of view, see Suzanne Kemmer, "Emphatic and Reflexive -self: Expectations, Viewpoint, and Subjectivity."

single referent takes two roles: here, agent (the person doing the shaving) and patient (the person being shaved). German uses the reflexive pronoun with some verbs that do not take the reflexive in English: for example, "Er fürchtet **sich** vor dem Donner"—"He is frightened of thunder"; "Sie hat **sich** versprochen" —"She has made a slip of the tongue"; "Ich habe **mich** erkältet"—"I caught a cold." In sentences like these, it is not clear that there is a single referent with two roles—agent and patient—at the same time. However, the subject in these sentences is really the patient of the action, not the agent, so the action of the verb in a way reflects back onto the subject.[5]

Philosophic German uses the reflexive pronouns in some important technical terms, such as "Ding an sich," which means a "thing-in-itself," and "Ding für sich," a "thing-for-itself." These terms have been translated into other European languages.

In French there are short forms of the reflexive that precede the verb (as in "Je me regards dans la glace"—"I look at myself in the mirror") and longer forms combined with "-même." These longer forms are most often emphatic, as in "Je couperai le pain moi-même"—"I will cut the bread myself"; but we have seen above that Descartes uses "moi-même" as a reflexive: "je pris un jour résolution d'étudier aussi en moi-même." French, like German, uses reflexives somewhat more than we do in English, so that the French equivalent of "to repent" is "se repentir," that is, "to repent oneself." The very beginning of Proust's *À la recherche du temps perdu* shows several of these reflexive forms, which I have put in bold letters:

> Longtemps, je **me** suis couché de bonne heure. Parfois, à peine ma bougie éteinte, mes yeux **se** fermaient si vite que je n'avais pas le temps de **me** dire: "Je **m'**endors."

Here is C. K. Scott Moncrieff's translation, which shows how English reduces the reflexive quality of the original:

> For a long time I used to go to bed early. Sometimes, when I had put out my candle, my eyes would close so quickly that I had not even time to say "I'm going to sleep."

The simple reflexive in French, like that in German, does not include anything like the English word "self." Nor does the compound form: the

---

5. But sentences like these may be better described as in the middle voice; see Suzanne Kemmer, *The Middle Voice*.

word "même" does not mean "self," but rather "same" or "the very." There is certainly a connection between sameness and selfness, since the self exists only if it is the same for some period of time; if it changes, if it is no longer the same, then it is no longer itself. (This connection can be coded in the vocabulary of a language: in ancient Greek, forms of "autos" are used for both "same" and "self.") Nonetheless, sameness and selfness are not the same.

I don't know of a French word that is quite the same as the English "self"; the closest is probably "soi," especially as a philosophic term, in combinations such as "en-soi" ("in-itself") and "pour-soi" ("for-itself"); these are built on the model of the German philosophic terms "an sich" and "für sich." But in any case, the forms "moi-même," "lui-même," and "elle-même" can't be divided into a possessive pronoun and "self," as the English reflexive can be divided, so the pun "I observe my self" doesn't really work in French.

II.

The reflexive pronoun is only one beast in a strange zoo of pronouns, all of which are connected to questions of the self. We generally think that a pronoun stands for a noun, and the pronoun thus needs an antecedent; but if so, then "I" and "you" may not really be pronouns at all.[6] The third-person pronoun almost always does need an antecedent: if I read "He was not old—verging on sixty—but he was failing perceptibly," I will probably feel that the statement is incomplete, since I don't know who "he" is. But if I read (in Amy Kelly's *Eleanor of Aquitane and the Four Kings*):

> Louis the Sixth, Louis the Fat, lay sick in his hunting lodge at Béthizy, whither his bearers had brought him from the unprecedented heat and the fetid odors of the summer in Paris. He was not old—verging on sixty—but he was failing perceptibly. (1)

Then the pronoun has its antecedent, and all is well.

Only rarely, however, do the pronouns "I" or "you" have a stated antecedent. It is not because of reference to an antecedent that you and I know who "I" am and "you" are, but because we are face-to-face, talking to each other. Of course there are exceptions. If, for example, the word "I" is not part of conversation but is part of a written text, then "you" and "I" are not face-to-

---

6. The first-person pronoun manifests the solitary Cartesian self, the second-person pronoun manifests the Hegelian double self, and the third-person pronoun manifests the Freudian third self.

face; in that case, the situation will not provide the antecedent, and the text will have to do the job—as in the first sentence of the ancient romance *Callirhoe:*

> I, Chariton of Aphrodisieus, secretary of the rhetor Athenagoros, will narrate a love story which took place in Syracuse.[7]

Robert Graves borrowed this feature of ancient style when he wrote:

> I, Tiberius Claudius Drusus Nero Germanicus This-that-and-the-other (for I shall not trouble you yet with all my titles), who was once, and not so long ago either, known to my friends and relatives and associates as "Claudius the Idiot," or "That Claudius," or "Claudius the Stammerer," or "Clau-Clau-Claudius," or at best as "Poor Uncle Claudius," am now about to write this strange history of my life....

Conversely, some writers use the third-person pronoun with no antecedent at the very beginning of a story, perhaps to plunge the reader into the middle of the situation, as Conrad does in *Lord Jim:*

> He was an inch, perhaps two, under six feet, powerfully built, and he advanced straight at you with a slight stoop of the shoulders, head forward, and a fixed from-under stare which made you think of a charging bull.

Or as Hemingway does in *For Whom the Bell Tolls:*

> He lay flat on the brown, pine-needled floor of the forest, his chin on his folded arms, and high overhead the wind blew in the tops of the pine trees.

Even in these special cases, the third-person pronoun eventually refers to some name, a post-cedent, if you will.

The peculiarities of pronouns are discussed in two classic papers by Émile Benveniste: "The Nature of Pronouns" and "Subjectivity in Language."[8] Although Benveniste's discussion concerns pronouns in general, it can be

---

7. The Greek text does not state the pronoun "I," which is expressed by the form of the verb; it is the form of the verb which makes it clear that the nominative subject of the verb, "Chariton of Aphrodisieus," is in the first person, an *I*; the English translation, however, requires an expressed subject of the verb.

8. Published originally in 1956 and 1958, respectively; both are reprinted in the volume *Problems in General Linguistics.*

applied specifically to Descartes' cogito. Benveniste defines *I* as "the person who is uttering the present instance of the discourse containing *I*," and *you* as the "individual spoken to in the present instance of discourse containing the linguistic instance *you*" (218). The person speaking defines *I* and *you* as the person speaking and the person addressed. But if a person quotes another person's speech, then it is the person quoted who defines *I* and *you*: "You should know that the boss said to me, 'I'd like you to finish the job before you leave for the night.'" Here one *I* is telling one *you* what another *I* said to another *you*, who happens to be the same person as the first *I*. Each pronoun is determined by the particular discourse in which it occurs; the reality to which these pronouns refer is solely "a reality of discourse" (218).

These first- and second-person pronouns take their meaning not from the language system (*langue*, in the terminology of structural linguistics) but from actual speech (*parole*); these "shifters," to use the term introduced by Roman Jakobson, function only when the speaker converts the system into a particular act of speaking (220).[9] As Benveniste says, these signs are in a sense empty, ready to be filled "as soon as a speaker introduces them into each instance of his discourse" (219).

These empty shifters are in a way like the Cartesian self, which has no properties in itself, beyond thinking; only after an extensive process of deduction could one perhaps link the Cartesian self to some particular person, a person with attributes and characteristics. Likewise, *I* has no properties until it is spoken by a particular person. When the speaker says *I*, there is a double effect: on the one hand, the empty pronoun begins to become filled with the speaker's attributes, and on the other, the speaker takes on subjectivity (220).

This subjectivity, according to Benveniste, is "the psychic unity that transcends the totality of the actual experiences it assembles and that makes the permanence of the consciousness" (224); here again we see the connection of "selfness" and "sameness," as well as the role of memory in the formation of the subject. This subjectivity, this psychic unity, is the result of taking a position within language, within a dialogue, in contrast to another subjectivity. Subjectivity is therefore necessarily reciprocal: "Consciousness of self is only possible if it is experienced by contrast. I use *I* only when I am speaking to someone who will be a *you* in my address" (224). And this *you* will become an *I* in its turn to speak, while *I* becomes *you*.

The subjectivity of the first-person pronoun can be seen very clearly in certain verbal constructions. If I say, for example, "I teach Latin," I am

---

9. The first- and second-person pronouns are part of a larger group of shifters, which also includes words such as "here" and "now." See Jakobson, *Shifters, Verbal Categories, and the Russian Verb*; see also Eco, *A Theory of Semiotics*, pp. 115–21.

describing a fact about myself, in just the way "James teaches Latin" describes a fact. If I say "James supposes that such-and-such," I also state a fact, based presumably on some objective evidence that James in fact supposes such-and-such. But if I say "I suppose that such-and-such," I do not have to refer to any objective evidence to prove that I suppose. I know subjectively that I suppose, so my statement is not a description but an action—the action of supposing.

This subjectivity is even clearer with verbs such as "promise," "guarantee," or "certify." A sentence using these verbs with a first-person subject constitutes an action: if you say "I promise that I will (do such-and-such)," you are not just saying something: you are actually making a promise. But these verbs with a subject in the third person form descriptions: the sentence "He promises that he will do such-and-such" is a description, not an action (229).[10]

Although Benveniste picks out phrases such as "I promise," it is possible to argue that any sentence at all implies the subjectivity of the person speaking. Even a simple description is also an act of assertion: "It's cold outside" implicitly says something like "I assert that it's cold outside." If a promise is performative, so is an assertion, and both require the first person, *I*, as the speaker.[11]

Subjectivity enters language in many other ways, as we can see by what little is left if we try to get rid of it. Wayne Booth, in *The Rhetoric of Fiction*, undertakes to see what remains of literary narrative if all traces of the author's subjectivity are removed—the same experiment could apply to any use of language. Booth begins by erasing all direct address by the author to the reader, all direct commentary (16). In addition to direct intrusions of the author's voice, there are also the author's implied judgments, which enter the story, for example, in the form of adjectives or adverbs (17). Nor have we finished: "the author's presence will be obvious on every occasion when he moves into or out of a character's mind...." (17). In fact, any inside view betrays the author's presence, since the contents of the character's mind are not objective facts available to an external observer (17). "For that matter, we

---

10. Benveniste here is discussing what we have come to call *performative verbs*, following J. L. Austin, who examined these at some length in his William James Lectures, *How to Do Things with Words*, delivered in 1955. Austin and Benveniste were working with very similar ideas at just the same time: something was in the air. But their approaches are different. Austin's account is more extensive and in many ways more detailed than Benveniste's, but he deals neither with the subjectivity involved in the performatives nor with pronouns and other shifters. Performatives as understood by Benveniste and Austin may be compared to Judith Butler's argument that gender is performative (see *Gender Trouble*, pp. 24–25 and 134–41), but performativity, as I use the term, precedes gender and includes many other aspects of subjectivity.

11. Austin discusses the performative aspect of assertion in lecture XI, pp. 133ff.

must object to the reliable statements of any dramatized character," because the reliability of a character is the author's judgment (17). Beyond characterization, every touch of style, every metaphor, every literary allusion—all these show the author's consciousness (18). Every dislocation of the natural sequence of events, or their proportion of duration, comes only at the will of the author (18). Even the author's choice of which story to tell is subjective (19). "In short, the author's judgment is always present, always evident, to anyone who knows how to look for it.... Although the author can to some extent choose his disguises, he can never choose to disappear" (19).

The author's subjectivity is only half the picture: there is also the reader's. Readers are real people, but they are also to some extent constructed by the author, by the text, and by the act of reading. Just as the author's *I* is both an empty grammatical marker and a real person, so is the reader's *you*. We can imagine the *I* subjectivity desperately seeking a compatible *you*: "Author, classicist, literary critic; hobbies: linguistics and philosophy, seeks reader with similar interests"—or perhaps: "I am: fit, fifty, funny, full of phrases; You are: warm and witty, welcoming new experiences, ready for strange travels and adventures; nonsmokers only." Of course the constructed self may not be exactly the same as the real person, on either side of this transaction.

Every communication has an author and an audience, and every sentence in every interaction implies not only the subjectivity of the first person, but also that of the second person. "It's cold outside" means "I [your mother] assert to you [my child] that it's cold outside [so you should put on a sweater]." The act of discourse will call out particular characteristics of the author and the audience, the *I* and the *you*, to fill the empty slots. Neither subjectivity is immutable; each adapts to fit the changing circumstances of the moment.

The empty first- and second-person pronouns are in some ways like the implied author and reader of a literary text.[12] The pronouns are filled in the act of discourse, while the implied author and reader are created in the act of writing and reading. Every use of language has an implied author and reader, each more or less like the real speaker and listener, and every conversation involves a constant exchange of these positions. We are always trying to meet in the middle, but our meetings, at least in language, are always virtual rather than real.

12. For a definition of the implied author, see Wayne Booth, *The Rhetoric of Fiction*, pp. 71–76; for a discussion of various theories of the audience, see Peter Rabinowitz, *Before Reading*, pp. 20–29. I take the implied author and reader to be theoretical ideals. As Rabinowitz notes, any reader must come with certain kinds of preknowledge, just as Descartes' *I* evidently knows the system of grammar through which it speaks.

But conversation is usually not simply the meeting and exchange of the first- and the second-person pronouns, and the two parties to the conversation are not simply the subject and object of discourse. Usually people are talking about something, and this something will be in the third person. "Have I got something to tell you!" Here the speaker is the first-person subject, the topic of discussion is the object, and the listener is in the dative case.[13]

III.

What if the speaker and the audience are the same person, the same self? What if the conversation is a conversation with oneself, Selbstgespräch?

Talking to oneself is very common; I suppose that everyone does it, and it may even be essential for mental well-being. The literary representation of Selbstgespräch is ancient. Often in the Homeric epics, a character will make a decision by staging an internal debate with himself; in Book Eleven of the *Iliad*, for example, Odysseus is alone on the battlefield, and he must decide whether to stay or retreat:

> Now Odysseus the spear-famed was left alone, nor did any
> of the Argives stay beside him, since fear had taken all of them.
> And troubled, he spoke then to his own great-hearted spirit:
> "Ah me, what will become of me? It will be a great evil if I run,
> fearing their multitude, yet deadlier if I am caught
> alone; and Kronos' son drove to flight the rest of the Danaans.
> But why does the heart within me debate on these things?
> Since I know that it is the cowards who walk out of the fighting,
> but if one is to win honour in battle, he must by all means
> stand his ground strongly, whether he be struck or strike down another.[14]

---

13. Note, for example the first words of Apuleius' novel *The Golden Ass:* "At ego tibi . . . varias fabulas conseram" ("But I for you . . . various tales will twine together"), where the narrator is in the first-person nominative, the reader is in the second-person dative, and the stories are in the accusative. In *Auctor et Actor*, John Winkler argues that this novel has no stable narrative self; different episodes seem to be told by different subjects, though they are all the same narrator, Lucius. I would argue that the reader's subjectivity must be equally labile.

14. The translation is by Richmond Lattimore, *The Iliad of Homer,* slightly revised. The line "And troubled, he spoke to then to his own great-hearted spirit" (Il.11.403) is a formula marking an internal conversation (see also Il.17.90, Il.18.5, Il.20.343, Il.21.53, Il.21.552, Il.22.98, Od.5.298, Od.5.355, Od.5.407, Od.5.464. The line "But why does the heart within me debate on these things?" (Il.11.407), closing the conversation, is also a formula, though it does not occur

In Greek tragedy, decision through debate with oneself can be highly elaborated, as also in Ovid's *Metamorphoses*.

Although Selbstgespräch is common, it is not therefore simple. A curious sort of reflexivity forces an entrance, since the same person is playing both roles in the sentence—author and audience, *I* and *you*—and *you* has become *myself*. This must be the situation of Descartes' cogito; if he is starting from scratch, basing his whole construction of the world only on his own existence, then who else is there to hear him? (When God said, "Let there be light," to whom was he speaking?) Descartes' cogito now becomes "I say to my self that I observe my self thinking, and therefore I know that my self exists." This situation initially seems contrary to Benveniste's claim that "Consciousness of self is only possible if it is experienced by contrast. I use *I* only when I am speaking to someone who will be a *you* in my address." In Selbstgespräch, there must be a contrast between the *I* of the speaker and the *myself* of the audience. The subjectivity of the author's *I* constructs, through the text, the subjectivity of a *myself*, so that there will be an audience that can understand what *I* is saying. And all this is in addition to the observed *self*, the object of the statement. Perhaps there is only one self here, but it has become (at least) a trinity of subjects.

IV.

The myth of Narcissus, as Ovid tells it, is all about the self-reflective self, the self in love with its own reflection. Narcissus was a beautiful young man, loved by many girls and boys, but too proud in his beauty to give himself to anyone. Finally one of his rejected suitors cursed him: "Thus may he himself love, thus may he not win over the one he loves" (*Metamorphoses* 3.405). The goddess Nemesis heard and brought about the destruction of Narcissus.[15]

> One day when Narcissus was weary from hunting he came across a pool in the forest. As he bent down to drink he saw his reflection in the water. He wanted to slake his thirst at the pool, but another thirst grew in him: he is captivated by the image in the water, he falls in love with an incorporeal hope, and what he thinks is a body is only water. He gazes at his own

---

in every instance of internal conversation (see also I1.17.97, I1.21.562, I1.22.122, I1.22.385). The words "spirit" and "heart" here translate a single Greek word, "thumos."

15. The following is my own rather free prose translation of Ovid, *Metamorphoses*, 3.413–68, with some lines left out; I have used the text of William S. Anderson, *Ovid's Metamorphoses, Books 1–5*.

eyes, his hair, his ivory neck, his mouth, the rosy color of his complexion mixed with the white of snow. He wonders at everything which is in himself wonderful. He desires himself, and the one who loves is himself loved, and while he seeks, he is also sought, he sets a fire and burns. How often he gave useless kisses to the cheating pool! He plunges his arms into the water, trying to embrace the neck he sees in there, but he cannot catch himself.

Stretching out his arms to the surrounding trees, he laments: "Has anyone loved more cruelly? What I see is pleasing to me, but what I see and what is pleasing, I cannot find: such a mistake holds my beloved! And what makes me more sad, it's not a huge sea which separates us, nor a road, nor mountains, nor the closed walls of a city: we are kept apart by a little water! He himself wants to be embraced! For as often as I bend down to kiss the flowing water, he reaches up towards me. You would think he could be touched: it is such a little thing stands between the lovers."

"Why do you flee when I seek you? Certainly it is not my beauty or my age that you flee. When I reach out my arms, so do you. When I laugh, you laugh. When I cry I have seen your tears. I am that fellow! My image does not deceive me. I am burned by my own love. I set the fire and I endure it. What is desire is myself! Abundance makes me poor. If only I could escape from my body! A strange prayer for a lover! I wish I were at a distance from what I love."

And now Narcissus begins to waste away: "Nor will death be hard for me, since as I die I will forget my grief. But I wish the one I love could live on! Now we die, two hearts in one soul." His tears troubled the water, and the image was clouded by the motion. As he saw it leave, he cried, "Where are you fleeing? Stay, don't desert me, your beloved! What I cannot touch, let me gaze at, feed my wretched passion!" And gradually he fades away, until nothing is left of him but a flower, the narcissus.

This passage dramatizes the fundamental dilemma of the reflexive self: the doubled sense of identity and distance, the unbridgeable tissue that divides the two aspects of the self. Even the grammar and the verse structure make the point. The passage is full of reflexive pronouns; many words are repeated, and these repetitions create alliterations; some repetitions form a mirror image:[16]

se cupit inprudens et, qui probat, ipse probatur (425)
[He rashly desires himself, and he who admires, he himself is admired]

16. Compare also 11.415, 424, and 464–67.

> dumque petit, petitur pariterque accendit et ardet (426)
> [And while he seeks, he is sought and he both sets a fire and burns]

The writing is extraordinarily witty, but the wit is not simply decorative. The form of the verse is an essential part of the meaning of the passage: the narcissistic self is reflexive, and the reflexive self is always at least potentially narcissistic.

V.

The reflexive self is the subject without an object, or at most the subject whose object is itself. This self is not the property of any one discipline; it can be regarded from the perspective of philosophy, psychology, literature, and linguistics, each of which has something to contribute to our understanding of the reflexive self. For Descartes, the reflexive self is simply the foundation on which he builds the rest of his system; he has no interest in it for itself; once he has observed himself observing himself, he moves ahead, leaving this self behind. Philosophy aspires to the general and the universal, but narrative does its work through exploration of the particular manifestations of general forms. In chapter 2, I will consider various literary versions of the Cartesian self.

CHAPTER 2

The Furniture of the Self
Montaigne, Highsmith, Dostoevsky

When the Cartesian self appears in narrative, it needs a world in which to exist and a cast of external characters through which and against which it can be defined. The reflexivity of the Cartesian self is shown by self-address and self-examination, but often the Cartesian self is lonely, even in the midst of society, and fragmentary. Beyond its pure existence, the self must be constructed from the world and from other selves. These characteristics of the Cartesian self are found variously represented in the *Essays* of Montaigne, in novels of impersonation such as Highsmith's *The Talented Mr. Ripley*, and in many memoirs, diaries, and autobiographies, both fictional and nonfictional. Dostoevsky's *Notes from the Underground* presents a vivid portrait of the lonely and fragmented self-reflexive self; at the end of the story there is a possibility that the hero will recognize another self in the world, but only for a moment.

I.

There is very little one can say about the pure Cartesian subject—the thinking substance which has no attributes except its own thinking and which thinks only about itself. This subject is like a virtual particle, always in danger of imploding or of disappearing into the void from sheer emptiness. In order to persist for any time at all, the Cartesian subject needs a world that can furnish it with attributes and with objects for its thought.

This furnishing of the Cartesian subject is one way to read Montaigne's *Essays*—even at the risk of anachronism.[1] The reflexivity of Descartes' thinking subject is already part of Montaigne's conception of himself, as he announces at the very beginning of the book, in the initial note "To the Reader" (I cite Montaigne's final version):

> You have here, Reader, a book whose faith can be trusted, a book which warns you from the start that I have set myself no other end but a private family one.

This first sentence of Montaigne's note explicitly states Benveniste's two subjectivities of discourse, the *I* (Montaigne) and the *you* (the reader)—and a third subjectivity as well, since it is not Montaigne who warns the reader, but the book, which seems to be able to speak for itself. Elsewhere, however, Montaigne identifies himself with the book he has written: "I have no more made my book than my book has made me—a book consubstantial with its author, concerned with my own self, a member of my life" (I.18); and "Everyone recognizes me in my book, and my book in me" (III.5).

The two subjectivities of discourse continue in the second sentence of the note, but then the *you* drops out:

> I have not been concerned to serve you nor my reputation: my powers are inadequate for such a design. I have dedicated this book to the private benefit of my friends and kinsmen so that, having lost me (as they must do soon) they can find here again some traits of my character and my humours.

Elsewhere, however, he says that he began writing for his own benefit, as a cure for his melancholy: his mind "gives birth to so many chimeras and fantastic monstrosities" that he "began to keep a record of them, hoping in time to make my mind ashamed of itself" (I.8). He wrote to make up for the

---

1. Montaigne was born in 1533 and died in 1592; the final edition of the *Essays* appeared posthumously in 1595; Descartes was born in 1596 and died in 1650. Descartes certainly knew and used the Essays. For Descartes' debt to Montaigne, see especially the fifth edition of Étienne Gilson's commentary on the *Discours de la méthode*, which includes twenty-nine index references to Montaigne. I was delighted to find that much of my thinking about Montaigne is consistent with Jean Starobinski's *Montaigne in Motion*, which I read only after this chapter was drafted. I have also consulted Frederick Ridder's *The Dialectic of Selfhood in Montaigne* and Hassan Melehy's *Writing Cogito: Montaigne, Descartes, and the Institution of the Modern Subject*. For discussion of differences between Montaigne and Descartes, see Steven Toulmin, *Cosmopolis*, pp. 36–44.

loss of his friend Étienne de la Boëtie: "He alone enjoyed my true image, and carried it away. That is why I myself decipher myself so painstakingly" (III.9). Exactly why such a private performance has been made public Montaigne does not say, but the reader is left in the position of a sort of eavesdropper.

The note concludes:

> And therefore, Reader, I am myself the material of my book ["je suis moy-mesmes la matière de mon livre"]: it is not reasonable that you should employ your leisure on a topic so frivolous and so vain.
> Therefore, Farewell.

The reflexivity of Montaigne's project could not be more clearly stated. Nor is this initial note the only occasion on which Montaigne indicates his reflexive attitude:

> Recently I retired to my estates, determined to devote myself as far as I could to spending what little life I have left quietly and privately; it seemed to me then that the greatest favour I could do for my mind was to leave it in total idleness, caring for itself, concerned only with itself, calmly thinking of itself. (I.8)

> And then, finding myself entirely destitute and void of any other matter, I presented myself to myself for argument and subject (II.8: "je me suis presenté moy-mesmes à moy, pour argument et pour subject").

> The world always looks straight ahead; as for me, I turn my gaze inward, I fix it there and keep it busy. Everyone looks in front of him; as for me, I look inside myself; I continually observe myself, I take stock of myself, I taste myself. (II.17)

> I study myself more than any other subject. That is my physics, that is my metaphysics. (III.13)

If Montaigne has to study himself, the reason perhaps is that his self is not immediately accessible to his own understanding: "the more I haunt myself and know myself, the more my deformity astonishes me, and the less I understand myself" (III.11). For Descartes, the self is the only thing that is immediately certain, but for Montaigne, the self is a mystery to itself.

Although Montaigne says that the *Essays* will be about himself, the essays announce themselves each as concerned with some external object: we find, for example, "On idleness" (I.8); "On educating children" (I.26); "On the Cannibals" (I.31); "On drunkenness" (II.2); "On coaches" (III.6). None of the titles in itself seems particularly reflexive, autobiographical, or self-referential, and there is no title of the form "Why I am such-and-such?" or "On myself as such-and-such." Even at his most subjective, Montaigne needs the world as a surface in which his subjectivity is reflected.

The early essays tend to be somewhat impersonal, with only a sentence or two of self-revelation sandwiched between anecdotes, but later essays vastly multiply these moments of self-portraiture.[2] In "On the affection of fathers for their children" (II.8), Montaigne tells us that 1) of all the vices, he is least able to understand theft; 2) he doesn't believe children should be punished (when he was a boy he was whipped only twice, and he himself has avoided corporal punishment in bringing up his own children); 3) he married at the age of thirty-three; 4) he has a rather bold way of speaking to other people; 5) he would rather be loved than feared by his children; 6) he is easily cheated by his servants; and so on. Each of these revelations is inspired by some example or anecdote. Montaigne liked a good story; he was interested in other people and their doings: but he always refers their behavior to himself. As he says in this essay:

> Whenever I hear of the state that some other man is in, I waste no time over that but immediately turn my eyes on to myself to see how I am doing. Everything which touches him touches me too. (II.8)

The external world provides examples which Montaigne can use to reflect upon himself and in which he is reflected for the observing reader.

But if Montaigne has an interest in observing others, he also insists on his own solitude:

> We should set aside a room, just for ourselves, at the back of the shop, keeping it entirely free and establishing there our true liberty, our principal solitude and asylum. Within it our normal conversation should be of ourselves, with ourselves, so privy that no commerce or communication

---

2. Montaigne's book went through several editions—including one that appeared shortly after Montaigne's death—and the book was altered at every stage, mostly by additions, many of which added personal touches, so that overall the text became increasingly subjective. Modern editions attempt to indicate the stages in the development of the text: in some editions, the parenthetical letter "A" indicates that a passage was present already in the first edition of 1580, "B" marks additions printed in 1588, and "C" marks additions printed in the posthumous edition of 1595; more-complex changes may be indicated in footnotes or commentary.

with the outside world should find a place there; there we should talk and laugh as though we had no wife, no children, no possessions, no followers, no menservants, so that when the occasion arises that we must lose them it should not be a new experience to do without them. We have a soul able to turn in on herself; she can keep herself company.... (I.39)

It would be wrong to expect the *Essays* to be consistent: Montaigne is providing a bouquet, not a dissertation. Some of the charm of the book is its openness to whatever strikes Montaigne to talk about. But in a sense, he is always talking about himself: he examines the various topics of the essays in order to reveal himself.

Montaigne's self as he presents it in the *Essays* is fundamentally derivative, dependent on other selves. No reader could fail to notice how much Montaigne quotes earlier writers, particularly the classic writers of Greece and Rome. If we take, for example, Essay I.20, "To philosophize is to learn how to die," we find that Montaigne begins by citing Cicero. Then in the third paragraph he quotes Seneca. A few paragraphs later, he refers to a passage in Hesiod. In the next paragraph there is a quotation from one of Horace's Odes; then another passage from Cicero (perhaps quoted from Erasmus' *Adages*); then passages from Horace, Claudian, and Lucretius. As we continue, we find many more borrowings, either by allusion or by direct quotation.

There is no feature of the *Essays* more typical or more consistent than these borrowings. Montaigne usually does not mention the source of a reference; some he probably expected the reader to recognize, but many are obscure. Some he certainly found for himself, but others he seems to have found in collections, such as the *Adages* of Erasmus. He doesn't really seem to care who the original author might have been:

> I leaf through books, I do not study them. What I retain of them is something I no longer recognize as anyone else's. It is only the material from which my judgement has profited, and the discourses and imaginations with which it has become imbued; the author, the place, the words, and other circumstances, I immediately forget. (II.7)

It is not the authority of a passage that impresses Montaigne but simply its excellence or, rather, its excellence in saying what Montaigne himself was thinking:

> (A).... if (as often happens) I chance to come across in excellent authors

the very same topics I have undertaken to treat ... I acknowledge myself to be so weak, so paltry, so lumbering, and so dull compared with such men, that I feel scorn and pity for myself. I do congratulate myself, however, that my opinions frequently coincide with theirs (C) and on the fact that I do at least trail far behind them murmuring "Hear, hear." (I.26)

He admits that "someone might say of me that I have here only made a bundle of other people's flowers, having furnished nothing of my own but the thread to tie them" (III.12). In fact, however, he has furnished more than the thread: the selection and arrangement of the flowers are his own as well. No one could imagine that any of Montaigne's essays is simply recapitulation; by collecting just these flowers, by arranging them just this way, and by tying them together with the thread of his own opinions and his own personality, he has created something new.

Still, it may seem odd that a writer who wants only to reveal himself speaks so often in the words of others. But this is how the self is constructed: these passages are the furniture of Montaigne's subjectivity.

Because the subject, for Montaigne, was formed through examining others, it is reflected in the external world, which provides examples both positive and negative. The self speaks with the voices of those who can express its thoughts better than it can itself. In addition, Montaigne's self is fragmented and inconstant. He divides himself into parts, and these parts have their own powers and desires. The mind is a faculty independent of the *I*:

> (B) But I am displeased with my mind for ordinarily producing its most profound and maddest fancies, and those I like the best, unexpectedly and when I am least looking for them. . . ." (III.5)

Here the mind is joined by the imagination:

> (B) Now I treat my imagination as gently as I can, and would relieve it, if I could, of all trouble and conflict. We must help it and flatter it, and fool it if we can. My mind is suited for this service; it has no lack of plausible reasons for all things. If it could persuade as well as it preaches, it would help me out very happily. (III.13)

Here the mind scolds the imagination, which has anticipated the pain of kidney stones before he actually developed the condition:

> (B) Fear of this disease, says my mind, used to terrify you, when it was

unknown to you; the cries and despair of those who make it worse by their lack of fortitude engendered in you a horror of it. (III.13)

Moreover, the soul is divided from the body, and both of these are divided from the self:

> (B) My mirror does not alarm me, for even in my youth I have more than once found myself thus wearing a muddy complexion and an ill-omened look, without any serious consequences; so that the doctors, finding inside me no cause responsible for this outward change, attributed it to the spirit and to some secret passion gnawing me within. They were wrong. If my body obeyed my orders as well as my soul, we should get along a little more comfortably. (III.13)

Montaigne's self is not only fragmented; it is also inconstant: "Myself now and myself a while ago, we are indeed two" (III.9); "(B) I have little control over myself and my moods. Chance has more power here than I.... (C) ... I do not find myself in the place where I look; and I find myself more by chance encounter than by searching and judgment" (I.10). The theme is important to him, and he devotes an entire essay to this topic: "On the inconstancy of our actions" (II.1). For example:

> (B) Not only does the wind of chance events shake me about as it lists, but I also shake and disturb myself by the instability of my stance: anyone who turns his prime attention on to himself will hardly ever find himself in the same state twice. I give my soul this face or that, depending upon which side I lay it down on. I speak about myself in diverse ways: that is because I look at myself in diverse ways. Every sort of contradiction can be found in me, depending upon some twist or attribute: timid, insolent; (C) chaste, lecherous; (B) talkative, taciturn; tough, sickly; clever, dull; brooding, affable; lying, truthful; (C) learned, ignorant; generous, miserly and then prodigal—(B) I can see something of all that in myself, depending on how I gyrate; and anyone who studies himself attentively finds in himself and in his very judgement this whirring about and this discordancy. There is nothing I can say about myself as a whole simply and completely, without intermingling and admixture. (II.1)

Montaigne is not entirely happy about the inconstancy and fragmentation of the self. When his body seems to rule his actions against his will, he tries to take control: "I want to be master of myself in every direction" (III.5: "je veus estre maistre de moy, à tout sens"). Grammatical reflexivity here raises a curious problem: if Montaigne is master of himself, is he also his own slave? But that question must be deferred until the next chapter, when we consider Hegel's account of subjectivity in his story of the Master and the Slave.

II.

We all learn by borrowing knowledge from others, but in the extreme Cartesian self, this manner of furnishing the self becomes pathological.[3] The pathological Cartesian self is unable to recognize other people as subjects in their own right; they become simply instruments or obstacles. The pathological Cartesian self is likely to be a con artist, in it only for himself, always looking out for number one—because there is no number two. At the same time, such a character may have a rather weak sense of self, and he may find himself appropriating for his own use not only other people's property but also other people's words and lives. The con artist becomes an imposter, an impersonator.

The hero of Patricia Highsmith's *The Talented Mr. Ripley* suffers from what might be called narcissistic self-loathing.[4] The circumstances of Tom Ripley's own life have given him nothing that he can admire, and so he lives the lives of other people. The novel is a complex plot of impersonation, as Tom takes on the persona of Dickie Greenleaf, whom he murders about a third of the way through the book. But Tom's fragile sense of reality is established at the beginning of the story. As the novel opens, Herbert Greenleaf, Dickie's father, asks Tom to help convince Dickie to come home from Europe, where he is wasting his life trying to become an artist rather than taking over the family business. In this conversation Tom claims that he has seen some of Dickie's drawings of ships, but, as the narrator tells us:

---

3. A healthier kind of self-formation is characteristic of the bildungsroman, but the heroes of most novels in this genre are too social to count as true Cartesian selves.

4. One might compare Thomas Mann's unfinished novel, *The Confessions of Felix Krull*; the theme of impersonation is present from the early part of the story—see, for instance, the episode when the young Felix pretends to be playing the violin (pp. 22–23)—and it culminates with the impersonation of the Marquis de Venosta, which dominates Part Three of the novel. Felix has a great deal of self-love, but no self-loathing, and he is not homicidal. To some extent he forms himself by taking on the words of other people: see Part Two, chapter 9, in which Diane Philibert compares him to Hermes, and Felix's later references to Hermes (e.g., p. 287); see also the discourse of Professor Kuckuck in Part Three, chapter 5, which Felix later appropriates at some length. If the novel had been finished, no doubt we would find many more such passages.

Tom had never seen them, but he could see them now, precise draughtman's drawings with every line and bolt and screw labeled, could see Dickie smiling, holding them up for him to look at, and he could have gone on for several minutes describing details for Mr. Greenleaf's delight, but he checked himself. (6–7)

Later, when he is having dinner with Mr. and Mrs. Greenleaf, he claims that he had attended Princeton. Again the narrator lets us in on the truth: "Tom had been very friendly last summer with a Princeton junior who had talked of nothing but Princeton, so that Tom had finally pumped him for more and more, foreseeing a time when he might be able to use the information" (17). Then Tom claims that he finished college in Colorado: "actually he had only finished high school there, but there had been a young man named Don Mizell rooming in his Aunt Bea's house in Denver who had been going to the University of Colorado. Tom felt as if he had gone there, too" (17–18).

At this point in the story, Tom is operating an extortion scheme in which he impersonates an employee of the Internal Revenue Service, but the scheme seems to be only an amusement because he can't cash the checks he receives. But this scheme shows us the strength of Tom's need to be someone else, so that when he takes over Dickie's life, we are not surprised.[5]

Herbert Greenleaf asks Tom to go to Italy to convince Dickie to come home, and Tom is happy to agree. Once in Italy, he falls in love not so much with Dickie himself but with Dickie's life and personality. A crucial moment comes when Tom tries on Dickie's clothes:

> He jerked Dickie's closet door open and looked in. There was a freshly pressed, new-looking grey flannel suit that he had never seen Dickie wearing. Tom took it out. He took off his knee-length shorts and put on the grey flannel trousers. He put on a pair of Dickie's shoes. Then he opened the bottom drawer of the chest and took out a clean blue-and-white striped shirt.
>   He chose a dark-blue silk tie and knotted it carefully. The suit fitted him. He re-parted his hair and put the part a little more to one side, the way Dickie wore his. (78)

He then pretends to be Dickie having an argument with Dickie's girlfriend Marge in which he ends up strangling her.

Some days later Tom and Dickie have an argument, and Tom's feelings

---

5. This scheme comes back into the story near the end (p. 251), as if to remind the reader that Tom's need to impersonate is a constant feature of his character.

reveal a great deal about Tom's Cartesian anxiety. He stares at Dickie's eyes, but he finds them empty, just "little pieces of blue jelly with a black dot in them," nothing more than "the hard, bloodless surface of a mirror." He feels that he and Dickie have never known each other, and that he has never known anyone: "each had stood and would stand before him, and he would know time and time again that he would never know them.... He felt surrounded by strangeness, by hostility" (89). For the pathological Cartesian self, other people are only hard reflective surfaces, no one ever knows anyone else, and the world is strange and hostile.

Shortly after this argument, Tom decides that Dickie is simply in the way. He kills Dickie, ties his body to weights, and dumps it into a lake. Then Tom starts to impersonate Dickie. He wears Dickie's clothes now for real, he signs Dickie's name to checks, and he books hotel rooms with Dickie's name. From time to time he must return to his own identity, but when he does, he feels that he is still playing a role: "It was a good idea to practice jumping into his own character again, because the time might come when he would need to in a matter of seconds, and it was strangely easy to forget the exact timbre of Tom Ripley's voice" (122). He goes to Paris in Dickie's persona: "This was the real annihilation of his past and of himself, Tom Ripley, who was made up of that past, and his rebirth as a completely new person" (127).

If his impersonation as Dickie is to work, he has to avoid anyone who knew Dickie; in a difficult moment he finds it necessary to kill one of Dickie's friends. Much of the rest of the plot is concerned with Tom's narrow escapes. After a while the deception becomes too dangerous, and he returns to his own persona:

> This was the end of Dickie Greenleaf, he knew. He hated becoming Thomas Ripley again, hated being nobody, hated putting on his old set of habits again, and feeling that people looked down on him and were bored with him unless he put on an act for them like a clown, feeling incompetent and incapable of doing anything with himself except entertaining people for minutes at a time. He hated going back to himself as he would have hated putting on a shabby suit of clothes, a grease-spotted, unpressed suit of clothes that had not been very good even when it was new. (192)

The self is superficial, something that can be put on or taken off at will, like clothing. This passage should be read along with the passage previously quoted in which Tom puts on Dickie's clothing. If Tom sees his self as a suit of clothes, then by putting on Dickie's clothes, he puts on Dickie's self, while his own self is like a suit that does not fit.

In the end, Tom escapes suspicion of the murder. Now that he is no longer impersonating Dickie, it seems that Dickie has disappeared, and eventually everyone concludes that Dickie has killed himself. Tom forges a will that gives all of Dickie's money to Tom, and this, too, is accepted as genuine: "It was his! Dickie's money and his freedom. And the freedom, like everything else, seemed combined, his and Dickie's combined" (294). Tom gains some sense of stability in his identity, but only through wearing the identity of someone else.

Montaigne and Tom Ripley are probably not the most obvious pair of literary characters. Montaigne is a model of the humane self in modernity, while Tom is a psychopath and a serial murderer. And yet they are united by an obsessive concern with the self, a self that is empty and must construct itself from what it can take from other selves. They differ, however, in the way they regard others. Tom hardly grants the existence of other people, except insofar as he fears them. Montaigne is certainly obsessed with himself and with self-examination, but he recognizes the existence and indeed the value of other selves. Tom is without true friends, but Montaigne began writing the essays to cure his melancholy after the death of his friend Étienne de la Boëtie. We must note, however, the reason for his melancholy: his friend was the only one who enjoyed the true image of Montaigne, and his death has carried that image away. Montaigne's response was not to write essays about his friend in order to preserve his memory, but to write essays about himself in order to preserve his own memory for his friends. Montaigne was not a psychopath, like Tom Ripley, but he was nonetheless very self-centered. Although the characters presented in Montaigne's essays and Highsmith's novel are very different, they are both versions of the Cartesian self.

III.

The Talented Mr. Ripley is narrated by an omniscient third-person narrator, but more often a Cartesian self is the first-person narrator of a diary, memoir, confession, or other autobiographical form. These are primary sites for the Cartesian self because they provide easy opportunities for self-regard and self-examination.

But for whom does the self-reflexive writer write?[6] Montaigne is a little

---

6. Many of the issues raised by what I am calling *reflexive narrative* are discussed by theorists of diaries and diary fiction; see, for example, Robert Fothergill, *Private Chronicles,* and Andrew Hassan, *Writing Reality: A Study of Modern British Diary Fiction;* each of these includes a good bibliography.

unclear about his audience, as we have seen: he writes for himself—no, he writes for his family and his friends—but then he publishes his book for the world to read, and he even addresses the reader. The personal diary can be the purest form of self-address, but a diarist may have a sneaking desire to be read by others. Most diaries, however, claim to be written simply for the writer, and many fictional diaries follow the convention, as we can see in Saul Bellow's *Dangling Man*:[7]

> There was a time when people were in the habit of addressing themselves frequently and felt no shame at making a record of their inward transactions. But to keep a journal nowadays is considered a kind of self-indulgence, a weakness, and in poor taste. . . . If you have difficulties, grapple with them silently, goes one of their commandments. To hell with that! . . . In my present state of demoralization, it has become necessary for me to keep a journal—that is, to talk to myself—and I do not feel guilty of self-indulgence. (9–10)

Reflexive narrative is about the writer, but it is more specifically about the writer's interior world of thoughts, opinions, and feelings. The writer's actions are of interest only insofar as they show something about the writer's self. Reflexive narrative is autobiographical, but not all autobiographical narrative is reflexive: the *Autobiography of Thomas Jefferson*, for example, is an interesting but most unreflective document. But the distinction between reflexive and nonreflexive narrative is graded: a work that is generally not reflexive may have reflexive passages, and vice versa.

The writer of a reflexive narrative is very likely to feel solitary or isolated, even in company:

> Now I'm back to the point that prompted me to keep a diary in the first place: I don't have a friend.
> Let me put it more clearly, since no one will believe that a thirteen-year-old girl is completely alone in the world. And I'm not. . . . No, on the surface I seem to have everything, except my one true friend.[8]

---

7. Even in a first-person novel, it can be difficult to imagine the identity of the person addressed by the narrator. Kazuo Ishiguro's *The Remains of the Day*, for example, is addressed to an impossible second person; perhaps, then, this second person is really the narrator's second self. Many diaries and memoirs, fictional and nonfictional, have some kind of editorial apparatus to explain how the book came to see the light of day, as in Leon Edel's Introduction to the *Diary of Alice James* or the pseudo-editors' note at the beginning of Sartre's *Nausea*.

8. Anne Frank, *The Diary of a Young Girl*, p. 6.

> I live alone, entirely alone. I never speak to anyone, never; I receive nothing, I give nothing. The Self-Taught Man doesn't count. There is Françoise, the woman who runs the "Railway Man's Rendezvous." But do I speak to her?[9]

The Cartesian self is solitary, but Cartesian narratives in general have a supporting cast.[10] Reflexive writers vary greatly in the interest they show in other people. Alice James loved gossip, and her *Diary* is full of wicked comments about the foolish behavior she has witnessed or heard about—indeed, other people often seem to exist merely to furnish targets for her barbs. But as she approached her death, her thoughts became increasingly concentrated on the personal. Sartre gives Roquentin a brilliant passage describing the Sunday promenade perambulations of the bourgeois of Bouville (40–54), but these other people are mostly a foil to display his own sense of estrangement.

The fragmentation of the self, which is very clear and emphatic in Montaigne's *Essays*, can be seen in some other reflexive narratives. The narrator of Bellow's *Dangling Man* talks of himself in the third person:

> Joseph, aged twenty-seven, an employee of the InterAmerican Travel Bureau, a tall, already slightly flabby but, nevertheless, handsome young man, a graduate of the University of Wisconsin—major, History—married five years, amiable, generally takes himself to be well-liked. But on closer examination he proves to be somewhat peculiar. (26)

He also has two conversations with an imaginary interlocutor he calls the Spirit of Alternatives; this must be a projection of his own inner indecisiveness.

Anne Frank at first addresses her diary as "you": the diary in effect becomes its own audience. She externalizes a part of herself and identifies it with the diary; the *you* of the diary is really herself. A little later she says, "To enhance the image of this long-awaited friend in my imagination, I don't

---

9. Jean-Paul Sartre, *Nausea*, p. 6.
10. A narrative with only a single character is theoretically possible—and Descartes' philosophical fable of the self comes close—but stories generally need at least two actants, two narrative roles, in order to provide the kind of conflict that turns a set of events into a story. These two roles may be parts of one character, or one role may be a part of nature rather than a person. Robert Heinlein's tour-de-force "All You Zombies" has only one primary character but two actants. William Golding's *Pincher Martin* at first seems to be an insistently Cartesian narrative with a single human character whose opponent sometimes is nature and sometimes his own memories—at least until the trick ending.

want to jot down the facts in this diary the way most people would do, but I want the diary to be my friend, and I'm going to call this friend Kitty" (7).

Thus the reflexive subject as Montaigne conceives it can be found in many diaries, memoirs, and other forms of literature. This subject is isolated and solitary, or at least it feels that it is all alone. The world of objects and other people exists primarily to reflect the solitary subject back upon itself. But this self-regarding self is necessarily fragmented into at least three parts: the subject speaking, the object spoken about, and the audience spoken to. In addition, the subject may project itself into the world by speaking to or through imagined characters; it may also form itself by borrowing the words or deeds of others.

IV.

Dostoevsky's *Notes from Underground* is both an example of self-reflexive narrative and its critique—a critique of the empty Cartesian self. This self is solitary; it is its own audience; it is full of self-love and self-loathing; it forms its identity by imitating the words of others. All of these are familiar features of the Cartesian self, as we have seen in our discussion. But at the end of the story, the Underground Man confronts another self, and we see the possibility of something beyond the Cartesian self, if only for a moment.

"Now what does a decent man like to talk about most?" the Underground Man asks near the beginning of his confessions. "Himself, of course. So I'll talk about myself" (Part One, II, 93). The Underground Man's Cartesian self, however, is empty and without definition: "I couldn't manage to make myself nasty or, for that matter, friendly, crooked or honest, a hero or an insect" (Part One, I, 92). As Mikhail Bakhtin notes:

> The Underground Man not only dissolves in himself all possible fixed features of his person, making them all the object of his own introspection, but in fact he no longer has any such traits at all, no fixed definitions, there is nothing to say about him, he figures not as a person taken from life but rather as the subject of consciousness and dream. (51)[11]

The self of the Underground Man has no intrinsic traits; it is formed by

---

[11]. In addition to Bakhtin, *Problems of Dostoevski's Poetics*, I have found Martinsen, "Of Shame and Human Bondage," particularly useful; also Jackson, *The Art of Dostoevsky*; Anderson, *Dostoevsky: Myths of Duality*; Wasiolek, *Dostoevsky: The Major Fiction*; Frank, "Nihilism and *Notes from Underground*."

imitation: thus, when he imagines in lurid detail all that might happen if he should challenge Zverkov to a duel, he realizes that all the details of his imagination were taken from stories by Pushkin or Lermontov (Part Two, V, 162). Furthermore, the Underground Man is his own audience:

> Now, in my case, I'm writing this just for myself, for even if I do address myself to imaginary readers, I do it only because it makes it easier for me to write. It's just a matter of form, nothing else. For as I said before, I'll never have any readers. (Part One, XI, 122)

Although the Underground Man pretends to have a conversation with his imaginary readers, typically he puts words in their mouths:

> I'd feel better if I could only believe something of what I've written down here. But I swear I can't believe a single word of it. That is, I believe it in a way, but at the same time, I feel like I'm lying like a son of a bitch.
> "Then why have you written all this," you may ask? (Part One, XI, 120)

These words, however, are not made up out of nothing:

> I've been listening to your words through a crack for forty years, while sitting in my hole under the floor. That was all I had to do. So, by now, I know them by heart, and it's no wonder I've been able to set them down like this, in literary form. (Part One, XI, 121)

Although he has been listening to these voices of other people, all he has heard is what they might say about him. He is unable to enter into any real dialogue: he takes the words he has overheard and constructs from them an imaginary conversation, which will never have any reader other than himself. As we will see, the Underground Man's inability to have any genuine relation to others is a persistent feature of his character. If Montaigne's *Essays* show a successful example of the furnishing of the self, then *Notes from Underground* shows the failure of the process.

The Underground Man is solitary partly because no one pays much attention to him. He tries to make others notice him, but with little success, and every attempt to be noticed turns into a conflict, at least in his fantasies. In the first episode of Part Two, he goes into a tavern where he inadvertently blocks the path of an officer, who simply moves him out of his way: "I could've forgiven anything, including a beating, but that was too much—to be brushed aside without being noticed!" (Part Two, I, 130). He nurses his grudge for years and finally manages to bump into the officer on Nevsky Avenue (Part Two, I, 135).

In the next episode, he goes to visit some old school friends, but they pay no attention to him: "Apparently I was something like a housefly in their eyes" (Part Two, III, 140). He manages to intrude himself into their party given in honor of his former schoolmate Zverkov, where he feels patronized, ignored, and generally humiliated, and he makes a great scene. The others leave to go to a brothel, and after a while he follows them, intending to challenge Zverkov to a duel, but by the time he arrives, they have left.

In the brothel, the Underground Man hires one of the girls, Liza; she, unlike the others, does pay attention to him: "I noticed that right next to me, two wide-open eyes were examining me curiously and insistently. The eyes looked at me with a cold, unsympathetic, sullen detachment that made me feel uncomfortable" (Part Two, VI, 164). They have a long talk in which he tries to make her feel the degradation and slavery of her life in order to exercise his power over her. But she engages with him in a way no one else does, and she provides the closest thing to a true dialogue in the story.

A few days later Liza comes to the Underground Man's apartment and tells him she wants to leave the brothel.[12] They have a great confrontation, in which Liza says very little, while the narrator rages at her. The result of his raging surprises him:

> What actually happened was that Liza, whom I had humiliated and crushed, understood much more than I had thought. Out of all I had said, she had understood what a sincerely loving woman would understand first—that I myself was unhappy. . . .
> Then she flung her arms around my neck and burst into tears, and I too lost all control and sobbed as I never had in my life before. (Part Two, IX, 197–98)

For a moment there is the hint of a naïve and sentimental ending—the two lost characters will save each other and live happily ever after. But, of course, that is not what Dostoyevsky has in mind: his narrator is too contemptible a creature for that. As Liza and the Underground Man are embracing and weeping, he realizes that this new situation is intolerable:

---

12. The story of Liza is interrupted by the Underground Man's description of his servant, Apollon; this serves to remind the reader of the Underground Man's hostile and subservient relation, and thus the importance of the possibility that his relationship with Liza will be different.

I began to realize, at first distantly, that it would be terribly awkward for me to lift my heard now and look Liza in the eyes. I'm not sure what I was ashamed of, but I was ashamed, all right. The thought also flashed through the turmoil in my head that we had definitely changed places, Liza and I, that she now had the heroic role, and I was the beaten-down, crushed creature she had been. . . . (Part II, IX, 198)

But as the Underground Man tells us, "for me, loving means bullying and dominating" (Part II, X, 199). He cannot bear Liza's gaze, and so he drives her away: "I wanted her to vanish. I wanted *peace*. I wanted to be left alone in my mousehole" (Part II, IX, 200). Once the story has demonstrated the emptiness of the Underground Man's Cartesian self and his inability to break out of that Cartesian self into any kind of mutual regard, the story has nowhere to go and must simply come to an abrupt end.

In this story, then, we see a second subject flash into existence, but only for a moment. We see the possibility of a more complex world of selves, but this world is in many ways no better than the solitary world of the Cartesian self. In this new world, the relation of one subject to another is seen as essentially violent: the second subject must be subjected; it must become an object in the narrator's consciousness. One or the other must be master. But to understand this struggle of two subjects, we must introduce Hegel's Dialectic of the Master and the Slave, the topic of the next chapter.

CHAPTER 3

The Dyadic Subject
Hegel, Aristophanes, Hemingway

The Cartesian self is essentially solitary, monadic; other selves may exist, but they are proved to exist only by deduction, and they exist only in relation to the Cartesian self. Dostoevsky's *Notes from Underground* challenges this Cartesian ideal of the self when a second and independent self flashes into being, if only for a moment. The Underground Man understands the relationship of two selves only as a struggle—a struggle that must end in the domination of one self and the slavery of the other. The Underground Man cannot bear the possibility that the world could contain two equal selves, and so the story breaks down and comes to a stop.

Many narratives, however, essentially concern the relationship of two characters. In this chapter I discuss two philosophic versions of this dyadic subjectivity: in Hegel's parable of the Master and the Slave, the two selves are antagonists; in Aristophanes' story of the divided self (as told in Plato's *Symposium*), the two selves are lovers. These two patterns can be combined in more complex patterns of conflict and affection, Thanatos and Eros, as seen in *The Epic of Gilgamesh* and *A Farewell to Arms*.

The Hegelian and Aristophanic models of the self mark an important change in what might be called narrative geometry. The previous models of the self all assume that the self is single: the ideal Cartesian self is a single point, in which the two I's of the cogito are identical; the self as described by William James distinguishes the I from the me, but both are aspects of a single identity, a single person; and Montaigne's self regards itself as if in a mirror. Dyadic plots, however, require two selves, two distinct points of subjectivity. Later chapters will describe more complicated narrative geometries.

I.

Hegel, like Descartes, uses a story to present his model of the self. This story, the Parable of the Master and the Slave from the *Phenomenology of Spirit*, sections 178 to 196, is one of the most famous and influential passages in all of Hegel's philosophy.[1] In this parable Hegel discusses the development of self-consciousness through the interaction of one consciousness with another. In brief, Hegel supposes that one self can become self-conscious only by confronting another self (section 178). In this confrontation, the two consciousnesses must be antagonists and must fight to the death (section 187).[2] One of these self-consciousnesses will surrender to the other, through its attachment to life. The victor becomes the master while the vanquished becomes the slave (section 189), but the position of the slave turns out to be the more favorable for further development of consciousness. The development of the master's self-consciousness is stymied, because the master is dependent on the slave both for recognition and for material satisfactions (section 190). The slave, however, through its experience of dread and through its work in the material world, comes to achieve an understanding of itself as self-consciousness (sections 193–94).

Although Hegel's parable does not present a complete account of subjectivity, Hegel's concept of the self introduces important elements not present in the Cartesian theory, first because it gives a role to desire in the development of self-consciousness, and second because it understands that the self needs company. The Cartesian ego is all alone, at least at the beginning. Other subjects can be deduced, but this deduction is a secondary development, after the self has established itself as a thinking substance, and these other selves are always supporting players to the Cartesian self's starring role. Hegel's self, however, lives in the world, feels desire, and comes into being only through its interaction with another self.

Hegel's model of self-consciousness based on the self and the other,

---

1. References (which are identified by section number rather than page number) are from A. V. Miller's translation of *The Phenomenology of Spirit*. Hegel's German title, *Phänomenologie des Geistes*, is sometimes translated as *The Phenomenology of Mind*, as in the translation by J. B. Baillie; Baillie's translation sometimes makes more sense than Miller's, but Miller's, so I understand, is closer to Hegel's German. Note that Miller uses the terms "lord" and "bondsman" where I use "master" and "slave." I have consulted several commentaries: Peter Singer's slim *Hegel*; Charles Taylor's massive *Hegel*; and *Hegel's Dialectic of Desire and Recognition*, a collection of articles edited by John O'Neill.

2. The two characters in the Hegelian parable will often correspond to the grammatical subject and object; the typical Hegelian sentence will therefore be transitive, whereas the typical Cartesian sentence is intransitive.

the subject and the object, has been extremely influential in later thought. In addition, we will see that many narratives seem to follow the Hegelian pattern more or less closely—even when it is clear that the storyteller was not influenced by Hegel: just as Montaigne anticipates the Cartesian self, many narratives before Hegel anticipate Hegel's model of subjectivity. Hegel's model is hardly the last word on the topic—as we will see, other models add important aspects of subjectivity that Hegel does not take into account. But he does describe a very common and very important narrative pattern.

Hegel's story does have a certain plausibility. It is easy to suppose that without any contact with others we would never achieve self-awareness. I do not mean to suggest, however, that Descartes' version of the solitary self is wrong while Hegel's version of the self in conflict with another self is right. For the student of narrative and the student of human nature, each of these stories of the self has validity, as do others which we will investigate in later chapters.

I do not claim to understand all of Hegel's parable, and I think the commentators I have consulted have not understood all of it, either; or at least they tend to leave certain difficult parts of the passage out of the discussion. The commentators do seem to agree more or less about the basic shape and also the overall moral of the story, as I have summarized it. Beyond this basic agreement, however, lie many difficulties of interpretation. For my purposes, two questions are most important: First, can the process as Hegel describes it occur within a solitary Cartesian self, or must there be a confrontation of two separate selves? Second, is this confrontation of two selves necessarily antagonistic?

According to the most obvious interpretation of Hegel's parable, the solitary Cartesian self cannot achieve self-consciousness; that is, consciousness by itself cannot achieve self-consciousness, and neither can consciousness achieve self-consciousness simply by becoming aware of external objects. In order to become self-conscious, consciousness needs to become aware of another consciousness, and it needs to be recognized and acknowledged by that other consciousness. Thus an individual person can become self-conscious only through interaction with another individual person who is also becoming self-conscious through mutual antagonism.

It is possible, however, that this confrontation of two consciousnesses facing each other may be located in one person rather than two, if consciousness within an individual can be divided. That is, self-consciousness may develop within a single self, if the self becomes aware of itself as a self.[3] This

---

3. Compare Norbert Wiley, *The Semiotic Self*, p. 37: "When Hegel analyzed the master-

process would be roughly the same as Descartes' meditation, in which the doubting self as subject becomes aware of the existing self as object: "I [first self-consciousness] think, therefore I [second self-consciousness] am" or "I [as subject] notice myself [as object]." Self-reflexive narratives, such as those discussed in the previous chapter, and also some stories of the double, such as Robert Louis Stevenson's *The Strange Case of Dr. Jekyll and Mr. Hyde*, could express this interpretation of the Hegelian process within a single person.

Another interpretation, however, would suppose that Hegel has in mind a sort of collective self-consciousness, which becomes manifest in the various self-consciousnesses which we think of as individual persons. This story is then not the story of an individual person coming to self-consciousness through self-reflection or through conflict with another individual consciousness; rather, it is the story of self-consciousness taking shape within the world through a process of emanation and division.

Still another interpretation would say that this parable is the story of God's creation of the world, and more particularly the creation of human beings. According to some theologians, such as the neo-Platonic philosopher Plotinus, God created the world from himself: the world is a sort of emanation of God's own being. In that case, the world comes out of God, and our individual and personal self-consciousnesses come out of God's self-consciousness. This story can include the previous two interpretations: in effect, God is the subject who says "I think, therefore I am," and the objective part of this realization is the created world; furthermore, God is the collective self-consciousness of which personal self-consciousnesses are emanations. One implication of this interpretation might be that God is not self-conscious until another self-consciousness has come into being; we are created in the image of God, and our creation allows God to become self-conscious.

It is primarily at the beginning of Hegel's parable that the number of individuals involved seems ambiguous; the later stages of the parable seem to locate more clearly the process of achieving self-consciousness in two individuals. In Hegel, the process of achieving self-consciousness is doubled, because two consciousnesses go through the same experience, each in relation to the other. In a sense, Hegel's parable grows out of and claims to supersede the Cartesian model. Narratives that deal with the conflict of two characters can be called Hegelian narratives, as opposed to Cartesian self-reflexive narratives, which concern one primary character.[4]

---

slave relationship, he was usually talking about something interpersonal, between two freestanding human beings. But at times, in a way that was confusing and never clearly explained, he was talking intra-personally, about the relation between parts of the self. . . ."

4. But we will see in section III of this chapter that there is another form of dyadic narra-

Why, then, does the relationship between the two Hegelian consciousnesses have to be antagonistic? The argument here partly depends on the distinction between "being" and "becoming": being is positive, while becoming is negative, because becoming involves change, and change involves negating what was before. Objects are negatively characterized because they are part of the world of becoming. Each consciousness initially takes the other consciousness as an object, and therefore not a subject. Where, then, does self-consciousness belong? Is it part of the world of being or the world of becoming? Is it negative (and therefore changing) or positive (and therefore unchanging)?

If self-consciousness is to be part of being, it must present itself by "showing that it is not attached to any specific *existence,* not to the individuality common to existence as such, that it is not attached to life" (section 187)—because, presumably, life is part of the world of becoming, not being. There must be, then, an antagonism between the two self-consciousnesses: "each seeks the death of the other" (section 187). In addition, each stakes its own life, presumably to demonstrate that it is not attached to life, to the world of becoming. "Thus, the relation of the two self-conscious individuals is such that they prove themselves and each other through a life-and-death struggle. They must engage in this struggle, for they must raise their certainty of being *for-themselves* to truth, both in the case of the other and in their own case" (section 187).

This life-and-death struggle consists of two parts: each self-consciousness needs to risk its own life, and it needs to seek the death of the other. First, "it is only through staking one's life that freedom is won; only thus is it proved that for self-consciousness, its essential being is not [just] being, not the immediate form in which it appears, not its submergence in the expanse of life, but rather that there is nothing present in it that could not be regarded as a vanishing moment, that it is only pure being-for-itself" (section 187). Each self-consciousness tries to demonstrate that it is not attached to the world of life, the world of becoming and the negative, but rather to the world of being and the positive. "The person who has not risked his life may well be recognized as a person, but he has not attained to the truth of this recognition as an independent self-consciousness" (section 187).

This requirement may seem extreme. Hegel does seem to allow that a person who has not risked his life can still be a person, but clearly he regards such a person as less than fully self-conscious. I would not reject this part of the story out of hand. In many times and places, the risking of life is not

---

tive, in which the two characters are linked by affection rather than by antagonism.

uncommon. In archaic and classical Greece, for instance, any man had to be ready to join in the defense of his city; and the danger in a woman's life is expressed by Medea, who said (in the play by Euripides) that she would rather stand in the battle-line three times than give birth once. In our time, some of those who risked their lives in the American civil rights movement reported a deep sense of freedom, and the risk was an essential part of that feeling. Freedom was won by people who were not simply attached to life.

But a second part of this process, according to Hegel, is that each self-consciousness must also seek the death of the other: "Similarly, just as each stakes his own life, so each must seek the other's death, for it values the other no more than itself" (section 187). Why does one self-consciousness, one person, need to show that it does not value the other? According to Hegel's argument, "its essential being is present to it in the form of an 'other,' it is outside of itself and must rid itself of its self-externality" (section 187). If the story is still a story about a single consciousness becoming aware of itself as an external object, or if it is about God and the world, the desire of each self-consciousness to destroy the other might have some justification as some kind of mystical unification in the world of being. But if the story is about two persons, I do not understand why one person has to seek the death of the other, and I am not prepared to defend this part of the story as philosophically adequate. It does, however, present one important aspect of subjectivity, and this aspect is often represented in narrative. We often feel that the world is full of conflict and that even our closest relationships are antagonistic. Hegelian narratives, therefore, abound in conflict and violence, as in crime novels or adventure stories.

If one self-consciousness needs to be recognized by another self-consciousness, then the death of one self-consciousness leaves the surviving self-consciousness without recognition. Thus, "self-consciousness learns that life is as essential to it as pure self-consciousness" (section 189). This is a crucial point in Hegel's thought. Though he is an idealist, he is also in a sense a materialist: the world of ideas is in some sense incomplete if it is not manifest in the material world.

In order to gain recognition, the one self-consciousness must somehow keep the other self-consciousness alive. But for some reason which I think Hegel does not clearly explain, these two self-consciousnesses cannot exist on an equal footing; as he says, "to begin with they are unequal and opposed . . . ; one is the independent consciousness whose essential nature is to be for itself, the other is the dependent consciousness whose essential nature is simply to live or to be for another. The former is lord, the other is bondsman" (section 189).

Evidently the life-and-death struggle has been stopped at the point where one self-consciousness is clearly the victor and the other is the vanquished. But the victor does not kill the vanquished. It is enough that the victorious self-consciousness has proved itself ready to die. Perhaps the vanquished has given up; then it has proved that it is not ready to die and thus it has proved that it is not pure self-consciousness. It now exists not simply for itself, but to give recognition to the victorious self-consciousness, the master.

In a sense, the slave is an object to the master's subject. And yet the slave cannot be merely an object, because the master needs the slave's recognition, and recognition can come only from another subject. So if the master is pure subject, the slave is a compound of subject and object. On the other hand, the master needs the slave, since he needs recognition from the slave, and thus the master is no more independent than the slave—perhaps less so. As Hegel says, the master is "a being-for-itself that is for-itself only through another" (section 190).

Hegel then considers the relationship of both the master and the slave to the world of things, the world of objects. The master lives in a world of the subject, while the slave lives in the world of objects. The master deals with this world only through the mediation of the slave—that is, the slave works for the master, and the master's material needs are satisfied through the work of the slave. For the master, the world of things is there simply to be enjoyed, without labor, whereas for the slave, the world of things is there to be worked on. The master's essential nature is to exist only for himself, whereas the actions of the slave are really the actions of the master, simply displaced onto the slave, who has become the master's instrument. (In the terms of my discussion in chapter 9, the slave has instrumental subjectivity.) For the slave, a material object has a measure of independent existence. In Hegel's terms, the slave can't simply annihilate the object; that is, he can't eat the cake he has made, since he has to give it to the master. Pleasure, in this story, is fundamentally consumption. If Hegel's theory of the master and the slave seems adolescent, his theory of desire and pleasure is infantile. Or, to take a more charitable view, Hegel here prefigures the symbolist aesthetic, as expressed by Villiers de l'Isle-Adam in *Axel*: "Live? Our servants will do that for us."

The master has become doubly dependent on the slave, subjectively and objectively: the master needs recognition from the slave, and he needs the things provided by the slave. Thus his position has become the reverse of his intentions (section 193). The position of the slave will also turn out to be reversed. This self-consciousness became the slave because it was afraid to die: "this consciousness has been fearful, not of this or that particular thing or just at odd moments, but its whole being has been seized with dread. In that experience it has been quite unmanned, has trembled in every fiber of its being, and everything solid and stable has been shaken to its foundations. But this pure universal movement, the absolute melting-away of everything stable, is the simple, essential nature of self-consciousness" (section 194). The experience of the slave is thus a deeper experience of self-consciousness than the experience of the master, who has not felt this fundamental dread. If philosophy is the preparation for death, then it is the slave who has become the philosopher.

Furthermore, through this feeling of dread, the slave comes to have a direct experience of the things in the world, through his labor for the master, while the master's relationship to things is indirect. The master's satisfaction of desire is only fleeting, since his relation to reality comes only through consumption: once he has eaten the cake, it's gone. But the slave sees himself changing the world, and he sees that the results of his labor have a certain permanence. In addition, some part of the world now is the result of the slave's own effort. Work, as Hegel says, "is desire held in check, fleetingness staved off; in other words, work forms and shapes the thing" (section 195).

Through labor, the slave comes to see that things have a certain independent existence, and thereby he comes to understand his own independent existence: "in fashioning the thing, he becomes aware that being-for-self belongs to him, that he himself exists essentially and actually in his own right" (section 196). At first, his labor seemed alienated, since it was labor for another, the master, but now it is through his labor that the slave comes to have a mind of his own. This level of self-consciousness the master never achieves.

Hegel's parable probably does not tell much us about slavery as it has actually existed in human society. No doubt many of the oppressed of the world understand something that the oppressors do not, but most often there is a degradation in slavery and other forms of oppression which hinders the full development of self-consciousness.

Nonetheless, something like the pattern of Hegel's parable is very common in narrative. The typical features of Hegelian narratives are, first, a pair of antagonistic characters; second, a conflict high in transitivity, especially including violence or death; and third, some kind of reversal of perspective. Stories with these features must tell us something important about how we sometimes think of ourselves and our relations with others.

II.

Various versions of the Hegelian pattern can be found in narrative, as we will see in this chapter and the next. Some Hegelian stories end in a fight to the death, particularly between doubles; in other stories, there is no fight to the death, but rather a permanent relationship of master and slave, though often the positions of the master and the slave are curiously the reverse of what one might expect. Sometimes the Hegelian pattern is implicit, to be teased out by the reader or the critic, but not infrequently even the characters within the story know what roles they are playing.

John le Carré's spy novel *Call for the Dead* ends with a fight to the death. The two principal characters are George Smiley and Dieter Frey. Smiley is an English spymaster; Frey had been an agent of Smiley's in Germany in the Second World War, but after the war Frey went east to work for the communists, and the two have not seen each other since. In the course of the story, Smiley discovers that Frey has been running agents in England, and eventually the two confront each other and fight. Although Frey is much the stronger, he holds back, and Smiley in his rage pushes him over a bridge and into a river, where he drowns:

> Dieter was leaning back and Smiley saw the clean curve of his throat and chin, as with all his strength he thrust his open hand upwards. His fingers closed over Dieter's jaw and mouth and he pushed further and further. Dieter's hands were at Smiley's throat, then suddenly they were clutching at his collar to save himself as he sank slowly backwards. Smiley beat frantically at his arms and then he was held no more and Dieter was falling, falling into the swirling fog beneath the bridge, and there was silence. No shout, no splash. He was gone; offered like a human sacrifice to the London fog and the foul black river lying beneath it. (141)

The Hegelian nature of Smiley's fight with Frey is brought out in a passage a few pages later, when Smiley is lamenting Frey's death:

> Dieter was dead, and he had killed him. The broken fingers of his right hand, the stiffness of his body and the sickening headache, the nausea of guilt, all testified to this. And Dieter had let him do it, had not fired the gun, had remembered their friendship when Smiley had not. They had fought in a cloud, in the rising stream of the river, in a clearing in a timeless forest: they had met, two friends rejoined, and fought like beasts. Dieter had remembered and Smiley had not. (144)

Stories are not illustrations of philosophic themes, and narrative patterns should not be expected to follow the philosophical forms exactly. Nonetheless, this passage seems impressively Hegelian. The diction places the events in a world of archetypes, as Frey and Dieter become beasts in a timeless forest. It is not clear who is the master and who is the slave, but it is clear that each desires mastery, and so they fight to the death. In the end, Frey proves that he is not wedded to life, not wedded to the world of becoming, and thereby he achieves a kind of purification through death. On the other hand, Smiley kills Frey in order to remain alive, and thereby he achieves a kind of superiority of tragic consciousness through pain, despair, and guilt—all elements of the world of becoming.

The other pattern, in which both characters live in a permanent relationship of master and slave, can be found in Roman comedy, where the tricky slave outwits his master, who is also in many ways dependent on the slave. Shakespeare adopts this pattern in the *Comedy of Errors* (which is closely based on Plautus' comedy *The Brothers Menaechmi*). In Denis Diderot's *Jacques the Fatalist and his Master*, written sometime in the second half of the eighteenth century and published in 1796, Jacques says:

> considering that it is just as impossible for Jacques not to know his ascendancy over his master as it is for his master to be unaware of his own weakness and divest himself of his insolence, it is therefore necessary that Jacques be insolent, and that for the sake of peace his master not notice.... It was ordained that you would have the title to the thing and I would have the thing itself. (161)

In Roman comedy and in Shakespeare's adaptation, as well as in *Jacques the Fatalist*, the relationship of master and slave, or lord and bondsman, is quite literal, but the same language can be used metaphorically to describe other kinds of human relationships, as we see in the following passage from *The Captive*, volume five of Proust's *À la recherche du temps perdu*. Marcel, the narrator, speaks of his relationship with Albertine in terms very like those of the narrator of *Notes from Underground*—though the tone is different, and there is an important twist at the end. At this point in the story, Albertine is living with Marcel, but he suspects that she has other lovers; he attempts to buy her fidelity with gifts and promises, and she responds with a great show of affection and obedience to his desires:

> The frocks that I bought for her, the yacht of which I had spoken to her, the wrappers from Fortuny's, all these things having in this obedience on

> Albertine's part not their recompense, but their complement, appeared to me now as so many privileges that I was enjoying; for the duties and expenditure of a master are part of his dominion and define it, prove it, fully as much as his rights. And these rights which she recognized in me were precisely what gave my expenditure its true character: I had a woman of my own, who, at the first word that I sent to her unexpectedly, made my messenger telephone humbly that she was coming, that she was allowing herself to be brought home immediately. I was more of a master than I had supposed. More of a master, in other words, more of a slave. (108)

Of course Marcel is not literally the master, nor is Albertine literally the slave; nonetheless, these are the terms in which Marcel thinks about the relationship. The master's domination, however, turns out to be an illusion and a paradox, because it depends on the obedience of the slave, purchased through gifts, which the master is privileged to give, in a reversal of Hegel's pattern. Both the master and the slave are bound by the rules of the relationship, but the slave is freer than the master, who depends on the obedience of the slave.

III.

Hegel's parable gives the model for an important and varied group of dyadic narratives, as we will see in chapter 4. There is, however, another group of dyadic narratives; the model for this group is another philosophical fable, this one written by Plato but put in the mouth of the Athenian comic playwright Aristophanes. In the *Symposium,* Plato presents a series of speeches by various Athenians on the topic of love, and in one of these, Plato has Aristophanes explain the origin of the human race. According to this story, what we now consider a whole person is just half of the original form; but the gods cut these double people apart, and now we go around searching for our other halves. Those who were part of a male/female double are heterosexual, while those who were part of a male/male or female/female double are homosexual. It's unlikely that Plato meant this story seriously—he put this fable into the mouth of the comic dramatist Aristophanes—but many people have found it compelling.

Freud, for example, in *Civilization and Its Discontents,* presents a model that must be based on Aristophanes' story: "The individual represents a fusion of two symmetrical halves; one of these, in the opinion of some investigators, is purely male, the other female. It is equally possible that each half was originally hermaphrodite" (chapter IV, 42–43n3). And as we will see in the next chapter, countless stories take the form of Aristophanes' fable.

There are thus two kinds of dyadic narratives. Hegelian stories are fundamentally antagonistic, and these lead to the defeat or death of one character. Aristophanic narratives, on the other hand, lead to some kind of merger of the two characters; the characters are joined by eros rather than by antagonism (though eros at times must be understood as something more inclusive than sex). In an Aristophanic story, each subject tries to find its mate, its double: "When a love relationship is at its height, the lovers . . . are self-sufficient as a pair. . . . In no other case does Eros so clearly reveal what is at the core of his being, the aim of making one out of more than one" (Freud, chapter V, 45).

The Hegelian and the Aristophanic forms of dyadic subjectivity are in a sense opposites—one is a story of antagonism and division, as two selves fight to the death, while the other is a story of affection and union, as two selves attempt to become one. One is the story of Thanatos, the other the story of Eros. And yet these two stories are in a way not only complementary but even in a sense the same. As Freud notes, "the two kinds of drive seldom—perhaps never—appeared in isolation, but alloyed with one another in different and highly varying proportions" (chapter VI, 56). And we find that even in simple Hegelian narratives of antagonism there is often an erotic connection between the antagonists, sometimes at the moment of death, while Aristophanic narratives of affection often involve an antagonism which can be resolved only through the erotic union of the pair.[5]

This ambivalence is clearly evident the ancient *Epic of Gilgamesh*.[6] The story begins as a fairly straightforward Hegelian narrative. Gilgamesh, the great king of Uruk, the mightiest of human beings, has become a tyrant, and the people ask the gods for help. The gods then create an opponent for Gilgamesh—the wild man Enkidu. The two fight; Gilgamesh wins the fight and Enkidu accepts Gilgamesh's supremacy.

At this point the narrative takes an Aristophanic turn, as Gilgamesh and Enkidu become the closest of friends; thus we see a shift from Hegelian conflict and a fight to the death to an Aristophanic close emotional bond.[7] In a

---

5. The grammar of antagonism and affection are similar as well: both can use reciprocal verbs which take the direct object "each other"; this object is sometimes implicit, as in the forms "they fought" and "they kissed."

6. I have used the translation by Andrew George, which I list under his name in the bibliography.

7. The erotic elements in the relationship are quite clear, for instance, in the dream interpretations offered by Gilgamesh's mother in I.262–97, pp. 10–11.

sense, the two opposing subjects form a new unity; this new unity can then find other opposing figures.[8]

Gilgamesh and Enkidu fight and kill the ferocious monster Humbaba, who protects the Cedars of Lebanon. Then the goddess Ishtar proposes to Gilgamesh, but he refuses her (partly because he fears the fate of mortal men who marry goddesses). In revenge Ishtar sends the bull of heaven against Gilgamesh, but he and Enkidu kill the bull, and Enkidu throws a piece of the bull at Ishtar. The gods kill Enkidu; Gilgamesh grieves for him, but his grief is mostly for himself, as Enkidu's death forces him to recognize his own mortality. The end of the story recounts the futile efforts of Gilgamesh to gain immortality and his final acceptance of death.

If this story had been a simple Hegelian narrative, Gilgamesh would have killed or subjugated Enkidu; we have seen this story pattern in le Carré's *Call for the Dead*, and we will see more examples in the next chapter. Instead, the two antagonists become close friends. Enkidu does eventually die, but not at the hands of Gilgamesh. It is through the death of his friend Enkidu that Gilgamesh comes to full self-consciousness and an acceptance of death. This realization comes only because of the mutual love of the two heroes; if Gilgamesh had simply killed Enkidu at the beginning, he might not have been forced to recognize his own mortality. But once they have become the closest of friends, the death of Enkidu is in a sense the death of Gilgamesh, or at least as close to his death as the death of another can be. So the Hegelian realization comes because of an Aristophanic merging of the two, which makes their Hegelian division in death only sharper. In the following section we will examine another version of this pattern in Hemingway's *A Farewell to Arms*.

IV.

The fundamental question raised in Hegelian and Aristophanic narratives is the nature of the self in a world that consists of two characters (rather than in the world of a single character investigated in Cartesian narratives). The Hegelian world is marked by division, conflict, mastery and submission, and finally death. The Aristophanic world, on the other hand, is a world of union rather than division, a world in which each character feels that it becomes a complete self only by uniting with its other half. But as we have seen in our

---

8. For discussion of Gilgamesh and Enkidu as doubles, see Van Nortwick, *Somewhere I Have Never Traveled*, chapter 1, pp. 8–38.

analysis of the *Epic of Gilgamesh*, a narrative may combine elements of both patterns. The point of analysis is not to check off points on one side or the other, but to understand how each narrative uses the various elements of the Hegelian and Aristophanic parables to present its particular view of the world of two selves.

Hemingway's *A Farewell to Arms*, like *The Epic of Gilgamesh*, is a combination of the Hegelian and the Aristophanic. It is both a war story and a love story, and one might expect the Hegelian elements to occur in the war story, and the Aristophanic elements to occur in the love story. (For that narrative geometry, however, we will wait until we examine narratives with three characters, in chapter 5.) Here, however, both the Hegelian and the Aristophanic elements occur in the love story, while the war story acts as counterpoint.

Almost from the beginning of their relationship, Catherine seeks to merge her self with Frederic: at the end of chapter 16, she tells him, "I want what you want. There isn't any me anymore" (100). In chapter 18, she tells him, "There isn't any me. I'm you. Don't make up a separate me" (107). In chapter 21, she says, "We really are the same one and we mustn't misunderstand on purpose" (129). At this early point in their relationship, however, Frederic does not express any desire for this kind of merging of their two selves.[9]

As the relationship develops, however, Frederic comes to share Catherine's sense that they have become a single self. The climax of this process comes in chapter 38, after Frederic has deserted from the army and after he and Catherine have escaped to Switzerland. This passage begins rather oddly, with a discussion of venereal disease, in which Frederic tells Catherine that he has never had syphilis but that he has had gonorrhea. Catherine says that she wishes she had had gonorrhea as well, so that she could have been just like him. Frederic tries to change the subject, but then Catherine suggests that they should have matching hairstyles: "let [your hair] grow a little longer and I could cut mine and we'd be just alike only one of us blond and one of us dark" (269). A moment later she says, "Oh, darling, I want you so much I want to be you too." And this time Frederic matches her: "You are. We're the same one" (270).

The end of the chapter, however, suggests that the merger of these two selves is not complete. One night Frederic wakes up and realizes that Cath-

---

9. As Daniel Schneider notes, "Like another Catherine, Brontë's Catherine Earnshaw, she *is* her lover: her temperamental affinity to Frederic is so marked that their right to each other is accepted almost from the first moment of meeting. Thus she is, in a sense, not a distinct character at all but Frederic's bitterness or his desire objectified" ("The Novel as Pure Poetry," p. 17). In this analysis Catherine is the objectification of Frederic's attitudes, but he is not the objectification of hers.

erine is also awake. After a short conversation, he says that they should go back to sleep, and she says, "Let's go to sleep at exactly the same moment." Catherine does go to sleep, but he does not. "I was awake for quite a long time thinking about things and watching Catherine sleeping, the moonlight on her face" (271). We can sympathize with his concern and his affection, if that is what is implied here, but we have to note that Frederic fails to fulfill Catherine's desire for complete union.

Catherine tends to subordinate herself to Frederic—that is, to put herself in the position of slave to his master. It is not clear that Frederic demands this submission, but he does little to discourage it. Catherine's submissiveness to some extent derives from her insecurity. For example, just before Frederic's operation, she asks him questions about other women he has been with: he says he has never loved another woman, that he has never been with another woman, and she says that she is not afraid of any other woman; the whole dialogue is a study in insincerity. Near the end of this passage Catherine tells Frederic, "I'll say just what you wish and I'll do what you wish and then you will never want any other girls, will you?" A moment later she says, "I do anything you want" and "I want what you want. There isn't any me any more. Just what you want" (100). Robert Lewis argues that Hemingway needed "a heroine who lacked a self":

> She doesn't care what they do or when they go; whatever Henry wants is fine with her; she will be what he wants, and they will never fight because if anything ever came between them they would "be gone"; she doesn't "live at all" when they are apart even briefly....[10]

Lewis may be exaggerating his case. Catherine is something more than a person without a self. She begins her relationship with Frederic by using him for her own purposes, as she makes him play the part of her dead fiancé in a somewhat morbid charade (34–35). She displays a good deal of courage and good humor during their escape to Switzerland. Moreover, as Sandra Whipple Spanier argues, Catherine at the beginning of the story understands what Frederic learns at the end, partly through her example:[11]

10. Robert W. Lewis, *Hemingway on Love*, p. 48. Millicent Bell calls Catherine "a sort of inflated rubber woman available at will to the onanistic dreamer" ("Pseudoautobiography and Personal Metaphor," p. 119), and Gerry Brenner argues that Catherine's desire "to merge her identity into his" shows "psychological dependency, not selflessness"; furthermore, "her fragile grasp of reality" shows that she is "a marginally neurotic woman who is more than a little out of her head" (*Concealments in Hemingway's Works*, p. 39 and p. 38).

11. Sandra Whipple Spanier, "Hemingway's Unknown Soldier: Catherine Barkley, the Critics, and the Great War," pp. 84–85. See also Sandra Whipple Spanier, "Catherine Berkley and the

Catherine had "realized" the war before the novel began. Her faith in traditional values was blown to bits offstage, along with her fiancé. She already knows what Frederic will learn. . . . Catherine has come to their relationship painfully wiser to the world than is the young man who happens into the war thinking it has nothing to do with him.

It has been easy for critics to see just one side or the other of this complex portrait, and consequently to blame the selfless doll or to praise the Hemingway code hero, but a proper understanding of her character and role must keep both aspects in mind.

The Hegelian parable insists that the two consciousnesses in the story are fundamentally antagonistic. At the very beginning of their relationship, Catherine and Henry do have a fight: he tries to kiss her and she slaps him hard enough to bring tears to his eyes. She apologizes, he feels that he has the advantage, and a few moments later they kiss (29–30). This fight is structurally similar to the initial fight between Gilgamesh and Enkidu, after which the two antagonists become fast friends.

And indeed, after this, Catherine and Henry do not fight; instead, they talk about how important it is that they do not and should not fight:

> "We both really are the same one and we mustn't misunderstand each other on purpose."
> "We won't."
> "But people do. They love each other and they misunderstand on purpose and they fight and then suddenly they aren't the same one."
> "We won't fight."
> "We mustn't. Because there's only us two and in the world there's all the rest of them. If anything comes between us we're gone and then they have us." (129)

This passage states a number of themes important for my argument: it shows the sense of the two selves against the world, the merger of these two selves into one, and the danger that fighting will destroy the merger of the selves.

As the passage continues, another important theme of the novel is stated, as Frederic tells Catherine, "They won't get us. . . . Because you're too brave. Nothing happens to the brave." This, of course, is in sharp contrast to the famous statement Frederic makes later on, in chapter 34, from his perspective as narrator looking back on the events of the story:

Hemingway Code: Ritual and Survival in *A Farewell to Arms*."

> If people bring so much courage to this world the world has to kill them to break them, so of course it kills them. The world breaks every one and afterward many are strong at the broken places. But those that will not break it kills. It kills the very good and the very gentle and the very brave impartially. If you are none of these you can be sure it will kill you too but there will be no special hurry. (226)

Death or the threat of death is an essential element in the Hegelian model of the self, because it is the knowledge of death that leads to self-consciousness and an understanding of the worlds of being and becoming. In the pure Hegelian story, the death or threat of death is caused by a conflict between the two selves; we have seen an instance of this pattern in the passage quoted above from le Carré's *Call for the Dead*, where Smiley gains a new understanding after he kills Frey. Death is certainly the crucial event in *A Farewell to Arms*, but here, as in *The Epic of Gilgamesh*, the death is not the direct result of the antagonism of the two characters.

Some critics, however, have argued that Frederic is glad that Catherine dies and that in a sense he is responsible for her death. In interpretations of this kind, the novel is deeply misogynistic, and it probably represents Hemingway's own hostility to women. According to Judith Fetterley, for example, "while the novel's surface investment is in idealization, behind that idealization is a hostility whose full measure can be taken from the fact that Catherine dies and dies because she is a woman." Furthermore, "[Catherine's] death, however much it may be shaped as biological accident, is in fact the fulfillment of his own unconscious wish, his need to kill her lest she kill him"; and "Her death is the logical consequence of the cumulative hostilities Frederic feels toward her, and the final expression of the connection between the themes of love and war." Fetterley goes so far as to call Frederic "the agent of her death."[12]

It would be an obtuse reader of this novel who would insist that there is nothing going on behind or beneath the words on the page. It would be wrong, however, to ignore the words, and any deep interpretation must somehow be based on the evidence of the words; otherwise, the critic can be accused of reading into rather than reading. I think there is good evidence for some tension and perhaps even hostility between Frederic and Catherine, particularly after they have escaped to Switzerland, both in her fear that he is

---

12. These quotations are from Judith Fetterley, *The Resisting Reader*, pp. 49, 53, 62, and xvi. Fetterley is not the first critic to have made this kind of interpretation; Robert W. Lewis Jr., for instance, argues that "There is a pseudo-tragic ring to the ending, for in the depths of his mind Henry is really glad that Catherine dies. . . ." (*Hemingway on Love*, p. 49).

dissatisfied and in his nervous insistence that everything is fine. It is another thing to argue that he is glad that she dies, and I do not see the evidence for this position.[13] But even if one believes that Frederic feels some (unexpressed) relief along with his sadness when first the baby and then Catherine dies, even if one believes that all his expression of grief is intended to deceive not only the reader but himself, it is another step to argue that Frederic is the direct cause or the agent of Catherine's death. In effect, Fetterley reads *A Farewell to Arms* as simply Hegelian, a story of hostility and conflict leading to death, with the added element of misogyny; I believe that such a reading reduces the complexity of the plot, which combines both Hegelian and Aristophanic elements, in somewhat the way these elements were combined in *The Epic of Gilgamesh*.

Fetterley's analysis, as James Phelan points out, fails to take into account the progression of the plot and the changes in the characters.[14] Most particularly, Frederic changes over the course of the story. He begins as "a callow, unreflective, self-centered youth, who is over his head both in the war and in his relationship with Catherine," but "[t]he progression traces Frederic's slow evolution into a mature man who both learns and faces up to what the narrative presents as the overwhelming truth of his existence" (172). This mature knowledge is "ultimately attained through his witnessing of the death of his child and especially the death of Catherine" (173). This is the knowledge expressed in the famous thematic summation in chapter 34, quoted above, and recapitulated at the very end of the story, in chapter 41, as Catherine is dying:

> Now Catherine would die. That was what you did. You died. You did not know what it was about. You never had time to learn. They threw you in and told you the rules and the first time they caught you off base they killed

---

13. It is perhaps worth noting that Frederic did not have to search for Catherine after he deserted from the army. I think this is partly the point of the conversation with Fergy in chapter 34 (p. 224), in which she says, "You had a love affair all summer and got this girl with child and now I suppose you'll sneak off." Hemingway is indicating what Frederic could have done but did not do. Moreover, Frederic expresses his fear and grief forcefully, for instance, in the "Please God" interior monologue near the end of chapter 41, as he is waiting to see Catherine in the hospital. Fetterley does not comment on this passage: it is not part of her reading of the novel.

14. Phelan finds three problematic methodological assumptions in Fetterley's argument: 1) "There is no significant progression in the book, except for its gradual revelation of male hostility towards women"; 2) "The male characters can be seen as reliably reflecting Hemingway's beliefs"; 3) "Efficient causes are actually final causes" (*Reading People, Reading Plots*, pp. 169 and 170). I might phrase point 3 the other way around, that Fetterley takes final causes to be efficient causes, or rather that she takes thoughts to be causes; but in any case I agree that there is a problem in Fetterley's view of causation in the story.

you. Or they killed you gratuitously like Aymo. Or gave you the syphilis like Rinaldi. But they killed you in the end. You could count on that. They would kill you. (293)

The achievement of self-consciousness through death or the threat of death is an essential part of the Hegelian parable, and in the parable this kind of self-consciousness is achieved through battle. Modern warfare does not typically offer the kinds of duels that would satisfy the Hegelian parable, the kinds of duels we see, for example, in ancient epic. Frederic, in any case, does not achieve self-consciousness through the war. He gains this knowledge and self-consciousness neither from his own injury, nor from observing the deaths of others, nor from participating in the killing of the sergeant, nor from his narrow escape from execution. He can learn this lesson only from the death of Catherine, his other self, just as Gilgamesh could learn only from the death of Enkidu. The Hegelian lesson is learned through an Aristophanic relationship. The war is a counterpoint to the love story because it shows all of the ways in which Frederic does not and cannot gain knowledge before we see the only way in which he can. Then, once he has learned this lesson, he can read it back into earlier experiences, such as the death of Aymo or Rinaldi's syphilis.

It is true, nonetheless, that this achievement comes at the cost of Catherine's death. As Fetterley says, "Catherine dies and dies because she is a woman" (49). In Hegelian stories, one of the two characters has to die or submit, and the same holds for combined Hegelian/Aristophanic stories. In *The Epic of Gilgamesh,* both characters are male, and therefore there is no gender disparity when Enkidu dies. Hemingway has chosen to write a heterosexual love story with a Hegelian ending, and in such a plot there is no escape from inequality.

One can legitimately ask, however, if the story could have been written the other way around, with the death of a male character leading to the achievement of self-consciousness by a female character. The answer of course is that this story has been written, by Hemingway, as a part of this novel: the knowledge Catherine has achieved at the beginning of the story she achieved because her fiancé was killed in the war. Thus there are really two Hegelian/Aristophanic plots in the novel: in the first, a woman gains self-consciousness through the death in war of the man she loves; in the second, a man gains self-consciousness through the death in childbirth of the woman he loves.[15]

---

15. We may remember here Medea's remark noted above that she would rather stand in the battle-line three times than give birth once.

This novel, in my opinion, is not without flaws. I find the characterization somewhat flat. I am not convinced that the events of the story support the theme; I am not convinced that the world has any special grudge against the very good and the very gentle and the very brave. At best I can see why the events make Frederic feels what he feels, but I am not moved by these events to agree with his feeling. The plot, however, has a complex symmetry and elegance which are essential to the meaning of the story and which must be taken into account in judging its success.

CHAPTER 4

Doubles and Doubled Doubles
Knowles and Austen

Narratives of the double reflect the common feeling of division within the self or the feeling that one person may have an essential affinity or antagonism with another. This chapter begins with a brief account of a proposed continuum of narrative doubles, followed by a more extended analysis of one particular doubled narrative, John Knowles's *A Separate Peace,* which I compare to *A Farewell to Arms.* In some stories, a character may have more than one double, and these doubled doubles can be used to define the extremes within which a central character sits, as in *The Lord of the Rings* or *Pride and Prejudice.* The doubled double plays a part in a kind of subjectivity that is found within narrative and without.

I.

Stories of the double can often be understood as Hegelian or Aristophanic narratives.[1] These stories can take the form of a single self divided against itself or, more often, two separate but closely linked individuals. Various arrangements are possible, and these may be arranged in a rough continuum, based on the closeness of the two halves of the double. The following list selects positions on this continuum. The order is not to be taken very seri-

---

1. There is a considerable body of scholarship on doubles in literature. I have found especially useful C. F. Keppler's *The Literature of the Second Self;* see also Ralph Tymms, *Doubles in Literary Psychology,* and John Herdman, *The Double in Nineteenth-Century Fiction.* Otto Rank's *The Double* ends with a psychoanalytic interpretation of the theme.

ously: other arrangements can be justified, and some narratives may belong to more than one position. A single example is given for each type, but the reader will be able supplement the list:

> The Divided Self: *The Strange Case of Dr. Jekyll and Mr. Hyde* (Stevenson)
> The Externalized Self: *Peter Schlemihl* (Chamisso)
> The Disguised Self: *The Scarlet Pimpernel* (Orczy)
> Conjoined Twins: "Those Incredible Twins" (Twain)
> Identical Twins: *The Comedy of Errors* (Shakespeare)
> Fraternal Twins: *Twelfth Night* (Shakespeare)
> Siblings: *The Master of Ballantrae* (Stevenson)
> Half-Siblings: *Oliver Twist* (Dickens)
> Identical Relatives: *The Prisoner of Zenda* (Hope)
> Identical Strangers: "William Wilson" (Poe)
> People Born on the Same Night: *Pudd'nhead Wilson* (Twain)
> Archenemies: "The Final Problem" (Doyle)
> Romantic Couples: *Pride and Prejudice* (Austen)

Each of these narratives presents some version of dyadic subjectivity. I discuss each briefly in section II of this chapter to suggest the range and variety of dyadic relationships possible in narrative. Each narrative can, of course, be read independently, but the narratives take on new meaning when they are seen in relationship to each other—just as a melody takes new meaning if it is heard, for instance, as one element in a theme and variations.

II.

The Divided Self

Stories of the divided self express the common idea that a person has two sides, one good, one bad. These stories often have an element of the fantastic or the uncanny. An obvious example is Robert Louis Stevenson's *The Strange Case of Dr. Jekyll and Mr. Hyde*. The idea of personal duality is clear in the structure of the story, but Stevenson makes it explicit particularly in the final section of the story, the short autobiography of Henry Jekyll. Even before his discovery of the potion that would allow him to turn himself into Mr. Hyde, he was "committed to a profound duplicity of life" (82). "With every day, and from both sides of my intelligence, the moral and the intellectual, I thus drew steadily nearer to that truth, by whose partial discovery I have been doomed to such a dreadful shipwreck: that man is not truly one, but truly two" (82). The potion reveals a duality that was always inherent in Dr. Jekyll and that Jekyll suggests is inherent in us all. This idea of the duality of the individual is latent in many stories of the double; even when the two halves of the double are clearly different individuals, there is often some sense that together they would make up a single whole person.

The Disguised Self

A single person can become double by adopting a disguise. Whereas the division within the self is usually involuntary, disguise is usually chosen. The best disguise, however, retains some of the duality of the divided self: that is, the two sides of the double are quite unalike or even opposites. An example is *The Scarlet Pimpernel,* by the Baroness Orczy. The hero of this story is a master of disguise. In his public persona he is a foolish English aristocrat, despised even by his wife. In secret, he is the dashing Scarlet Pimpernel, who cleverly manages to help French aristocrats escape from the terror of the French Revolution. At the end his true character is revealed, and he wins the love of his wife.

The disguised self and the divided self are in a sense two versions of the same story: one version is a nightmare, in which the secret self is fundamentally evil, whereas the other is a fantasy of wish fulfillment, in which the secret self is powerful and heroic. (Other disguised selves include Patroklos in the *Iliad* and Sidney Carton in *A Tale of Two Cities;* these belong to a subgroup one might call the *sacrificial double.*)

The Externalized Self

Adelbert Chamisso's short novel, *Peter Schlemihl,* written in German and published in 1814, tells the story of a man who sells his shadow for endless wealth. As soon as he has made the sale, he realizes he has made a disastrous mistake. He tries to keep other people from seeing that he has no shadow. Those who learn the truth are horrified, and eventually he must flee from the company of all others, except for his faithful dog. Evidently, the shadow is a symbol, but exactly what it means is difficult to determine, since it derives its effect from its vagueness. However, in part it seems to represent an externalization of the soul or the self.

Peter Schlemihl is not, I think, much read today, but in its time it was popular and influential. It was quickly translated into the other major European languages, and it probably influenced other writers, including E. T. A. Hoffmann ("Story of the Lost Mirror Image," "The Sandman," and *The Devil's Elixirs*) and also Hans Christian Andersen ("The Shadow").

Twins: Conjoined, Identical, and Fraternal

Twins are common in myths and legends, many of which show at least some of the features of the Hegelian fable. The narrative patterns in these stories of twins vary, but it is common for the twins to be rivals or to represent two different ways of life. Amphion and Zethus were the twin sons of Zeus and Antiope; Amphion became a musician, while Zethus became a herdsman, and in a lost play by Euripides they evidently debated the merits of their respective ways of life. Twins in myth may have different fathers: Herakles had a twin brother, Iphikles; Herakles is the child of Zeus, whereas Iphikles is the child of Amphitryon.[2] In one version of Zoroastrian theology, the supreme god, Ahura Mazda (Wise Lord), had twin sons, Spenta Mainyu (Beneficent Spirit) and Angra Mainyu (Destructive Spirit). The history of the cosmos is the battle between these two forces.[3] Jesus, according to both Matthew 13:55 and Mark 6:3, had brothers, one of whom was named Judas or Jude. In the apocryphal *Gospel of Thomas*, Thomas Judas is called the twin brother of Jesus. According to C. F. Keppler (21–22), some medieval myths identified this person with Judas Iscariot, so that Jesus was betrayed by his twin brother. Literature also has its share of twins. I have already mentioned Shakespeare's *Comedy of Errors*, based largely on Plautus' *Brothers Menaechmi*. Mark Twain's "Those Incredible Twins" involves conjoined twins of different personalities and even different appearance: one is dark and bad, the other is good and fair. (In the novel he developed from this story, *Pudd'nhead Wilson*, these twins are separated, but another doubled pair is added, as I will discuss shortly.)

Fraternal twins are less clearly manifestations of the Hegelian or Aristophanic forms of dyadic subjectivity; on the other hand, unlike identical twins, they can be of opposite sex. Even so, the point is often made that the fraternal

---

2. Herakles also has a female double: in one version of the myth, he spent some time as the slave of Queen Omphale of Lydia, who made him wear women's clothing, while she wore his lion's skin and carried his club. There are many other instances of twins in ancient myth, including Kastor and Polydeuces, Romulus and Remus, and Jacob and Esau. In *The Divine Twins: An Indo-European Myth in Germanic Tradition*, Donald Ward offers a general background to the world mythology about twins, as well as to Indo-European and German myth in particular.

3. A good account of dualistic religion, from Zoroastrianism to the Middle Ages, can be found in Yuri Stoyanov, *The Hidden Tradition in Europe*.

twins are in some sense identical or that they make up a single person, as in Shakespeare's *Twelfth Night* or Arundhati Roy's *The God of Small Things*.

The fascination of twins is easy to understand. In reality, twins often have a special kind of closeness, a way of being that is quite unlike that of a singleton; in literature, identical twins allow all the possibilities of the divided self, including both affection and rivalry, but in a somewhat less fantastic form.

Siblings: Full and Half-

Siblings who are not twins also can be doubles. An ancient example is the story of Cain and Abel, but there are innumerable examples. In Robert Louis Stevenson's *The Master of Ballantrae,* the two brothers, James and Henry, are rivals for the affection of their cousin Alison; I will have more to say about this complex romance later on. Oliver Twist has an evil half-brother, Edward Leeford, known as Monks, who tries to cheat Oliver out of his rights. Of course everything turns out well in the end. Oliver's story is based on a variation of the idea that Birth Will Out: Monks, though legitimate, is the child of a bad marriage; he is morally bad, physically deformed, and subject to fits. Oliver, though illegitimate, is the child of true love; he is morally pure and physically handsome. Again we see the theme of the good aspect and the bad aspect of the double, which we have seen in the story of the divided self and which recurs in so many stories of the double, no matter the relationship.

Identical Relatives

The hero of Anthony Hopes's *The Prisoner of Zenda* is Rudolf Rassendyll, a young English aristocrat of some energy but no ambition. He happens to be the spitting image of a distant relative, Rudolf Elphberg, who is about to be crowned the king of Ruritania. But Rudolf Elphberg is kidnapped, and Rudolf Rassendyll takes his place—and wins the love of the king's intended bride. At the end of the story, Rudolf Elphberg is restored to his position and to his bride, while Rudolf Rassendyll returns to England—and no one is ever the wiser.

Identical Strangers

Edgar Allan Poe's story "William Wilson" has two characters by this name.

(The initials of the name are "Double You, Double You.") The first is the narrator. While he is a student at an English boarding school, the narrator discovers that there is another student there with the same name; as it happens, the two were born on the same day, they arrive at the school on the same day, and they look very much alike. The double imitates the narrator's dress, his physical mannerisms, and even his voice. Some of the students in the school have the impression that the two are brothers. The narrator is a rather willful character, but his double had a practice of interfering in his affairs—not so much directly, but through hints and insinuations. Although, as the narrator admits, his double's suggestions were always for the better course, the narrator most often rejected them with repugnance.

Eventually the narrator flees the school and enters into a life of reckless vice and dissipation. But he finds his debaucheries frustrated by uncanny appearances of his double. Ultimately, he forces his double into a duel and kills him. The double tells him, as he dies:

> "You have conquered, and I yield. Yet henceforward art thou also dead—dead to the world, to Heaven, and to Hope! In me didst thou exist—and, in my death, see by this image, which is thine own, how utterly thou hast murdered thyself." (469)

In this story, then, we find the two sides of the double, the fight to the death, a final reversal, and, perhaps, the increase in self-awareness of the Hegelian parable.

People Born on the Same Day

Mark Twain's novel *Pudd'nhead Wilson* was developed from the story "Those Incredible Twins," which I have mentioned above. In this version, the conjoined twins are divided into two whole people, who play, however, only a minor role in the story. As a kind of compensation, Twain added another set of doubles—two children born on the same day. One of these is white, and the other is legally black, but white in appearance, thirty-one thirty-seconds white in ancestry, and a slave. Roxy, the mother of the slave child, is also the nurse of the white boy. The father of Roxy's child is never named in the story, but there is a hint that the two children have the same father, Roxy's owner; if so, the boys are half-brothers. Roxy fears that her child will be sold into harsher conditions down the river, so she switches the boys, and no one notices. The one born into slavery grows up free, and the one born free grows up a slave. In this Hegelian story, the characters are literally master and Slave, though the positions of their birth have been reversed. The results are complex and hard to summarize, but it is fair to say that the novel is in part a meditation on race and racial essentialism.

Eventually the truth about the birth of the two boys is revealed, and everything works out badly. The child born a slave but raised free becomes a slave and is sold down the river; the child born free but raised as a slave is unable to adjust to his new status as a free man.

The Hegelian pattern is clear. The two boys are two selves confronting each other. They are nearly as close as two people can be: born on the same day, perhaps sons of the same father. And yet their relationship is fundamentally unequal, antagonistic, and violent. The one raised as a slave is shown in a sense to be superior to the master. And there is a reversal, since the master becomes a slave and the slave becomes a master.

Archenemies

Crime fiction and thrillers often feature a hero and his archenemy. A clear example is found in Sir Arthur Conan Doyle's story "The Final Problem," in which Sherlock Holmes and Professor Moriarty fight to the death. As Dr. Watson reports, "An examination by experts leaves little doubt that a personal contest between the two men ended, as it could hardly fail to end in such a situation, in their reeling over [the Reichenbach Falls], locked in each other's arms." These doubles annihilate each other in the embrace of death, whereas the contest in le Carré's *Call for the Dead* leaves Smiley alive, but in despair.

Romantic Couples

Romantic couples count as doubles when the two subjects are seen to be halves of a complete person. Sometimes there is an explicit statement of the doubling: in *Wuthering Heights*, for instance, Catherine says to Nelly Dean, "It would degrade me to marry Heathcliff, now; so he shall never know how I love him; and that, not because he's handsome, Nelly, but because he's more myself than I am. What ever our souls are made of, his and mine are the same..." (121). And then a page later, "My love for Heathcliff resembles the eternal rocks beneath—a source of little visible delight, but necessary. Nelly, I am Heathcliff..." (122).

It may seem that Hegelian antagonism rather than Aristophanic eroticism dominates in these examples of dyadic subjectivity, with the erotic relegated only to romantic doubles. At all points on the continuum, however, there can be a mixture of the two drives; thus the eroticism of *Wuthering Heights* is surely combined with antagonism, whereas, on the other hand, antagonism is mixed with a certain hint of eroticism in *Call for the Dead*, "The Final Problem," and even *The Strange Case of Dr. Jekyll and Mr. Hyde*.[4]

This quick summary shows the great variety found in Hegelian and Aristophanic stories of the double, and also the similarity in fundamental narrative geometry. These stories should not be taken as illustrations of Hegel's parable or of the myth in Plato's *Symposium*: narrative is an independent way of thought, legitimate in its own terms. But all these narratives of the double, taken both individually and as a group, seem to be concerned with the same question raised by Hegel and by Plato: what is it like to be in a world that essentially consists of two selves?

The various narrative investigations of this question tend to deploy the same few themes and devices. These include the ideas that 1) the person is a duality, part good and part bad, or else that one person needs another person as a complement; 2) the two parts of the double engage in a struggle, often to the death; 3) in this struggle both parts may be annihilated, locked in the embrace of death; 4) if one part survives, survival is a dubious victory; and 5) this victory may be an increase in self-awareness, sometimes explicit, but often enough left to the reader to understand and appreciate. And yet each story presents these elements in its own way and creates its own experience of reading. In the following section I turn to a more extended interpretation of one narrative, John Knowles's *A Separate Peace*, and this discussion leads in section IV to patterns of greater complexity.

III.

The events of *A Separate Peace* take place in the summer of 1942, at a prep school in New England. The story is narrated fifteen years later, by one of the students, Gene Forester, who has returned to revisit the places and remember

---

4. Many stories of the romantic double involve a third subject as a further complication; I will discuss stories of this type in chapter 5.

the events with new and more mature understanding. At the time of the story, Gene and Phineas (Finny) are two sixteen-year-old students (Upper Middlers in the school's terminology), best friends and roommates. Ordinarily, students would not be at school during the summer, but special sessions have been arranged to prepare the students more quickly for military service.

The basic situation of the story is somewhat reminiscent of the early parts of Poe's "William Wilson," which also takes place at a boys' school. Gene and Finny are almost as close as the two William Wilsons, but not quite: they are the same height, but Finny weighs five pounds more; they both have birthdays at the end of the summer, but there is no suggestion that they were born on the same day; they occasionally wear each other's clothing, though they do not look particularly alike; Finny is the better athlete, Gene the better student; Finny is the dominant character, and in some ways he tries to influence Gene, just as the second William Wilson tries to influence the narrator of Poe's story.

In the first incident of the story, Finny decides to jump off a tree into the river that runs through the campus. It's a risky jump, and no Upper Middler has ever tried it; only Finny would be crazy enough to dare. He makes the jump, and then Gene, despite his fears, goes next. Gene makes a good jump, but the other boys refuse: "'It's you, pal,' Finny said to me at last, 'just you and me'" (16). On their way back to the dorm, they start to tussle. First Finny trips Gene and sits on him. Then Gene jumps at Finny, and they wrestle. Then Gene attacks again; they seem to be equally matched. Finny, as Gene says, is especially pleased that Gene will fight him (18).

Certainly many adolescent boys like to wrestle with their friends, but there is more here than an affectionate romp. Or perhaps there is more to any affectionate romp than shows on the surface. Gene and Finny are best friends, but gradually Gene begins to feel that they may be the deepest of enemies.

Gene resents Finny's attempts to take him away from studying. Finny has won a series of athletic prizes, and Gene wants to win the academic prizes: "If I was head of the class on Graduation Day and made a speech and won the Ne Plus Ultra Scholastic Achievement Citation, then we would both have come out on top, we would be even, that was all. We would be even . . ." (60). Gene has a sudden realization that Finny is deliberately trying to sabotage his academic work: "He minded, despised the possibility that I might be the head of the school" (61). In his misery, Gene finds a single sustaining thought:

You and Phineas are even already. You are even in enmity. You are both coldly driving ahead for yourselves alone. You hate him for breaking that school swimming record, but so what? He hated you for getting an A in every course but one last term. You would have had an A in that one except for him. Except for him. (62)

But sometime later, Gene's hatred for Finny is shaken. One of the other boys has summoned up the courage to try a jump from the tree into the river, and Finny comes to take Gene to be a witness. Gene protests that he needs to study for a French test. To Gene's surprise, Finny agrees that Gene should study:

> "We kid around a lot and everything, but you have to be serious sometime, about something. If you're really good at something, I mean if there's nobody, or hardly anybody, who's as good as you are, then you've got to be serious about that. Don't mess around, for God's sake." He frowned disapprovingly at me. "Why didn't you say you had to study before? Don't move from that desk. It's going to be all A's for you." (69)

Gene is completely overwhelmed by Finny's response: "He had never been jealous of me for a second. Now I knew that there never was and never could have been any rivalry between us. I was not of the same quality as he" (70).

Gene now insists on going to witness the jump from the tree. When they get to the river, Finny suggests that he and Gene jump from the tree together. They climb the tree and stand on the overhanging limb:

> "Come out a little way," he said, and then we'll jump side by side." [. . .] Holding firmly to the trunk, I took a step toward him, and then my knees bent and I jounced the limb. Finny, his balance gone, swung his head around to look at me for an instant with extreme interest, and then he tumbled sideways, broke through the little branches below and hit the bank with a sickening, unnatural thud. It was the first clumsy physical action I had ever seen him make. With unthinking sureness I moved out on the limb and jumped into the river, every trace of my fear of this forgotten. (70–71)

Finny's leg is shattered and his athletic career is over. The second half of the story works out the consequences of this fall.

Gene and Finny are in a sense almost two aspects of a single person: their near identity is demonstrated while Finny is in the infirmary. Gene tries on Finny's clothes and looks in the mirror:

> I was Phineas, Phineas to the life. I even had his humorous expression in my face, his sharp, optimistic awareness. I had no idea why this gave me such intense relief, but it seemed, standing there in Finny's triumphant shirt, that I would never stumble through the confusions of my own character again. (73–74)[5]

The merging of Gene and Finny is a continuing theme. When Finny comes back to school, in the middle of the fall term, he knows that his athletic career is over, and he trains Gene to take his place (145); and Gene in turn starts to tutor Finny (147): "Finny and I, to our joint double amazement, began to make flashing progress where we had been bumblers before" (147).

Late in the story, some of the other boys stage a sort of kangaroo court to determine what caused Finny to fall. Brinker, the boy who has taken on the role of prosecutor, asks Finny to tell in his own words what happened:

> "What own words?" said Phineas, grimacing up at him with his best you-are-an-idiot expression.
> "I know you haven't got many of your own," said Brinker with a charitable smile. "Use some of Gene's then." (209)

And a little later, Gene himself tells us that "Phineas had thought of me as an extension of himself" (224).

Before the kangaroo court can deliver its verdict, Finny runs out of the room and falls down a flight of stairs. He breaks his leg again, and in the operation to set the bone he dies. In a sense Gene has killed him—or at least he was killed by the sequence of events initiated by Gene—but it must be an important part of Knowles's conception of the story that Finny was not directly killed by Gene. Responsibility is not simple or direct.

Gene does not cry when the doctor tells him that Finny is dead:

> I did not cry then or ever about Finny. I did not cry even when I stood watching him being lowered into his family's strait-laced burial ground outside of Boston. I could not escape a feeling that his was my own funeral, and you do not cry in that case. (242–43)

---

5. The wearing of another person's clothing is a common episode in stories of the double; we have already seen an example in Highsmith's *The Talented Mr. Ripley* in chapter 2. Tom and Dickie, however, are not doubles; in a story of the double, the two characters have a rough equality, as Gene and Finny are equals, but Dickie is only a tool for Tom's fantasy. The idea of the self as a suit of clothes returns in the final chapter of this study.

Clearly Gene and Finny are doubles.[6] Moreover, the Hegelian narrative geometry is clear—or rather the oscillation of the Hegelian and the Aristophanic patterns, an oscillation we have also seen in *A Farewell to Arms* (and in *Call for the Dead* and *The Epic of Gilgamesh*). The two principal characters are complements, almost, in fact, the same person, both in life and in death. They are the best of friends and also the deepest of enemies, and the difference between these two relationships is difficult to discern. They struggle, and in that struggle, one is killed, while the one who is left alive gains some kind of increased awareness.

A Separate Peace is not, I think, particularly obscure or difficult. By and large the critics agree that the theme has something to do with maturity and the loss of innocence.[7] I do not disagree, but as a reader I am more interested in the gradual working out of the relationship between Gene and Finny and in the complex of affection and hatred that drives the events. This may be a story about Gene's loss of innocence, but before it is that, it is a story about two people. If Gene does mature, if he does come to an increased awareness, it is only through the death of his friend and enemy, and through his own responsibility for that death.

No doubt the story makes its point when read in isolation. But when the story is read alongside other Hegelian stories, it becomes clear that it is built with pieces from a stock of traditional themes and devices. The originality of the story, of course, is not diminished when it is seen in this way. No one could say that *A Separate Peace* is the same story as *A Farewell to Arms*; even if they share a fundamental narrative geometry and use many of the same motifs, and even if their themes are somewhat similar, each story moves in its own way through its own situations and its own characters and their very particular relationships. But both stories are explorations of dyadic subjectivity. If the Hegelian parable or the fable Plato puts in the mouth of Aristophanes have philosophic value as accounts of the dyadic self, then so do these various stories of the double.

---

6. The point has been recognized by critics; see, for example, Hallman Bell Bryant, *A Separate Peace: The War Within*, pp. 63–65.
7. Thus according to Marvin E. Mengeling, Gene's maturation "will come by his siphoning off bits and pieces of the Phineas spirit and world view, incorporating their stuff into himself, and thus rendering himself whole" ("*A Separate Peace*: Meaning and Myth," pp. 1323–33); and according to James M. Mellard, the theme is "the growth to maturity through the loss of adolescent innocence and the acceptance of adult experience" ("Counterpoint and 'Double Vision' in *A Separate Peace*," p. 127). These themes are similar to, but hardly the same as, the theme of *A Farewell to Arms*, which is more concerned with the acceptance of death.

IV.

In my analysis of *A Separate Peace*, I have concentrated on the relationship of Gene and Finny as doubles, but this account is a simplification. In truth, even stories of the double usually have more than two characters. Sometimes these other characters are simply there to move the furniture, as it were, but some play a role in the narrative geometry, as further doubles, doubled doubles. Doubled doubles often are used to define the extremes within which a central character negotiates the problems of the narrative. These doubled doubles thus function as narrative devices, but they also reveal a kind of subjectivity that moves beyond the Hegelian and Platonic dyads.

Gene and Finny are not the only characters in *A Separate Peace*. The most important, after Gene and Finny, is without question Edwin Lepellier, known to the other boys as Leper. At the beginning, he is simply one of the witnesses to Finny's and Gene's first jump from the tree. He is next mentioned as the oldest boy in the class, and therefore the first to become eligible for the draft. A little later in the story, it is Leper who declares that he will try to jump from the tree. Leper never does make the jump, but he is the only other character who even suggests that he will try. Leper is a dreamy character; he collects snails and sketches birds and trees in his school notebook; he goes cross-country skiing to look for a beaver dam. When an army recruiter shows the class a movie of the ski troops, Leper is enthralled, and he decides to leave school to enlist in the army before he is drafted, so that he can join the ski troops. But he breaks down from the rigors of boot camp and deserts. He sends a telegram to Gene, which he signs "Your very best friend." Gene goes to visit Leper, and this visit is by far the longest episode in the book without Finny. Near the end of the story Leper turns up on campus again, and he plays a role in the crucial final episode of the story, the mock trial, because he was a witness to Finny's fall.

If Finny and Gene are doubles, Leper is a doubled double. Finny and Gene are best friends, and in his telegram Leper calls himself Gene's very best friend. Both Finny and Leper dress oddly, but Finny wears his strange clothing with style and bravado, while Leper just looks awkward. Finny desperately wants to join the army, but he can't because of his injury; Leper joins the army, but he becomes a psychological casualty. Finny jumps from the tree willingly; Gene jumps because Finny has; Leper says he will give it a try but he never does. Thus Finny and Leper define two extremes of style, individualism, daring, and alienation, while Gene is in the middle.

Leper can be seen as a device of narrative, but the doubled double reflects a phenomenon also found outside narrative. We often judge ourselves by reference to flanking characters: "I may not be as rich as X, but I am richer than Z." Thus the world of the principal character is defined not simply in reference to a single Hegelian or Platonic double, but in reference to two doubled characters who flank the principal character. If subjectivity is understood as a role taken by a self, then each of the three subjects in this relationship has its own kind of subjectivity, though perhaps only the middle position normally takes on awareness of itself in the pattern, and perhaps only the middle position will be the hero of a story.

Doubled doubles can be multiplied, as in J. R. R. Tolkien's *The Lord of the Rings*. It is obvious enough that Gollum is Frodo's double: they are both bearers of the Ring; on much of the journey Gollum is Frodo's shadow; and at the last moment, Frodo and Gollum fight over the Ring. But Sauron is another double. Sauron is the Lord of the Rings; Pippin calls Frodo the Lord of the Rings, and although Gandalf quickly rebukes him, he can't keep the reader from hearing. Sauron wants to possess the Ring to enslave the world, while Frodo (until the last moment) wants to destroy the Ring to free the world from Sauron's power. Sauron lost the Ring when his finger is cut off, and Frodo loses the Ring when Gollum bites off his finger. Again we find two doubles at the two extremes—Sauron is at the high point of power in the story, and Gollum is at the low point—while the hero is in the middle.

This elegant pattern is complicated by the presence of a third double, Sam Gamgee. Sam and Frodo are master and servant doubles, but Sam and Gollum are also doubles. In the later parts of the journey, Gollum is the negative version of Sam—the bad servant, the faithless servant, the servant who must be driven by force. For a short while, Sam, too, bears the Ring, but while Gollum is mastered by his desire for the Ring, Sam gives it back to Frodo willingly. Thus the figure is a sort of inverted Y, with Sauron at the top, Frodo in the middle, and Gollum at one of the lower points and Sam at the other.

Scholars have tended to emphasize the psychological aspect of narrative doubles, and perhaps for this reason the doubles at the top of my list—divided selves—may seem more clearly doubles than those at the bottom—romantic doubles. According to the psychological interpretation, doubles express the duality within the individual; and even when this duality is externally manifest in two different characters, this division is a narrative convenience to express symbolically the two sides of one self. This version of doubling would take the Hegelian parable as an intrapersonal process.

Another reading of the parable, however, sees the two selves as independent and antagonistic; and in the Aristophanic fable, even though the two selves were originally one, now they are two separate individuals looking for each other. According to this reading, a self comes to self-consciousness only through interaction with another self, different from itself. This is the situation, for example, in *A Farewell to Arms* and *A Separate Peace*: even if one character or the other desires a merger, the two characters never lose their individuality, and the death at the end leaves one character alive and alone.

A double, in addition to its psychological aspect, may be a narrative device—though, of course, narrative devices usually also have thematic implications. In *A Separate Peace* the doubled doubles act to place Gene as the middle point between extremes, and in *The Lord of the Rings* the three doubles place Frodo in a slightly more complicated geometry. Jane Austen's *Pride and Prejudice* has a more complicated geometry still, as Elizabeth Bennet and Mr. Darcy are the central double in a complex network of doubles. Some readers may resist the idea that what I describe as doubles in *Pride and Prejudice* are really doubles at all. In a sense I am not concerned about defending the word; I think it is clear that Elizabeth and Mr. Darcy sit on the bottom end of the continuum that I have sketched above. Some readers will want to restrict the term "double" to the upper part of the continuum, though exactly where to place the division is not an easy decision, and those who grant that Heathcliff and Catherine are doubles may find it hard to state a principle that would exclude Elizabeth and Mr. Darcy.[8] I grant that Elizabeth and Mr. Darcy are not psychological doubles in the way that Dr. Jekyll and Mr. Hyde or even in the way that Catherine and Heathcliff are psychological doubles—partly because Austen is interested in a different kind of psychological analysis, partly because her use of doubles is more clearly a narrative device, and partly because this narrative device has social rather than psychological implications. Austen's understanding of the self is social rather than individual, and her doubles, therefore, are social doubles, married couples, rather than psychological doubles. (I will have more to say about the social self in chapter 5.)

The center of *Pride and Prejudice,* in this analysis, is the erotic double formed by Elizabeth Bennet and Mr. Darcy. But radiating out from these two principal characters are several additional doubles, and all of these characters set up a complex network of social and moral attitudes and actions.

Elizabeth's first double is her sister Jane. They are close in a way that neither is close to any of the other Bennet children; and they have somewhat

---

8. In chapter 18, Elizabeth (somewhat sarcastically) tells Mr. Darcy that they are very alike; then in chapter 50, Elizabeth "began now to comprehend that he was exactly the man who, in disposition and talents, would most suit her" (p. 325). They complement each other, as doubles often do, though they do not show any great need to merge their identities. But there are many doubles who show no desire to merge: Sherlock Holmes and Dr. Moriarty, Oliver Twist and Monks.

similar ideas about love and marriage, but they have very different personalities. Jane falls in love with Mr. Bingley, who doubles Mr. Darcy, but while Mr. Bingley is always charming and good, Mr. Darcy is, at first, proud and unfriendly. Jane and Mr. Bingley are a pair doubling a pair.

Mr. Collins also doubles Mr. Darcy. These are the two men who propose to Elizabeth, but two characters could hardly be more different in their attitudes to love and marriage. For Mr. Collins, marriage is simply a social and financial transaction, and given the right situation one person can substitute for another. Almost as soon as Elizabeth refuses him, he proposes to Elizabeth's friend, Charlotte Lucas, who accepts him. Elizabeth also rejects Mr. Darcy, but his reaction is very different; rather than changing the object of his attention, he changes himself. If Mr. Collins doubles Mr. Darcy's double, then Charlotte doubles Elizabeth—her attitude to marriage allows her to accept Mr. Collins, whereas Elizabeth could not. So while Jane and Mr. Bingley double Elizabeth and Mr. Darcy on one side, Charlotte and Mr. Collins double them on the other side.

Mr. Darcy is also doubled by Wickham. He has all the social graces that Mr. Darcy lacks, but none of Mr. Darcy's virtues. "We were born in the same parish," Wickham tells Elizabeth; "within the same park, the greatest part of our youth was passed together; inmates of the same house, sharing the same amusements, objects of the same parental care" (124). Wickham eventually elopes with Elizabeth's foolish sister Lydia. Again we find a pair of doubles: Wickham and Darcy, Lydia and Elizabeth.

Of course this analysis simplifies very complex characters and situations, but it shows a pattern that is part of the meaning of the story. Austen has created a set of eight characters: Elizabeth and Mr. Darcy stand, as it were, in the center of a circle, with three spokes radiating from them: Jane and Mr. Bingley, Charlotte and Mr. Collins, and Lydia and Wickham. Jane and Mr. Bingley are separated only by external forces and do not need to develop or to learn in order to achieve their happiness. Charlotte reasons that it is best to settle for security in a loveless marriage, while Lydia acts simply from passion and ends up with what will be a loveless marriage with no security. Thus each of these pairs comments on the same situation, each in a different way. The narrative is complex; but the geometry of doubling is simple and elegant, and this geometry is a fundamental part of the meaning of the narrative, which depends on moral discriminations within society, as shown through this pattern of doubles. Austen's doubles are social because her understanding of the self is social rather than individual, and in Austen's world social stability comes through the creation of couples.

CHAPTER 5

Freudian Thirds
Heinlein, Stevenson, Forster, Wharton

The Hegelian and Aristophanic doubles are formed through separation and division of two subjects within the Cartesian monadic self. As the distance between the two subjects increases, a space is created which may be filled by a third subject. In this narrative geometry, there are three distinct but interdependent selves, each of which plays a distinct role as a subject. The third subject, however, is not a double to either of the two Hegelian or Aristophanic subjects but often serves as the medium through which the conflict of doubles is expressed. Often the third subject plays a role in one of the family dramas described by Sigmund Freud: the Oedipal story, here represented by Robert Heinlein's *Double Star*; or the story of fraternal conflict over a woman, here represented by Robert Louis Stevenson's *The Master of Ballantrae*. A story of the Freudian third may concentrate on the rivalry between the doubles, with the third character functioning simply as the channel of this rivalry; but the focus may be on the figure in the middle, as we see in E. M. Forster's *A Room with a View*. Other configurations are found which often can be seen as variants of the Freudian patterns. Moreover, in literature, as in life, all these narrative positions may be taken by substitute figures—a father figure rather than a father, for example. The character in the middle position is neither subject nor object, in the ordinary binary use of these terms; thirdness is a particular kind of subjectivity which must be understood in its own terms.

I.

The Oedipal model as Freud described it in *On the Interpretation of Dreams* can be understood as a development of Aristophanes' fable: the two divided parts of the original self have found each other, and if they are a heterosexual romantic couple, they may have offspring. But now the roles shift: the father and son become doubles, and the mother becomes the mediating figure in their conflict. (In the classic form of the story, there are two characters in the older generation and one in the younger, but we will see other configurations in a moment.)

Oedipus, of course, did not have an Oedipus complex. Although he killed his father and married his mother, he did so without knowing the family relationships. His reaction, however, when he learned the truth, suggests that these crimes against his parents did have a considerable psychological power for him. In any case, even if Oedipus did not suffer from his complex, the play does, and so do we as the audience or else we would not be affected by the story as we are. But Sophocles' play does not manifest the model I am describing in this chapter, since the conflict between Lauis and Oedipus is represented only by report, and Jocasta is never in the middle and never mediates the conflict.

Many narratives show some version of the Oedipal situation. In the myth of Hippolytus, as told in the eponymous play by Euripides, Phaedra, the young wife of Theseus, falls in love with her stepson, Hippolytus. When Hippolytus finds out about her passion for him, he is disgusted and outraged. Phaedra kills herself and leaves a note for Theseus claiming that Hippolytos has raped her. Theseus curses Hippolytus, who is then attacked by a miraculous bull that emerges from the sea. At the end of the play, the goddess Artemis tells Theseus what really happened, and Hippolytus dies knowing that his father knows the truth. In this version, the mother (or here, a close substitute, the stepmother) falls in love with the son, and the father kills the son.

Another variation is shown in Robert Heinlein's science-fiction novel *Double Star*. The principal character, who is also the narrator, is Lorenzo Smythe, or Larry Smith, an out-of-work actor with an attitude. He is hired to impersonate John Joseph Bonforte, who has been kidnapped by his political enemies. Bonforte is the leader of the opposition in the Planetary Empire and the head of the Expansionist coalition; one of his goals is to bring the Martians into the Empire. Bonforte is about to be adopted into a Martian nest, and his failure to show up for the ceremony would constitute a serious interplanetary crisis: thus the kidnapping, and thus the plan to have Smythe take his place.

In short, leaving out a series of complications, Smythe's impersonation succeeds. Then, shortly after the adoption ceremony, Bonforte is found, but he is in very bad shape. Bonforte's inner circle persuade Smythe to continue the impersonation until Bonforte can recover. An election is called, and Smythe, impersonating Bonforte, leads the party to victory.

All this time, Bonforte is slowly recovering, but Smythe decides to stay away from him, for fear of hurting his characterization:

> I had made the terrible mistake of going to my father's funeral; for years thereafter when I thought of him I saw him dead in his coffin. . . . I was afraid of something like that with Bonforte; I was now impersonating a well man at the height of his powers. . . . I was very much afraid that if I saw him ill, the recollection of it would blur and distort my performance. (101)

Of course it is also the author who decides to keep Bonforte away from the reader. But in any case, the identification of Bonforte and Smythe's father is clear here and elsewhere.

The real Bonforte suffers a stroke, but gradually his health improves, and by election day his handlers believe that he will be able to take over his own life again, and Smythe will be able to drop the role. Bonforte asks to see Smythe perform his impersonation, and on election night the meeting is staged. Bonforte is brought into the room in a wheelchair and placed on a couch before Smythe makes his entrance:

> He looked like my father! Oh, it was just a "family" resemblance; he and I looked much more alike than either one of us looked like my father, but the likeness was there—and the age was right for he looked *old*. I had not guessed how much he had aged. He was thin and his hair was white. (119)

Bonforte is impressed and amazed by Smythe's impersonation; as he says, "It is an odd thing to see one's own self" (120). Smythe is Bonforte, who in turn is Smythe's father.

They win the election, but the excitement is too much for Bonforte, who has another stroke and dies. Smythe is now left with a final decision: should he quit now that Bonforte is dead, and leave the party and the politics to the professionals, or should he continue the impersonation forever—should he really become John Joseph Bonforte? All Bonforte's inner circle want him to stay, and finally, at the urging of Bonforte's secretary, Penelope Russell, he agrees. The novel is narrated from a time twenty-five years after the events of the story. Smythe/Bonforte has had a long and successful career; he has been elected Supreme Minister three times, and he has brought the extraterrestrials into the Empire.

Double Star is an extremely clever narrative of the double, in which the two subjects finally merge. In addition, however, there is a very clear Oedipal theme. Smythe often mentions his father, who was certainly the formative influence in his life. And then, as we have seen, when he sees Bonforte, he sees his own father. So when he takes Bonforte's place, when he becomes Bonforte, he becomes his own father.

The third character in the geometry of this story is Penelope Russell. She is Bonforte's personal secretary, and at the beginning of the story she is clearly in love with her boss. She deeply resents Smythe's impersonation, and for a time she finds it hard even to be in the same room with him. Smythe himself, however, is immediately taken with her. Gradually she seems to come to terms with the situation; she realizes that her cooperation in the impersonation is the only way to help Bonforte, and she sees that Smythe is doing a very good job, as he manages through his own cunning to get them out of a number of very sticky situations in which he is almost unmasked.

After Bonforte is found, Penelope suffers greatly from the contrast between Bonforte and Smythe: "The poor girl was going almost out of her mind from visiting the sickroom of the man she hopelessly loved—then going straight in to work closely with a man who looked and talked and sounded just like him, but in good health. She was probably beginning to hate me" (110). Of course that's wrong: she is beginning to love Smythe in his role as Bonforte. And when Bonforte dies, what convinces Smythe to continue the impersonation is Penelope's desire that he do so.

The resolution of this relationship is delicately managed, in the narrator's afterword:

> I wrote all of the above twenty-five years ago to try to straighten out my own confusion. I tried to tell the truth and not spare myself because it was not meant to be read by anyone but myself and my therapist, Dr. Capek. It is strange, after a quarter of a century, to reread the foolish and emotional words of that young man. I remember him, yet I have trouble remembering that I was ever he. My wife Penelope claims that she remembers him better than I do—and that she never loved anyone else. So time changes us. (127)

Smythe ends up marrying the beloved of his double—the double who was in turn the double of his father—that is, he ends up marrying his mother. Although Smythe often mentions his father, never once in the story does he mention his mother. That position must be kept open for Penelope.

Lorenzo Smythe and John Joseph Bonforte are the subject and the double in this story—though exactly who is which can be debated: Smith is hired to be Bonforte's double, but since Smith is the principal character of the story, he should count as the central subject, so Bonforte is Smythe's double. In any case, Penelope is the Freudian third. Heinlein is rather fond of the Oedipal character structure; he uses it, more or less obviously, in *Spaceman Jones*, *Citizen of the Galaxy*, *Time for the Stars*, *The Star Beast*, and *Tunnel in the Sky*, to name books only from his early period. He is completely aware of his interest in Oedipal stories, as we can see from a direct reference to Freud in *The Puppet Masters*. Nor is this simply Heinlein's idiosyncrasy—the same sort of Oedipal configuration in a narrative of a double can be found, for example, in the movie *The Mask of Zorro*—which has a double, an impersonating double, and a Freudian third—and in many other narratives as well. Any of these narratives can be read (or watched) on its own, but a larger view sees that all these narratives are variations on a theme. Each performance is individual, but each takes its full meaning only when it is seen against the underlying pattern. I would not claim that *Double Star* has any profound theme, but it is a superb performance within its type; and for those willing to take it as it is, it is deeply satisfying, partly because the doubling and the Oedipal situation are managed so cleverly. The appreciation of technical skill is not the lowest form of aesthetic pleasure.

The geometry of *Double Star* has a character in the place of the father, a character in the place of the son, and a character in the place of the mother; the father dies, the son takes the place of the father and marries the mother, all in the classic Oedipal manner, though with substitutes. But other triads can occur. Many folktales, for instance, tell about a young hero who survives a test set by the father of a princess; the boy wins both the princess and the kingdom, in effect taking the place of the father through marriage with the daughter. In Greek myth we find the story of Oinomaos, King of Pisa, who did not want to give up his daughter Hippodameia. In some versions of the story there was a prophecy that he would be killed by the successful suitor; in other versions he desired Hippodameia himself. He set a test: a suitor would take Hippodameia away on his chariot and Oinomaos would chase after them; if he caught them, he would kill the suitor and take Hippodameia back home. After Oinomaos had killed twelve suitors—in some versions he nailed their skulls to the front of the palace—the thirteenth suitor, Pelops, bribed Oinomaos' servant to replace the bronze axel-pin with one made of wax; when the race began, Oinomaus's chariot crashed, and he was thrown from his chariot and killed. Pelops married Hippodameia.

Here the geometry has one figure in the older generation and two in the younger.[1]

Another variation is found in Balzac's *Eugénie Grandet*, in which the wealthy Grandet will not allow his daughter Eugénie to marry her cousin Charles, who has become poor because of his father's bankruptcy. Charles goes to the West Indies and makes his fortune, but when he returns to France, he has become as materialistic as old Grandet and breaks his engagement to Eugénie for what he erroneously thinks is a better match.[2]

II.

In *Totem and Taboo,* Freud presents another form of the family triad. Here he attempts to explain the link between totemism and incest prohibitions by postulating stages in the development of primitive societies (though I don't think he commits himself to the historical reality of these stages). He begins with a description of the primal horde, in which "[t]here is only a violent, jealous father who keeps all the females for himself and drives away the growing sons" (182). But, according to Freud, "[o]ne day the expelled brothers joined forces, slew and ate the father, and thus put an end to the father horde. . . . This violent primal father had surely been the envied and feared model for each of the brothers. Now they accomplished their identification with him by devouring him and each acquired a part of his strength" (183). This murder solves one problem, but it creates another:

> Though the brothers had joined forces in order to overcome the father, each was the other's rival among the women. Each wanted to have them all to himself like the father, and in the fight of each against the other the new organization would have perished. For there was no longer any one stronger than all the rest who could have successfully assumed the role of the father. Thus there was nothing left for the brothers, if they wanted to live together, but to erect the incest prohibition—perhaps after many difficult experiences—through which they all equally renounced the women

---

1. The story of Cupid and Psyche, in Apuleius' *Golden Ass,* has the same form, but the characters are a mother (Venus), a son (Cupid), and an outsider (Pysche). Perhaps because Psyche is female, she is passive and Cupid is the active suitor; but it is still Psyche who must pass the tests.

2. The plot of Henry James's *Washington Square* is somewhat similar, though the characters are very different; see also James Joyce's story "Eveline" from *Dubliners.*

whom they desired, and on account of whom they had removed the father in the first place. (185–86)

There are difficulties in this theory, both historical and logical; nonetheless, it provides another important model of the narrative third. Freud takes this story primarily as a manifestation of the Oedipal conflict, as the sons kill their father. He is less concerned with the rivalry of the brothers, but this situation is equally interesting, and it shows up in many narratives; indeed, it may be more common than the classic Oedipal pattern. A good example of the type is Robert Louis Stevenson's romance *The Master of Ballantrae*. The plot of this story is rather complex, but the details matter, and I will summarize the story at some length.

This story begins in 1745, the year of the Jacobite Rebellion, when the exiled Bonnie Prince Charlie made an attempt to return to Scotland and claim the throne, only to be defeated at the battle of Culloden in 1746. The principal characters of the story are four—or perhaps five. The eighth Lord of Durrisdeer, the father of the family, has become prematurely aged, and he spends his time at the chimney side, reading. His older son, James Durie, the Master of Ballantrae, is twenty-four at the time of the Rebellion; he is dissolute, but charming and well liked by many. The second son, Henry, is "neither very bad nor yet very able, but an honest solid sort of lad" (11). Living with them is Miss Alison Graeme, "a near kinswoman, an orphan, and the heir to a considerable fortune" (11). In many ways she is almost a daughter of the family. Alison and James are expected to marry. The fifth character is the principal narrator, Ephraim Mackellar, the land steward of the family estate. (I will have more to say about Mackellar in chapter 8.)

At the news of Prince Charlie's landing in Scotland, the Duries, like many other Scottish families, must decide which side to take, and, like many other families, they decide to hedge their bets—one son will go with Prince Charlie, and the other will remain loyal to King George. Both sons want to follow the Prince, but finally James is chosen by the toss of a coin.

After the Battle of Culloden, the family get the news that James has been killed. The father now wants Alison to marry Henry. Meanwhile, the people of the area begin to remember James as if he had been a kind of romantic hero, and they blame Henry for his death and for their own hardships. Alison agrees to marry Henry out of pity, but her heart remains in mourning for James.

Some years pass, and Henry and Alison have a child, Katherine. Then the family receives word that James is not, in fact, dead. After a series of adventures, which demonstrate both his quick wits and his cruel amorality, he has managed to reach France, by way of New York, and he sends word that he needs money. Henry complies, though he has to mortgage the estate. Again and again James asks for money; the family is nearly bankrupt when finally Henry refuses. James now returns in person (the year is 1756); he claims that his return puts him in danger of his life, but it later comes out that he has changed sides and has been acting as a spy for the English.

His diabolical cleverness is now devoted to tormenting his brother. Among the family he feigns brotherly affection, but he taunts Henry in private. He pays court to Alison, who obviously is still in love with him, and he even wins the affection of Henry's daughter Katherine. Finally Henry can bear no more, and he strikes James. They fight a duel, which Henry wins. He thinks he has killed James, and he runs into the house in despair. But when Mackellar goes to look for the body, he finds that it has disappeared; evidently some smugglers, friends of James, have found him and carried him off—whether dead or alive, the family does not know.

After the duel, Henry suffers some sort of illness; he recovers, but he seems permanently weakened in mind and body. For a time after his recovery, he avoids discussion of the duel, but one day he asks Mackellar where James's body has been buried. When Mackellar tells him that James disappeared and that they have hopes that he did not die in the duel, Henry says, "nothing can kill that man. He is not mortal. He is bound upon my back to all eternity—to all God's eternity!" (118).

The Lord of Durrisdeer has also been affected by the duel between his sons; he seems to have suffered a stroke, and after a short illness he dies. Then a second child is born to Henry and Alison—a son, Alexander.

The family hear no more of James until 1764, when once again James returns. He has spent much of the intervening time in India, and now he has brought back with him an Indian servant, Secundra Dass. After a quick family council, Mackellar and Alison convince Henry that their best course is to depart secretly and immediately, with the children, to go to New York, where Alison owns some property. Mackellar is to be left behind to keep a sort of guard on James.

It takes James only three weeks to discover where his brother has gone, and he follows after, taking with him Secundra Dass. Mackellar goes along as well. When they arrive, James finds that Henry has taken some precautions: he has explained the situation to the governor, who, as it happens, had suspicions about James from his earlier visit to New York. Henry gives James a small allowance, on condition that he not communicate with the family. James sets himself up as a tailor in order to shame the family, but he gets little work.

The story now continues with an intrigue that is complex and not relevant to this discussion. In short, James leaves New York to search for treasure he had buried in the northern wilderness of the territory on his earlier visit. He takes with him a crew of thugs and thieves, including a character named Mountain, but eventually he discovers that this crew is actually in the pay of Henry; he then dies, and Secundra Dass buries him. The others are now killed off by Indians, one by one, except for Mountain and Secundra Dass. Secundra Dass disappears into the woods.

Henry, meanwhile, has followed James as far as Albany and then into the woods. He comes across Mountain, who tells him what has happened, but he refuses to believe that James is dead. He makes his way to the place where James was buried, and there he finds Secundra Dass digging up the grave. James has only faked his death, using a trick taught him by Secundra Dass, who now tries to revive him. As Henry sees his brother's eyes open, he falls to the ground. But the resurrection of James fails; the two brothers die together.

The Master of Ballantrae is not exactly like Freud's myth from *Totem and Taboo*, but the fundamental structure of characterization is very close: a father, sons, and a woman who is the object of sibling rivalry. In Stevenson's tale, the Oedipal and incestuous themes have been somewhat modified, but nonetheless they cast a shadow over the story. In Freud's myth, the sons kill the father to gain access to the women; James and Henry do not directly kill their father, but as Mackellar says, "to any considering mind, the two sons had between them slain their father" (121). Alison is not the biological sister of the sons, though she is near kin, and as Henry says, "we were all brought up like brother and sister" (31). In a way she is also a mother figure; Mackellar says that her affection for Henry "was that rather of a mother than a wife" (125); the brothers' biological mother is absent from the story and is mentioned only briefly.

Freud's myth emphasizes the conflict between the father and the sons. In Stevenson's tale the role of the father has become secondary; it is the rivalry of the brothers that dominates the story. James and Henry are not simply brothers—they are doubles, and James even has the habit of calling himself "Esau" and calling Henry "Jacob." In Freud's myth, the woman is hardly a person, but only the object of desire. In Stevenson's tale, Alison is perhaps secondary to the brothers, but she is an independent subjectivity—she, rather than the father, is the third of the story, and thus all the principal characters are in the same generation.[3]

3. Graham Greene's *The Quiet American* is another story of this type, with two Hegelian figures (Thomas Fowler and Alden Pyle) and a third character who mediates the conflict between the doubles. But the third figure in this story is almost vacant; she has almost no inde-

In a sense the Freudian third is developed from the two characters in a double. That is, in the Hegelian process whereby two self-consciousness become differentiated, a space is created which can be filled either with objects, as Hegel suggests, or with another consciousness, which is both an object and potentially a subject in its own right. Thus in *Double Star,* Penelope is the link that binds Smythe and Bonforte and through which they finally merge; in *The Master of Ballantrae,* Alison is the object of the antagonism between James and Henry.

III.

In *The Master of Ballantrae,* the woman in the triangle is subordinate, the physical manifestation of the rivalry that forms between the two Hegelian subjects as they confront each other. She is nonetheless a subject, and in general we can note that the third figure has a kind of subjectivity that is different from the kind of subjectivity of either half of the double. And sometimes the third character, the mediator, can become the principal subject of a story, the center of subjectivity.[4]

In E. M. Forster's *A Room with a View,* the central character is a young English woman, Lucy Honeychurch. When we first meet Lucy, she is a tourist in Italy, chaperoned by Miss Charlotte Bartlett. The story takes place in the first decade of the twentieth century, and the social forms of the time are an important element in the story. In Florence, Lucy meets a young Englishman, a rather brooding character named George Emerson, who goes so far as to kiss her while they are on a picnic. Lucy is not so sure what she thinks of George and the kiss, but Miss Bartlett considers the kiss a serious act of sexual aggression. Lucy and Miss Bartlett agree not to tell anyone about the unfortunate incident.

Once back in England, Lucy becomes engaged to another young man, Cecil Vyse. She has refused his proposals twice, but when he asks for a third time she agrees. Cecil is characterized mostly in rather negative terms. For example, Lucy's younger brother Freddy doesn't like him much: "Cecil praised one too much for being athletic.... Cecil made one talk in his way, instead of letting one talk in one's own way.... And Cecil was the kind of fellow who would never wear another fellow's hat" (91–92). Cecil's gravest

---

pendent subjectivity. And, of course, the doubles are not brothers, but only friends.

4. Compare the comment of Claude Lévi-Strauss (1969, p. 496): "woman could never become just a sign and nothing more, since even in a man's world she is still a person, and since in so far as she is defined as a sign she must be recognized as a generator of signs."

fault is no doubt his attitude toward women: "Cecil . . . always felt that he must lead women, though he knew not whither, and protect them, though he knew not against what" (140).

Not long after the engagement, George Emerson and his father, by coincidence or by fate, rent a house near Lucy's home in the country. George is still somewhat morose, but his good qualities begin to manifest themselves: he has good taste in books and he reads German philosophers in German. Moreover, he and Freddy hit it off. They go skinny-dipping in a nearby pond, and when Lucy surprises them, George ends up wearing Freddy's pants. (Here we are reminded that any motif must be interpreted not in the abstract but within its own story. The sharing of clothes in other stories we have examined is a marker of the double, but here it is not; it is only a sign of a particular kind of good fellowship, in contrast to Cecil's rigidity of character.)

Of course, by the end of the book Lucy has broken off her engagement with Cecil and has married George; the steps in the dance need not be described in detail. But what is important here is that in this version of the plot, the central subjectivity belongs to Lucy. The narration is in the third person, but for the most part the story is told from Lucy's perspective, as if the narrator were standing beside her, and it is her thoughts and feelings that the narrator presents to the reader. And the choice of suitors finally is hers. Cecil is not even aware that he has a rival until long after the engagement is broken. There is just a hint that George thinks that he is involved in a contest; near the end, when he finally professes his love to Lucy, he catalogues Cecil's faults: "Every moment of his life he's forming you, telling you what's charming or womanly; and you, of all women, listen to his voice instead of to your own[;] . . . therefore I settled to fight him" (177). But the fight never develops. All the struggle takes place inside Lucy.[5]

The abstract narrative geometry of *A Room with a View* is thus rather like the plot geometry of *The Master of Ballantrae*—two men interested in the same woman, only one of whom can win her—and of many other similar stories; but the fleshing out of the geometry is very different. In *The Master of Ballantrae*, the two men are brothers, whereas in *A Room with a View* they hardly know each other. In *The Master of Ballantrae* the conflict is open and ultimately fatal to both, whereas in *A Room with a View* there is hardly any direct conflict between the two rivals, and no one dies. And in *The Master of*

---

5. The same plot geometry can be found in Margaret Atwood's first novel, *The Edible Woman*. The moral question posed by the two stories is the same: do men have a right to control women? But the question and the solution seem clearer and simpler in *A Room with a View*: although the two sexes have not yet entered the garden, as George puts it, someday they will if they work together. *The Edible Woman*, however, is deliberately ambiguous.

Ballantrae the third character, Alison, is a secondary character, whereas in *A Room with a View* Lucy is the center of the story.

In *The Master of Ballantrae* and in *A Room with a View*, a woman is the middle figure between two men; in Edith Wharton's *The Age of Innocence*, however, the triangle consists of a man caught between two women. At the beginning of this novel, Newland Archer has just become engaged to May Welland, when May's cousin, the Countess Ellen Olensky, returns to New York from Europe. Ellen's marriage has failed, she is separated from her husband, and her position in good society is rather dubious and insecure. As they are presented in the story, May and Ellen are clearly doubles. Of course Newland falls in love with Ellen. This is a novel of renunciation, however, so he gives up the great love of his life and stays with May.

Newland is the central character of the story, but in a sense the decision is taken out of his hands. The battle is really between May and Ellen, and Newland is the prize. They fight with hints rather than swords, but the struggle is nonetheless fierce, and when May finally wins, her eyes are "wet with victory" (343). Thus there is a Hegelian contest between the doubles, with Newland as the prize.

IV.

The geometry of the Freudian third can appear in many variations, and the tradition of narrative literature seems to have an urge to fill every possible niche in the ecological system. But narrative geometries, and the philosophic fables associated with them, are by their very nature somewhat abstract. They are not, however, Platonic ideals, nor are they essentially prior to the narratives I have examined—logically, chronologically, or in any other way. The geometries are useful primarily as schemes that may help us understand the stories. Most often the artists were there before the philosophers (and, as I hope to show in Part Two, the storytellers have developed understandings of subjectivity as yet unthought by the philosophers).

I have been reading these narratives as stories of the self, as stories that explore what it is to be a self—the monadic, dyadic, or triadic self. It is useful to place the stories within the groups, but it is then equally important to keep in mind the differences that make each story unique. Both judgments are necessary. Once we have a sense of the groups and the narratives within the groups, then we can begin to compare and interpret on the basis of comparison. In somewhat the same way, there is only so much to say about any piece of music just as a piece of music; interpretation is richer when we interpret a piece as a fugue, as a sonata, or as a twelve-bar blues. But in music, as in literature, the forms are developed by artists before they are analyzed by theorists. (And, of course, there are many possible cross-categorizations; reading narratives as representations of the self is only one among many interpretive approaches.)

It would be improper, therefore, to require an absolute fit between any scheme and any particular story. Indeed, the particular effect of any story is determined by the details of its telling. Any scheme can accommodate many different themes. It is only a beginning to say that a story represents a monadic, dyadic, or triadic view of subjectivity; we need to examine the details of the presentation of the scheme. Thus, a monadic subject may be more or less comfortable in its loneliness (*The Confessions of Felix Krull, Notes from Underground*); the relative strengths of the Hegelian and Aristophanic patterns may vary (*A Farewell to Arms, A Separate Peace*); a Freudian third may be male or female (*The Age of Innocence, A Room with a View*); and the Freudian third may be a secondary character or the central consciousness of the story (*The Master of Ballantrae, A Room with a View*). The schemes of narrative geometry, then, do not determine the themes of a narrative, but they do present the framework within which themes are developed.

V.

The character sets examined so far are structured in ones, twos, and threes; these numbers, however, have a disconcerting habit of changing before our eyes as subjects split and merge. Sets of one are found in reflexive narratives, but the reflexive self can split into two parts: the observing subject and the observed object, as in Descartes' *Meditations* and Montaigne's *Essays,* or in Dostoevsky's *Notes from Underground* and Sartre's *Nausea*. The two parts of one self can shade into two characters, as in Stevenson's *Dr. Jekyll and Mr. Hyde,* or two distinct subjects can merge, as in Highsmith's *The Talented Mr. Ripley.* Then, as the space between two subjects increases, a third subject may appear, often as a figure mediating the relationship between two parts of a double, as in Heinlein's *Double Star* and Wharton's *The Age of Innocence.*

The philosophical fables of Descartes, Hegel, Plato, and Freud have provided models for these monadic, dyadic, and triadic forms of subjectivity, but the narrative tradition presents stories with more positions than these fables can supply. The theory of the social self, as presented in George Herbert Mead's *Mind, Self and Society from the Standpoint of a Social Behaviorist,* may provide a better model for these more complicated structures and for the selves expressed by these structures.[6]

According to Mead, the self is not innate, but develops gradually through social interaction (135). Mead notes that the self is both subject and object to itself; the word "self" expresses this duality through its reflexivity (136). To become a self, the individual must experience itself not as a subject but as an object, and not directly but indirectly, "from the particular standpoints of other individual members of the social group as a whole to which he belongs" (138). The individual becomes an object to himself "by taking the attitudes of other individuals toward himself within a social environment" (138). Thus the mirror in which one sees oneself is made up of the attitudes of others.

In the Hegelian and Platonic fables, the self develops in company with just one other consciousness. But for Mead the self develops in society as a whole, and "the unity and structure of the complete self reflects the unity and structure of the social process as a whole" (144).

Mead's social theory of the self leads to a particular conception of the difference between the *I* part of the self and the *me* part of the self. The Cartesian self is divided into an *I* and a *me* by self-reflection; but in Mead's theory of the social self, the *me*, the part of the self that is an object, represents the "group of attitudes which stands for others in the community" (194). That is, the expectations and understandings of one's place and role in society constitute the *me*. The subjective side of the self, the *I*, is "the response of the individual to the attitude of the community as this appears in his own experience" (196). That is, although there may be social expectations, which constitute the *me*, exactly how a person will respond to these expectations is not known until the person acts (197). At times it is the *me* that is important, particularly when one is maintaining a role or position in society; at other times it is the *I* that comes to the fore. But both aspects of the self, the subjective *I* and the objective *me*, are essential: the individual must belong to a group, but it must also have individual responses to the expectations of the group (199–200).

Mead takes organized games as his a model for the interaction of society and the individual self. In organized games, the child "must be ready to take the attitude to everyone else involved in that game" (151). Life, in effect, is like a game of baseball: each person is part of the team, and the various selves are formed through a mutual interest in the outcome of the game. If you are playing first base, you have to anticipate what the shortstop may do, what the

---

6. Norbert Wiley, *The Semiotic Self*, presents a theory of the self based on G. H. Mead and C. S. Peirce.

runners may do, and so on, just as you understand that they have to anticipate what you might do. This process of anticipation involves taking on the roles of the other characters and seeing your own role from the perspective of others.

If we adopt Mead's athletic model, then a Cartesian narrative is a game with one player, like solitaire, whereas Hegelian and Platonic narratives are games with two players, like chess. Games with two players can be combined in various ways—some are like simultaneous chess matches, some are like chess played on intersecting boards, and some are like tag team wrestling—but the similes begin to fail. In these narratives, although many people are involved, they are all involved in two-player games, but these games overlap. This is Jane Austen's view of marriages in a social world. In three-player games, the third is the prize of the contest, the pot in the poker game, but a prize that takes on subjectivity for itself.

But there are many games with more than three characters. In baseball, for instance, there are nine players on the field, one at the plate, and perhaps others on base. Each of them has a role, and each has a name. Each understands its role and takes its sense of itself from the game as a whole and from the roles of the other players on the field. If we are to understand the roles of characters in more complex narratives, we need a terminology richer than any I have seen named by the philosophers. In order to explore these more complex narrative positions, we need a new model, which I take from the linguistic theory of deep-structure semantic roles. These roles provide the framework for second part of this study.

PART TWO

The Case of the Subject

CHAPTER 6

Introduction to Part Two
Deep Subjectivity

The narrative geometries discussed in Part One fit more or less easily into a familiar set of binary oppositions: the *self* and the *other*, the *subject* and the *object*, the *agent* and the *patient*, where the *self* is the *subject* is the *agent*, while the *other* is the *object* is the *patient*. These oppositions have become part of how we think before we think. The Cartesian self, then, is a solitary subject, and everything else is object to that subject. The Hegelian self is a subject coming to terms with an object that has its own subjectivity. When two Hegelian subjects fight, the prize at stake may be the Freudian third, which can take on its own kind of subjectivity. At this point, however, the dichotomy begins to become questionable: the relation between the Hegelian subject and its opponent is not the same as its relation to the prize, the Freudian third: the dichotomy has developed into a triad.

Mead's model of the social self, as described briefly at the end of Part One, allows for an indefinite roster of selves, all defined in relation to each other. The binary oppositions are no longer sufficient. In order to think beyond these oppositions and to analyze narrative geometries of greater complexity, we need a richer theory and terminology; these can be found, I believe, in the linguistic model called *Case Grammar*.[1] In this chapter I briefly summarize this model, which I then apply in the remaining chapters of Part Two.

---

1. For a rather different account of Case Grammar and its possible application to the study of narrative, see David Herman, *Story Logic*, pp. 133–69.

I.

The naturalness of the subject/object or agent/patient opposition derives in part from the way we usually think about English sentences. Most students learn the opposition of grammatical subject and object in school, and this grammatical opposition seems to correspond to something in the world—on the one hand there are agents in the world, people who do things (subjects), and on the other there are the objects acted on by these agents. The link between the subject/agent and the object/patient is the action, the verb. According to the *Canadian Oxford Dictionary*, a subject may be "a word or phrase in a sentence indicating who or what performs the action of a verb or upon which a verb is predicated"; the examples given are "we" in the sentence "we ate ice cream" and "my dog" in the sentence "my dog is clever"; in the first example, the subject "we" performs the action of eating the ice cream, and in the second, the verb phrase "is clever" is predicated on the subject "my dog."

This dictionary definition does not consider passive sentences such as "The ice cream was eaten by us." In the sentence "we ate ice cream," "we" is the subject of the verb and the agent of the action, and "ice cream" is the object of the verb and the patient of the action. In the sentence "The ice cream was eaten by us," "the ice cream" is the subject of the verb, but it is the patient of the action, and while the agent of the action is "us," it is also the object of the preposition "by." Evidently, the subject of the sentence and the agent of the action may be different.

The subject of a sentence in English is normally the topic of the sentence—what the sentence is about—and the rest of the sentence is a comment on the topic. In an active transitive sentence the topic is normally the agent ("John ate the ice cream"); in a passive sentence the topic is normally the patient ("All the ice cream has been eaten"). The primary function of the passive construction in English is precisely to allow the patient to be the topic.[2] A grammar that distinguishes only subject and object does not tell us all that we need to know about the structure of a sentence.

An intransitive sentence has a subject, which may be related to the verb in various ways. In the sentence "Sam shouted," Sam is the agent of an action, but the action performed has no object, or else the object is internal to the verb—that is, if Sam shouted, what he shouted was created by his shouting;

---

2. In inflected languages, such as Latin or Greek, the accusative object of an active sentence may come first if it is the topic, as in the beginning of the *Aeneid*: "Arma virumque cano" 'Arms and a man I sing'; topicalizing inversions are possible even in English: "John, I like, but Frank, I don't like."

it did not exist beforehand. The subject of an intransitive verb can also be a patient, as in the sentence "Sam tripped"—tripping is not something you do, but something that happens to you. An agent subject and a patient subject can usually be distinguished by the questions that correspond to the affirmative forms: the question corresponding to "Sam shouted" is "What did Sam do?" but the question corresponding to "Sam tripped" is "What happened to Sam?" (If Sam is habitually clumsy, we may ask something like "What did Sam do now?" implying that Sam is responsible for tripping because of his clumsiness.)[3]

The verb "to trip" is one of a group of verbs in English that can take as subject either an agent or a patient, depending on the form of the sentence: in the transitive sentence "John tripped Sam," the verb takes an agent as subject and a patient as object, and the corresponding question is "What did John do?" But in the intransitive sentence "Sam tripped," the subject is a patient, and the corresponding question is "What happened to Sam?" If John tripped Sam, then Sam tripped.

These examples remain within the opposition of subject and object, agent and patient, but another kind of intransitive sentence seems to require a new term. In the sentence "Sam dreamed," Sam is neither the agent nor the patient, but something else, which is most often called the *experiencer*. Dreaming is neither something you do, as shouting is something you do, nor something that is done to you, as being hit is something that is done to you. It is an experience you have. Transitive sentences can also have experiencer subjects; in the sentence "Sam listened to the song," Sam is probably an agent, but in "Sam heard the song," Sam is probably an experiencer.[4]

The question test most often seems to align experiencers with agents; the question corresponding to "Sam dreamed" is probably not "What happened to Sam?" but "What did Sam do?" Informants, however, do not always agree about which form of the question is best; sometimes experiencers may be closer to agents, sometimes closer to patients. A second test seems to align experiencers with patients: "Sam ran" has a corresponding imperative, "Sam,

---

3. More precisely, the verbs "do" and "happen" form a binary opposition in which "do" is unmarked and "happen" is marked; that is, "do" has wider application and can serve either meaning if no contrast is needed, but it also can contrast with "happen," which is used only in the narrower application.

4. There seem to be three common situations in which the subject of an intransitive verb is the agent rather than the experiencer or patient: 1) if the verb has an object that has been omitted because the point of the sentence is the agent's doing of the action rather than the effect of the action on the object: "Yes, I ate already" rather than "Yes, I ate dinner already"; 2) if there is an actual or potential internal object created by the action: "I shouted," "I wept"; and 3) if the action of the verb affects the agent or part of the agent's body: "I jumped," "I nodded."

run!" but "Sam tripped" and "Sam dreamed" do not have corresponding imperatives—"Sam, trip!" or "Sam, dream!"—at least not with meanings corresponding to the usual meanings of the active forms.[5]

The grammar of English, and of most European languages, groups together the subject of an active transitive sentence, the subject of a passive sentence, and the subject of an intransitive sentence. In English this grouping shows up most clearly in pronouns, which show case. Thus English uses the same subject pronoun in the sentences "I hit the ball," "I was hit by the ball," "I ran," and "I dreamed." The pronoun object of a transitive sentence and also the agent in a passive sentence take a different form: "The ball hit me" and "The window was broken by me." English no longer marks these distinctions on nouns, but in many other languages, such as Greek or Latin, all nouns carry these case markings, among others.

In the notation used by Bernard Comrie, the subject of an intransitive sentence is symbolized by the letter S, the subject of a transitive verb by the letter A, and the object of a transitive verb by the letter P; A stands for agent, P stands for patient, and S stands for subject.[6] In English and almost all other European languages, the grammatical case of S is the same as the case of A—both are expressed in the nominative case—while P is different—expressed in the accusative case: in short, S = A, while P is different. That is, agents and experiencers are grouped together, and patients are in another category.

This alignment of semantic functions with cases may seem proper and natural to native speakers of English and the other major European languages, but in fact another arrangement is possible. Some languages group together the subject of an intransitive sentence and the object of a transitive sentence, but use a different case for the subject of a transitive sentence: S = P, while A is different. That is, patients and experiencers are grouped together, and agents are in another category. The case of A is called the *ergative* case (the case of the doer), and the case of S and P is called the *absolutive* case. Languages with this arrangement of cases are called *absolutive-ergative* languages (or *ergative* languages, for short), while languages where S = A, and P is different, are called *nominative-accusative* languages (or *accusative* languages, for short).[7] In an accusative language, a person who experiences

---

5. The subject of many copulative constructions is best thought of as an experiencer, as in "George was hot," but the subject of a sentence such as "My dog is clever" is probably not an agent, or a patient, or an experiencer. Some linguists use the term "theme" for such subjects.

6. See Comrie, *Language Universals and Linguistic Typology*, pp. 110–11. Comrie's analysis raises problems which need not detain us here; in brief, his terminology seems to conflate grammatical and semantic categories. Moreover, the subjects and objects of English sentences can play various semantic roles, which Comrie's terminology tends to elide.

7. A majority of the world's languages are nominative-accusative, but absolutive-ergative

something is felt to be like a person who does something, but in an ergative language, a person who experiences something is felt to be like a person to whom something happens. If English were an ergative language, we would say "I swung the bat," "The pitch hit me," and "Me fell down."[8]

The contrast between accusative and ergative languages shows that the binary opposition of subject and object in English and most other European languages covers a ternary opposition of S, A, and P. The ternary opposition can be divided in two different ways: either [A, S] and [P], or [A] and [S, P]. A few languages have a three-way division, where S, A, and P each has a distinct form. But since S will never occur in the same clause with either A or P, it is more efficient to use only two forms, one of which will cover S and either A or P, with a different form for the remaining term.

The boundary between agency and experience is not altogether firm. In the sentence "The boy hit the ball," it seems clear that the subject is an agent and the object is a patient. But transitivity is graded, and the subject of a verb low in transitivity may be an experiencer: in the sentence "I smelled the roses," the subject may be either an agent or an experiencer, depending on how active and voluntary the smelling was. The boundary between experience and patience is likewise somewhat fuzzy. In the sentence "I vomited," the subject certainly had an experience, but the experiencer was also a patient—and perhaps also the voluntary agent, if the vomiting was self-induced.[9]

II.

We have seen that the subject of a clause may be an agent, a patient, or an experiencer. The relation between semantic role and grammatical function is not absolute. The subject of an intransitive clause is often an experiencer

---

languages are not uncommon. Some languages usually classified as absolutive-ergative are Basque, Dyirbal, Inuit, and Tagalog. Ergativity is not all-or-nothing; in many languages, some constructions are ergative while other constructions are accusative.

8. In the West Greenlandic sentence "Oli eats meat," Oli is an agent, and he is in the ergative case, while the meat he eats is in the absolutive case. But in the sentence "Oli sleeps," he is an experiencer, and he is in the absolutive case, like the meat. Sleeping is more like being eaten than it is like eating (Manning, p. 3).

9. In Tsova-Tush the subject of some intransitive verbs may be either ergative or nominative. (The nominative here is more or less equivalent to what Comrie calls the *absolutive*.) In general, the more agency the intransitive subject has, the more likely it will be in the ergative case. Thus the Tsova-Tush sentence equivalent to "I fell" will have an ergative subject if I want to indicate that the falling was my fault, but a nominative subject otherwise; see Holisky in Dixon, *Studies in Ergativity*.

("Sam slept"), but it could also be an agent ("Sam sang") or a patient ("Sam fell"). The subject of an active transitive clause is often an agent ("Sam kicked the ball"), but it could also be an experiencer ("Sam enjoys football"). And the subject of a passive clause is often a patient ("The ball was kicked through the goalposts"), but it could also be an experiencer ("Joe was entertained by Sam's antics") or even an agent ("Sam was generally feared because of his ruthless actions").

Although these three roles are the most frequent subjects and objects, they do not exhaust the semantic universe, as we can see from sentences such as these:

> We gave **George** the money.
> This **key** opens the door.
> The **Yukon** is cold.
> Sam ran a good **race**.
> This book costs **ten dollars**.
> I heard the **trumpet**.

"George," "This key," "The Yukon," "race," "ten dollars," "trumpet"—none of these is an agent, a patient, or an experiencer. What roles do these words play in their sentences? How should we analyze the semantic functions of these words? How many semantic functions should we admit? And how many of these semantic functions can be used as models for narrative roles?

As a methodological principle, we can begin with the semantic distinctions that are marked by the grammatical structures of language itself.[10] But the marking of semantic distinctions is complex and various, and grammatical relations do not map directly onto semantic functions; moreover, no one language will mark every interesting semantic distinction. Nonetheless, we can safely assume that any grammatical structure that is observed in a fair number of languages is likely to have some cognitive importance.

In English, some of the basic grammatical relationships are shown by the usual order of the words in a clause: subject, verb, object; or with a verb of giving, subject, verb, indirect object, direct object. (There are, of course,

---

10. Compare Suzanne Kemmer, *The Middle Voice*: "Recurring instances of different meanings being expressed by the same formal or structural means is an indication that the meanings in question are related. Furthermore, the more direct the semantic relationship between two meanings, the more likely they are to be subsumed under a single form of expression, both within and across languages" (p. 4); "Of all potential semantic relationships that one could trace, the ones most significant for linguistic analysis are those which languages actually do collapse under one form" (p. 6).

exceptions, such as questions.) English also indicates many semantic functions with prepositional phrases. Instead of "Sam gave Mary the flowers," we can say "Sam gave the flowers to Mary."

In addition to word order and prepositional phrases, English also uses case marking, but only in a rather minor way. English nouns have two cases: the genitive case, which functions most typically as a possessive,[11] and an unmarked case (which one might call the "non-genitive") for most other grammatical relations. So we say "the king's crown" (genitive: possessive), but "The king has a crown" (non-genitive: subject), "I saw the king" (non-genitive: direct object), "They gave the king an ovation" (non-genitive: indirect object), "Don't stare at the king" (non-genitive: object of the preposition), and so on.

English pronouns have three cases: the nominative (or subjective), the accusative (or objective), and the genitive (or possessive). Thus we say "I laughed" (nominative: subject), "Sally saw me" (accusative: direct object), "Sally gave me a present" (accusative: indirect object), "Sally stared at me" (accusative: object of a preposition), "This book is mine" (genitive: possessive), and so on.

In some other languages, such as Latin, the order of the words in a clause is relatively free, and grammatical relations are shown mostly by case markings on words rather than by word order in the sentence. Latin has six cases, which are distinguished in nouns and adjectives as well as in pronouns. These cases are nominative, vocative, genitive, dative, accusative, and ablative. (Not all grammarians consider the vocative to be a true case, since a noun in the vocative stands outside of any clause; moreover, most Latin nouns use the nominative form for the vocative function, so most nouns have only five case forms.) There are several classes of nouns (declensions), and each class has a different set of case endings, but all the classes have the same six cases.

Each case has a variety of functions, but usually one function is considered primary. The nominative is used for the subject of the sentence, as in "**dominus** ambulat" 'the master is walking'; the vocative is used in direct address, as in "**domine**, docê puerôs" 'master, teach the boys'; the genitive is used as a possessive, as in "liber **dominî**" 'the master's book'; the dative is used for the indirect object, as in "puer dedit **dominô** pecuniam" 'the boy gave money to the master'; the accusative is used for the direct object, as in "servus amat **dominum**" 'the slave loves the master'; and the ablative is used with some prepositions, as in "puer ambulat cum **dominô**." 'the boy is walking with the

---

11. But some genitive functions are not possessive; for example, "the elephant's trunk," "the rockets' red glare," "the car's engine," and so on.

master." These are only the primary case functions; I will discuss other case functions below.

Latin is a member of the Indo-European family of languages, along with most of the other European languages and also the Indo-Iranian languages, such as Persian and Sanskrit, and their modern descendants, Farsi and Hindi. The Indo-European languages are all descended from a single language, usually called Proto-Indo-European, which was spoken perhaps five or six thousand years ago. Comparative analysis has shown that Proto-Indo-European had eight cases: the six found in Latin, plus two more: the instrumental and the locative. The instrumental case was used to mark the instrument with which an action was carried out, and the locative was used to indicate various spatial relationships.

Latin has lost the instrumental and the locative cases; Classical Greek has also lost the ablative; and English nouns have only two cases, the genitive and the non-genitive. When a case is lost, its functions may be taken over by other cases, so that the Greek genitive, for example, has taken over many of the functions of the Indo-European ablative.

There are far more semantic functions than cases, even in a language with a relatively developed case system, such as Proto-Indo-European. Consequently, each of the various cases must serve several semantic functions. Most often one of these semantic functions will seem to be central or prototypical, and the case will probably derive its name from the prototypical function. Most native speakers of English, for example, if they have thought about it at all, probably think that the genitive is simply the case of possession; many grammar books use the term "possessive" for this case, as if that were the only function it can express. Many English speakers would probably equate the functions of the genitive in "the teacher's car" and "the car's engine," as if the car somehow owned its engine, just as the teacher owns her car.

A good grammar book will make some attempt to indicate the various semantic functions of the cases, though most grammar books don't give an account of any theoretical basis for the analysis.[12] The Latin dative can be used, for example:

---

12. "Typically the rationale for separating meanings or functions is not made explicit. Some distinctions seem to have a syntactic basis, but others are semantically based and in the absence of explicit criteria there is the possibility that the distinctions are based on the intuition of the grammarian. In fact this is more than a possibility given that different writers come up with different classifications of the meanings and functions of a particular system" (Blake, *Case*, p. 30).

- as the indirect object, both in the narrow sense of the recipient: "do **tibi** librum" 'I am giving you the book,'" and in extended senses, as in "monstro **tibi** librum" 'I am showing you the book,' or "hoc **tibi** dico" 'I am saying this to you.'
- as the complement of certain verbs: "noceo **tibi**" 'I am injurious to you.'
- as the complement of certain compound verbs: "inico terrorem **tibi**" 'I cast fear into you.'
- as the complement with certain impersonal verbs: "licet **mihi** hoc facere" 'it is allowable for me to do this.'
- as a possessive: "est **mihi** liber" 'a book is to me,' that is, 'I have a book.'
- as the person for whose advantage or disadvantage something is done: "**tibi** me exorno" 'I am decking myself out for you.'
- as the completion of certain adjectives: "homo amicus **tibi**" 'a man friendly to you.'

In addition, there is the dative of the person judging, the ethic dative, the dative of the agent, the dative of purpose and result, and so on. This proliferation of uses of the dative is not abnormal: Smyth's *Greek Grammar*, for instance, lists about thirty functions of the genitive case in ancient Greek. It is very unlikely that a speaker of Latin thought much about the various uses of the dative or that a speaker of ancient Greek thought about the uses of the genitive: they simply used the language they learned as children, just as we do.

The proliferation of case functions and the variety of cases manifest in different languages raise some questions: How many cases could there be? Is it possible that every semantic role could have its own case? Thus, to take only some of the functions of the Latin dative, could there be a distinct case for the recipient, another for the person advantaged or disadvantaged, another for the person judging, another for purpose and result, and so on? Could there be a distinct case for each of the thirty-some uses of the ancient Greek genitive?

Clearly, such a profusion of cases would be unwieldy. The meanings expressed by language are almost without limit; it is therefore a general rule that any one grammatical form will serve many semantic functions. The various semantic roles expressed by any particular grammatical form tend to have some kind of connection, but different languages will make different groupings—and different numbers of groups as well. Only inspection of actual languages will show which distinctions actually occur.

III.

Natural languages show a wide variety of case systems. Although the various Indo-European languages have varying numbers of cases, all these case systems seem to derive from the basic set of eight Proto-Indo-European cases. But languages in other families can have case systems that are quite different.[13] Greenlandic Eskimo, for example, has eight cases: ergative, equative, instrumental, nominative, ablative, allative, perlative, and locative. The equative case is used in sentences which state that one thing is the same as another thing; the allative is used to express motion to a place; and the perlative expresses motion through, across, or along (Blake 38).

Kalkatungu has nine cases: nominative, ergative, dative, locative I, locative II, aversive, allative I, allative II, and ablative. According to Blake (41–42), "The aversive case is used to express what is to be avoided ('Keep away from the fire!') or the indirect cause ('sick from (eating) bad meat')." Blake does not go into detail about the two locative cases and the two allative cases, but locative case I seems to express simple location, while locative II means "facing"; allative case I seems to express motion to a place, whereas allative II expresses motion toward a place.

Most languages seem to have between two and a dozen cases, but a few languages have more extensive systems. Avar, a language of the Northeast Caucasian, has twenty-seven cases; twenty of these are cases of location, leaving seven for the other grammatical and semantic relationships. The twenty cases of location can be arranged in a grid of four markers of position (locative or simple location, allative or destination, ablative or source, and perlative or path) multiplied by five markers of orientation (on top of; at; under; in or among; in a hollow object) (Blake 151). Thus there are cases for position on top of, destination on top of, source from the top of, and path on the top of, as well as cases for position in a hollow object, destination to a hollow object, source in a hollow object, path in a hollow object, and so on. In general, extensive case systems like that in Avar seem to come about through elaboration of cases of location (Blake 151).

Blake names about twenty-five cases, but it would not be practical to make a census of all the various cases in all languages of the world: not all languages have been described, and linguists disagree about the proper analysis of those which have been described. Different names are used for the same or similar cases, and a term in one case system does not necessarily equate precisely with the same name in another case system.

---

13. The information in this and the following paragraphs is taken from Barry Blake, *Case*.

Many of the cases translate into English as prepositional phrases. The genitive often translates as "of," the dative as "to" or "for," the ablative as "from," the allative as "to," the comitative as "with," the perlative as "through," and so on. It seems, then, that English prepositions can be seen as doing more or less what case forms do.

It may be that the various ways of marking semantic functions are superficial manifestations of deeper structures of meaning; these deep structures would be the same for any language. At this deep level, we might assume, for example, a set of (unordered) semantic roles such as agent, patient, action, tense, and recipient, in no particular order. These semantic roles could then be specified in a particular instance: agent = teacher; patient = book; action = give; tense = past; aspect: perfect; recipient = boy. Then each particular language would apply a particular set of rules to produce a surface structure. In Latin, the rules would mark the semantic roles through various morphological forms of the words—"Magister puero librum dedit." In English, the semantic functions would be marked by word order—"The teacher has given the boy a book"—or by a prepositional phrase—"The master has given a book to the boy."

If this argument holds, it may be that every language has a set of semantic roles at the level of deep structure, and these semantic roles can then be manifested in various ways at the level of surface structure. Thus Latin shows a dative case in its surface structure, and this dative case can express any of several semantic roles. English at the deep level has the same semantic roles expressed by the Latin dative, but in the surface structure of English, these roles are manifested through word order or through prepositional phrases.[14]

According to this argument, the deep-level semantic roles are universal: that is, they are the same in every language. It seems plausible that the semantic roles agent, patient, and recipient would be present in every language; it is less plausible that every language would have a deep semantic role for motion through a hollow object, although we have seen that such a case function is marked at the surface level in Avar.

We need, then, some reasonable list of the universal deep semantic roles. Different linguists have come up with different lists, and as usual there is also variation in terminology. Fillmore (1968) began with an inventory of six cases, but later (1971) he expanded his inventory to eight. Longacre (1976) lists ten cases. Blake (67–69) lists fourteen cases which have been most

---

14. The seminal article here is Charles Fillmore's "The Case for Case." See also Blake, *Case*, chapter 3, "Modern Approaches to Case." A well-developed system of Case Grammar is found in Longacre, *An Anatomy of Speech Notions*.

frequently proposed as universal.[15] There is some overlap in these lists, often disguised by subcategorization and differences of terminology. From these lists I derive the following generous inventory of eighteen possible universal semantic roles:

1. *Agent:* the entity that performs an activity or brings about a change of state. **George** kicked the football.
2. *Patient:* an entity viewed as affected by an action. George kicked **the football.**
3. *Theme:* an entity viewed as existing, as in a state or undergoing change, or as located in a place or moving. **The sea** is calm. **The bird** is in its nest.
4. *Experiencer:* an entity experiencing an emotion or perception. **George** was angry.
5. *Recipient:* an entity that receives the action of the verb. John gave **George** the money.
6. *Beneficiary:* an entity on whose behalf an activity is carried out. John mowed the lawn **for his neighbor.** Sally cut **me** some flowers.
7. *Possessor:* an entity that possesses another entity. John used **George's** lawnmower.
8. *Factitive:* a thing made. George built **a canoe.**
9. *Range:* the specification of the action of the verb. George ran a **race.**
10. *Instrument:* the means by which an activity or a change of state is carried out. George opened the door with **a key. This key** opens the door.
11. *Locative:* the position of an entity in space or time. George is **at home.** We visit **every Tuesday.** It's cold **in the Yukon.**
12. *Source:* the point in space or time from which an entity moves or derives. I heard the song **of the loon.**
13. *Path:* the course in space or time over which an entity moves. We walked along **the road.**
14. *Destination:* the point in space or time to or toward which an entity moves or is oriented. George went **to Paris.**
15. *Purpose:* the purpose of an action. We went to the store **for ice cream.**
16. *Manner:* the way in which an activity is done or the way in which a change of state takes place. George acted his part **with panache.**

15. Fillmore (1968): agentive, instrumental, dative, factitive, locative, and objective; Fillmore (1971): agent, experiencer, instrument, object, source, goal, place, and time; Longacre: experiencer, agent, instrument, range, goal, source, patient, measure, locative, and path; Blake: patient, agent, instrument, experiencer, location, source, path, destination, recipient, purpose, beneficiary, manner, extent, possessor.

17. *Extent:* the distance, area, or time over which an action is carried out or over which a state holds. Patsy ran **ten miles.**
18. *Measure:* the measure, price, or value of an entity. This box weighs **ten pounds.**

The theory of deep-structure semantic roles accounts for the sentences I presented earlier in this chapter. In "We gave George the money," "George" is recipient; in "This key opens the door," "This key" is instrument; in "The Yukon is cold," "The Yukon" is theme (or perhaps locative; see discussion below); in "Sam ran a good race," "race" is range; in "This book costs ten dollars," "ten dollars" is measurement; and in "I heard the trumpet," "trumpet" is source.

This list of deep-structure semantic roles is both too long and too short. It is too short because it collapses distinct semantic functions. For example, the role of possessor would probably include such constructions as "the teacher's book," "the car's engine," "the elephant's trunk," and "the government's authority." Only the first of these is clearly a possessive, but the others have to find their place in this category. As always, the challenge is to find generalizations that do not excessively violate the richness of nature. On the other hand, this list of eighteen possible universal semantic roles may be too long, and it may not generalize enough: an inventory of eight or ten cases would be easier to manage. It is not clear, however, which eight or ten of these roles should be kept, and which rejected. It might be possible, for example, to combine factitive and range, or theme and patient, or recipient and beneficiary, though there are also good reasons to keep them all separate. But these are problems for linguists to solve.

IV.

There is no direct relation between the deep semantic roles and the cases that show up at the surface. The familiar names of most of the Indo-European cases are notably absent from the list of deep-structure roles. There is no deep-structure nominative, no genitive, dative, accusative, or ablative; these are cases only at the surface. (The locative and the instrumental, however, are present at both levels.) In general, a case (or a grammatical function) at the surface level may manifest any of several deep-structure roles; thus the surface-structure nominative (subject) case can manifest the deep-structure agent, patient, or experiencer. We can distinguish these deep-structure roles through comparison to corresponding questions or imperatives; similar tests can demonstrate the reality of the other deep-structure roles.

Many deep-structure roles can manifest as subjects at the surface level. The sentences "John broke the window" and "A baseball broke the window" have the same surface structure: noun phrase subject + transitive verb + noun phrase direct object. In deep structure, however, "John" and "a baseball" are in different roles; thus, it seems odd to make a conjunct subject of the two: "*John and a baseball broke the window." Furthermore, it is possible to say "John broke the window with a baseball," but it is not possible to say "*A baseball broke the window with John." "John" is the agent in these sentences, and "a baseball" is the instrument; so we may conclude that English allows the instrument to be the subject of a verb, at least in some situations.

The patient may be the subject not only in a passive sentence but also in some active constructions. In the sentence "Dad is cooking the roast beef now," "the roast beef" is the patient, and it must still be the patient in "The roast beef is cooking now." In the sentence "John broke his arm in the accident," the subject is probably a possessor; compare "John's arm was broken in the accident." But in "John broke all the dishes in his rage," "John" is clearly the agent.[16] In the sentence "It's windy in Chicago," the phrase "in Chicago" is locative, as it is in the sentence "Chicago is windy" (Fillmore, "The Case" 25). We may also compare such sentences as "Dallas is hot," "Tom is hot," "It's hot in Dallas," "*It's hot in Tom": "Tom" is experiencer, but "Dallas" is locative.

These examples show that the subject of an English verb can take many different semantic roles; it is simply wrong to identify the subject with the agent, or even with the core functions agent, patient, and experiencer. More often than not, the subject is the topic of the clause, and more often than not, the topic of a clause will be someone who is doing something, but the exceptions are too many to ignore.

The object of a verb can also take many semantic roles. In the prototypical transitive sentence, the subject is the agent, and the object is the patient of the action: "George frightened Sam." But other sentences do not conform to this model: in "Sam feared George," the subject is the patient, and the object is probably the agent. Verbs of making or producing take a factitive object: "Sam built the table." The sentence "Sam scratched the table," where "the table" is the patient, has a corresponding question, "What did George do to the table?" But the question "What did George do to the table?" would

---

16. As Fillmore says, "The superficial nature of the notion 'subject of a sentence' is made apparent by these examples in a particularly persuasive way, because in the possessor-as-subject cases, the 'subject' is not even a major constituent of the sentence; it is taken from the modifier of one of the major constituents" (Fillmore, "The Case," p. 23).

be very odd if the corresponding sentence were "George built the table." Likewise, "What George did to the table was to scratch it" is acceptable, but "What George did to the table was to build it" is odd. It is one thing to say "George paints nudes" and something very different to say "What George does to nudes is to paint them."

In "This book costs ten dollars," the object "ten dollars" is measurement. In general, measurement objects cannot become the subject of a corresponding passive construction: "*Ten dollars is costed by this book." If, however, the verb "to cost" means something like "to make a judgment concerning the price to be charged for an item," then the passive does work: "George costed these dresses" can be transformed to "These dresses were costed by George."

In the typical three-place clause, the subject is the agent, the object is the patient, and the indirect object is either the recipient or the beneficiary, as in "We gave the teacher a cake," which can also take the form "We gave a cake to the teacher"; but other deep-structure roles can occur in the third position. In "He blamed his parents for everything," "his parents" is the patient, and "for everything" may be range; in "He blamed everything on his parents," the object "everything" is presumably still range. In "John smeared the wall with paint," "the wall" is the direct object and probably patient, while "with paint" is instrument; the point of the sentence is that something happened to the wall, and paint was used to do it. But in the sentence "John smeared paint on the wall," the focus of the action is "the paint," which in this instance may be the patient, while "on the wall" is presumably locative; the point is that something was done to the paint, and the wall was where it was done. Whatever is used as the direct object seems to take on a sense of being acted upon, no matter what its deep-structure case; the surface-structure grammatical role is not beside the point in the interpretation of the sentence.

Most of the sentences I have been discussing so far have been simple sentences in the active voice, and even in these sentences we have seen both the subject and the object take on several different semantic functions. But English grammar has other resources for moving semantic functions into different grammatical or discourse roles.

The passive voice is most often used to move the patient of a transitive verb into the subject position. Instead of "Sam killed George," we may say "George was killed by Sam." The passive demotes the active subject from the topic position and places in that topic position whatever had been the direct object of the active sentence. Most often, it will be the patient of the verb that becomes the new topic, though we will see some exceptions to that pattern.

The first model of transformational grammar proposed by Noam Chomsky included a detailed description of the transformation from the basic active form to the derived passive. Some later models derive active and passive sentences independently, but one of the great attractions of the early model was its ability to describe the relationship between these two forms of the sentence.[17]

The most common sort of passive transformation in English moves the subject of a transitive clause into a prepositional phrase: If the subject is a pronoun, its surface case is changed from the nominative to the accusative, and the direct object is moved into the position of the subject. If the new subject is a pronoun, its case is changed from the accusative to the nominative. Certain adjustments are then made to the verb. The result is that a sentence such as "We killed them" is changed to "They were killed by us." The prepositional phrase may now be deleted: "They were killed."

The mechanics of the passive transformation as described by Chomsky seem very simple and elegant, but in practice the passive is more complex. Some sentences that on the surface seem to be transitive nonetheless resist the passive transformation, and others produce passives that are possible but awkward. In the sentence "We feared the tyrant," the subject is patient and the object is agent, but still the sentence can be transformed to "The tyrant was feared by us." The sentence "I spent ten dollars on this book" can be transformed to "Ten dollars was spent on this book," but the agent phrase "by me" will almost certainly be deleted; in any case the sentence seems slightly odd. Larger amounts make a better passive: "Ten million dollars was spent on this building!"[18]

Passive constructions are more likely to be successful if the subject is a real patient—that is, if the subject is directly and physically affected by the agent—or if the situation is general. In the sentence "Susan knows a lot of Canadian history," the phrase "a lot of Canadian history" is probably range rather than patient; the passive "A lot of Canadian history is known by Susan" is perhaps possible, but awkward. A more general agent produces a better passive: "Canadian history is better known by this generation than by our parents' generation." "This bridge has been passed under by a pedestrian" is awkward, but "This bridge has been passed under by countless generations of lovers" is better. "The army was deserted by the soldier" is unlikely, because the army was probably unaffected the desertion, but "The army was

---

17. See Chomsky, *Syntactic Structures*, pp. 42–43. See also Lasnik, *Syntactic Structures Revisited*, for an evaluation of the early model from a perspective many years later. For a general account of developments in the theory of transformational grammar, see Horrocks, *Generative Grammar*, and for a description of the most recent model, see Chomsky, *The Minimalist Program*.

18. These examples are based on the discussion of passives in Longacre, pp. 90–95.

deserted by all its generals" seems to be acceptable; "He was deserted by his wife" is successful.

English allows some indirect objects to become the subject of a transformed passive. The sentence "George gave John the book" thus has two passive transformations: "The book was given to John by George" and "John was given the book by George." Some dialects (not including mine) allow "The book was given John by George." Some languages, such as German, ancient Greek, and Latin, do not allow an indirect object to become the subject of a passive sentence; in these languages, the indirect object has a dative case marker in surface structure, and perhaps this marker somehow blocks the transformation. English, of course, does not mark the dative, and so the transformation is not blocked.

English, in fact, allows any deep-structure role to be the topic of a statement by means of what is called a cleft construction.[19] In a cleft construction the constituents of the simple sentence are divided into two parts, one of which is placed in the main clause while the rest of the sentence is in a subordinate clause. For example, given the simple sentence "Sam killed George," the cleft construction would be "It was George that Sam killed." The effect of the transformation is to emphasize whatever item is placed in the main clause. In this example, the cleft construction tells us that we are talking about George, not Sam. There is also a cleft construction with the original subject in the main clause: "It was Sam who killed George." This sentence is most likely to occur if there has been some question about who killed George—was it Sam, or someone else? The simple sentence "Sam killed George" is a possible answer to the question, but the cleft is more emphatic—"It was Sam who killed George." Cleft sentences can also occur with a passive construction in the subordinate clause: "It was George who was killed by Sam."

The cleft construction allows almost any case function to become the topic. For example, the sentence "Peter carried a black flag at the demonstration just to annoy Sue" can produce the following cleft sentences:

It was Peter who carried a black flag at the demonstration just to annoy Sue.
It was a black flag that Peter carried at the demonstration just to annoy Sue.
It was at the demonstration that Peter carried a black flag just to annoy Sue.
It was the demonstration that Peter carried a black flag at just to annoy Sue.
It was just to annoy Sue that Peter carried a black flag at the demonstration.
It was Sue that Peter annoyed by carrying a black flag at the demonstration.

---

19. For topicalizing constructions in other languages, see Palmer, chapter 8, "Topic and Inverse Systems."

Any of the deep-structure cases can be emphasized in a cleft construction:

Agent: It was Smiley who killed Dieter Frey.
Patient: It was Dieter Frey that Smiley killed.
Theme: It was the sea that was calm. It's the bird that's in its nest.
Experiencer: It was George who was angry.
Recipient: It's George that John gave the money to.
Beneficiary: It's Mary that John built the deck for.
Possessor: It's George whose lawnmower John used.
Factitive: It was a canoe that George built.
Range: It was a ballad that George sang. It's algebra that Mary learned.
Instrument: It was a crowbar that John opened the window with.
Locative: It's Chicago that's windy. It's Tuesday that we go home.
Source: It was a loon whose song we heard. It's Winnipeg we came from.
Path: It was the bridle-path that we walked along.
Destination: It's Paris that George went to.
Purpose: It's the money that I work for.
Manner: It was with grace that George accepted the award.
Extent: It was ten miles that Patsy ran.
Measure: It was ten dollars that this book cost.

Not all of these are equally successful, at least in isolation, but I think that contexts can be imagined in which any of them could be quite acceptable.

The dichotomy of the subject and the object, the agent and the patient, cannot do justice to the richness and flexibility of expressed meaning. The whole range of deep-structure semantic functions is needed; and these are only the most general and most useful of the possible distinctions. The task of the following chapters is to see if these semantic roles have narrative counterparts.

CHAPTER 7

Agents, Patients, and Experiencers
le Carré, Weldon, Kesey, Woolf

In chapter 6, I summarized the elements of Case Grammar, a linguistic theory of deep semantic functions and their surface realizations in various natural languages. In the rest of Part Two, I will discuss narrative analogues of some of these semantic functions. Most clauses show more than one function, as do most narratives, but often one function or another dominates in a narrative. In this chapter, I examine the narrative analogues of three cases: narratives of the agent, in which someone does something (le Carré's *Call for the Dead*); narratives of the patient, in which something is done to someone (Kesey's *One Flew Over the Cuckoo's Nest*); and narratives of the experiencer, in which someone experiences something (Woolf's *The Waves*).

I.

The division of the world into subject and object, self and other, seems fundamental and pervasive, as we can see in this passage from Ernest Fenollosa:

> Light, heat, gravity, chemical affinity, human will, have this in common, that they redistribute force. Their unit of process can be represented as: term from which, transference of force, term to which. If we regard this transference as the conscious or unconscious act of an agent we can translate the diagram into: agent, act, object.[1]

1. Ernest Fenollosa, *The Chinese Written Character as a Medium for Poetry*, p. 12.

Typically, agents are people, and objects are things; but sometimes people can be objects—or at least they can be treated as if they were objects, even if we believe that treating a person as an object is morally wrong. Certainly one does not want to be treated as an object:

> The Zionist revolution was meant to liberate Jews from the age-old ghetto mentality of the weak, helpless victim. It set out to prove that Jews were not doomed to be objects, but they could be subjects—that this people whose reality and destiny were always defined for them by external forces could become a community of choice, with the power to construct their own political history.[2]

It is very easy to find collocations of the terms "self" and "other," or "subject" and "object," or "subjective" and "objective"—indeed, it is difficult to avoid them. Even those who wish to deny the opposition of subject and object are likely to deny it in its own terms. Thus the following passage suggests that everyone is both subject and object, agent and patient, because acting is also being acted upon, or suffering; but both action and suffering are part of a pattern of ultimate stillness:

> You know and do not know, what it is to act or suffer.
> You know and do not know, that acting is suffering,
> And suffering action. Neither does the actor suffer
> Nor the patient act. But both are fixed
> In an eternal action, an eternal patience
> To which all must consent that it may be willed
> And which all must suffer that they may will it,
> That the pattern may subsist, that the wheel may turn and still
> Be forever still.[3]

The grammar of the subject is related to the philosophy of the subject. In most European languages (as we saw in chapter 6), the intransitive subject S (often the experiencer) and the transitive subject A (often the agent) have the same form, while the transitive object P (often the patient) has a different form. Western philosophy has likewise usually assumed an opposition of the subject and the object, in which the subject is both experiencer and agent, while the object is different.[4]

---

2. Thomas L. Friedman, *From Beirut to Jerusalem*, p. 273.
3. T. S. Eliot, *Murder in the Cathedral*, pp. 40–41.
4. The conflation of agent and experiencer can also be found in psychoanalytic theory,

In the Cartesian cogito—"I think, therefore I am"—the Cartesian subject is the S of an intransitive sentence; it is an experiencer.[5] The Hegelian subject is characterized by action rather than by experience, through its struggle with an opposing self-consciousness; it is an agent. If Descartes and Hegel are talking about the same subject, then the subject can be either experiencer or agent, just as the subject of a sentence in most European languages can be either experiencer or agent. But if the major European languages were ergative rather than accusative, if the Cartesian subject S were identified with the Hegelian object P, but distinguished from the Hegelian subject A, then the philosophy of the subject might have developed in a different way, with clear distinctions between the subject acting, the subject acted upon, and the subject experiencing. All three of these subjectivities find expression in the narrative tradition.

II.

Literary analysis, like grammatical analysis, is incomplete if it distinguishes only two subjectivities. In addition to the narrative agent and the narrative patient, there is also the narrative experiencer: sometimes the subject acts, sometimes the subject is acted upon, and sometimes the subject sees, hears, feels, and so on. We should not expect, however, that the narrative experiencer will always show up as the subject of an intransitive verb. Even within the grammar of the sentence, semantic roles do not always match grammatical functions; in narrative, things can get even more complicated. Nor should we expect any passage of much more than a sentence to be strictly confined to one mode of subjectivity. Even within a short passage, subjectivity can shift. In chapter 3, I examined the description of a fight from John le Carré's *Call for the Dead* to illustrate the Hegelian pattern of self-consciousness and conflict; this fight also shows the complexity of shifts of subjectivity, a com-

---

as noted by Stolorow, Brandchaft, and Atwood, in *Psychoanalytic Treatment: An Intersubjective Approach*, pp. 17–18: "Paradoxically, the concept of the 'self' is without a doubt the most problematic one in the theory of self psychology. A conceptual imprecision that has pervaded the self psychology literature . . . is the use of the term *self* to refer both to a psychological structure (an organization of experience) and an existential agent (an initiator of action)."

5. An early critique of the Cartesian cogito objected that Descartes might as well have said "I walk, therefore I am," rather than "I think, therefore I am." The subject of "I walk" is an agent, while the subject of "I think" is an experiencer. Descartes, however, rejected this proposed reformulation of the cogito. He could have merely imagined that he was walking—indeed, any action could be illusory—but an experience, or experiencing, is incontrovertible, and thinking is the fundamental experience. So the Cartesian subject must be an experiencer.

plexity we all follow without effort: before the fight actually gets going, le Carré presents an account of Smiley's physical and emotional experience:[6]

> Smiley was out of breath. His chest was burning from the bitter, rank fog, his mouth hot and dry, filled with a taste like blood. Somehow he summoned breath, and he shouted desperately:
> "Dieter!"

In the first sentence of the passage, Smiley is the subject, but he is certainly neither an agent nor a patient: he is neither doing something, nor is something being done to him. Being out of breath is a condition, an experience.

The account of Smiley's experience continues in the next sentence. Here, however, Smiley's subjectivity has been transferred to parts of his body, and it is these parts of his body that are the grammatical subjects.[7]

The third sentence is a conjunction of two transitive clauses, and Smiley is the subject and agent in both. The action of breathing is usually automatic and spontaneous; the verb "to breathe" can be intransitive, and the person breathing is not really an agent: "He was breathing heavily." Here, however, the normally spontaneous action of breathing takes an effort; the transitive verb "to summon" takes an object and also an agent. When an ordinarily spontaneous action takes an agent, the agent is probably in trouble.

It is not only the subjects and objects of verbs that can express the subjectivity of the experiencer. In this third sentence, the adverb "desperately" could be considered a transformation of a copulative clause—"he was desperate"—with an experiencer as subject.

The passage now moves into a more active mode:

> Frey looked at him, nodded, and said:
> "*Servus*, George," and hit Mendel a hard, brutal blow with the pistol.

Frey begins as the agent of three verbs of low transitivity: we could take "to look" as an intransitive verb, or "to look at" as a transitive phrasal verb. In either analysis the object is not affected by the action; nonetheless, the verb "to look" or "to look at" does take an agent, in contrast, say, to the verb "to see," which takes an experiencer; "looking at" is an intentional action. The

---

6. All of the following are from le Carré's *Call for the Dead*, p. 141.
7. Some languages have a construction called the *accusative of respect*, or *retained object* in a passive construction, in which the subjectivity remains that of the person, and the part affected is in the accusative case, as if one were to say: "Smiley was burning (with respect to) his chest from the bitter, rank fog"; see Smyth, *Greek Grammar*, p. 360.

verb "to nod" can be intransitive, as it is here, or it can take an internal object of the part of the body, "to nod the head"; although nodding is an action, and thus takes an agent, the agent is acting only on himself. The object of the verb "to say" is what is said, so the verb is factitive.

The last verb phrase in the sentence is highly transitive, even violent. As the first clause unfolds, it seems for a moment that the object of the verb is "Mendel"; certainly "he hit Mendel" would be perfectly grammatical, with Mendel as the direct object and patient. But as the clause continues, it seems that the verb "hit" takes the (internal) direct object "a hard, brutal blow," while Mendel is the indirect object, as if the clause were "he gave a hard, brutal blow to Mendel." The effect is to emphasize the blow, which has been nominalized and is therefore an existing thing rather than just a momentary action. The prepositional phrase "with the pistol" is instrumental. The word "brutal" in "[Frey] hit Mendel a hard, brutal blow" probably expresses the experience of Mendel as well as the judgment of the narrator.

Once the fight begins, there are more highly transitive verbs with an agent as subject and a patient as object. But even during the fight, Smiley's experience and emotion remain part of the story. In fact, mixtures of the three subjectivities—experiencer, agent, and patient—are probably more common than not, at least over any extended narration, and readers seem to have no difficulty negotiating these shifting subjectivities.

All of these three modes of subjectivity will be found in any extended narrative, but often one form dominates, and thus we can have narratives of action, narratives of patience, and narratives of experience. Often, however, shifts in subjectivity within a dominant mode lead to more-complex narrative structures. The following sections explore these modes and their complexities.

III.

A story about a perfect agent would be boring: that's why there are so few good novels about God. Every superhero needs his kryptonite. Working down from gods and superheroes, we find some secret agents—such as Ian Fleming's James Bond—and some detectives—such as Rex Stout's Archie Goodwin—who seem competent in almost any situation. A part of their appeal is their sophistication and their sexual success. They are, in a word, cool. Being cool is largely a question of agency—the person who is cool is always in control, never under the control of someone else.

Bond's agency, however, is oddly ambiguous and compromised. Though he is an agent, he is not his own agent: he is an agent of the Queen, and he takes his orders from M. Moreover, Bond is hardly invulnerable; from time to time he is injured, and occasionally he is even tortured by some villain into whose clutches he has fallen—though when tortured, he can control his reactions to deceive his torturer. Between assignments he often falls into a state of lethargy, depression, and even impotence. At the beginning of *On Her Majesty's Secret Service,* he tells his doctors, "I feel like hell. I sleep badly. I eat practically nothing. I drink too much and my work has gone to blazes. I'm shot to pieces. Make me better" (25). In a sense, the stories show Bond struggling to establish his sense of agency through danger. He is not happy unless he is the subject of some highly transitive verbs.[8]

George Smiley, John le Carré's secret agent, seems designed almost as an anti-Bond, as we see in the second paragraph of the beginning of *Call for the Dead:* "Short, fat, and of a quiet disposition, he appeared to spend a lot of money on really bad clothes, which hung about his squat frame like skin on a shrunken toad" (7). The contrast between Bond and Smiley is even more direct in *A Murder of Quality:* "Obscurity was his nature, as well as his profession. The byways of espionage are not populated by the brash and colorful adventurers of fiction" (83). Nor is Smiley successful with women. It is true that he managed to marry a great beauty, Lady Anne Sercomb, but in the first paragraph of *Call for the Dead,* we find out that she has left him for a Cuban motor racing driver.

By the end of each of the stories, of course, Smiley has shown himself to be an agent, a far better agent than Bond ever is, but unlike Bond he gets no satisfaction from his agency. The reader's satisfaction is probably complex. One the one hand, we are pleased to think that a person of no obvious distinction can be heroic, but on the other hand, we are left with Smiley's feelings of disappointment and betrayal.

The clearest forms of agency are expressed in verbs of high transitivity, such as hitting and killing, but there are many other kinds of less transitive agency: convincing someone of something, building something, finding or hiding something, traveling somewhere, and so on. Moreover, behind every action there is the decision to act. Sometimes it is the action that is important, sometimes the decision.

The internalization of agency is perhaps most characteristic of the modern period, but it occurs even in ancient epic. The crucial moment in the plot of the *Iliad* is Achilles' decision to return the body of Hector to Priam.

---

8. For an interesting discussion of the Bond phenomenon, see Tony Bennett and Janet Woollacott, *Bond and Beyond.* I must admit that I am mystified by Bond's popularity; I find the books and movies not only offensive but also boring.

The final event of the *Aeneid* is a death, as Aeneas kills Turnus in battle; what matters most, however, is not the killing but the decision to kill. Epic decision making can also be found in modern fiction: at the climax of *The Lord of the Rings*, Frodo must decide either to destroy the ring or to use it; he makes the wrong decision, but then the matter is, as it were, taken out of his hands.

These epic decisions either derive from or lead to actions of high transitivity. In many modern narratives, the decision remains, but the action has become attenuated or even negative. At the end of Henry James's *The American*, Christopher Newman decides not to take revenge on his fiancée's family; in Edith Wharton's *The House of Mirth*, Lily Bart decides not to reveal some incriminating letters that have come into her possession.

Women, of course, have usually had less access to agency than men, both in life and in literature.[9] The first sentence of Wilkie Collins's *The Woman in White* describes the typical division of literary labor: "This is the story of what a Woman's patience can endure, and what a Man's resolution can achieve." According to Sandra Gilbert and Susan Gubar, "assertiveness, aggressiveness—all characteristics of a male life of 'significant action'—are 'monstrous' in women precisely because 'unfeminine' and therefore unsuited to a gentle life of 'contemplative purity'" (28). Following Simone de Beauvoir, they note that

> the human male's "transcendence" of nature is symbolized by his ability to hunt and kill, just as the human female's identification with nature, her role as a symbol of immanence, is expressed by her central involvement in that life-giving but involuntary birth process which perpetuates the species. (14)

Men are the subjects of verbs of high transitivity, whereas women are the involuntary patients of a process they do not control. As Lucy, the heroine of Forster's *A Room with a View*, asks:

> Why were most big things not ladylike? Charlotte had once explained to her why. It was not that ladies were inferior to men; it was that they were different. Their mission was to inspire others to achievement rather than to achieve themselves. Indirectly, by means of tact and a spotless name, a lady could accomplish much. But if she rushed into the fray herself she would be first censured, then despised, and finally ignored. (45)

9. Here I can only touch on a topic that has received extensive discussion. See, as a beginning, Showalter, *A Literature of Their Own*; see also Gilbert and Gubar, *The Madwoman in the Attic*.

An adventurer can be someone to admire and emulate, but an adventuress is disreputable. The "sensation" novelists of the 1870s, for example—writers such as Mary Braddon, Rhoda Broughton, and Florence Marryat—show female characters as active subjects:

> Sensation novels expressed female anger, frustration, and sexual energy more directly than had been done previously. Readers were introduced to a new kind of heroine, one who could put her hostility toward men into violent action.... In many sensation novels, the death of a husband comes as a welcome release, and women escape from their families through illness, madness, divorce, flight, and ultimately murder.

But the narrative conventions still "demanded the erring heroine's destruction."[10]

Issues of female agency are often played out through doubles. The female double, like the male, often consists of a good side and a bad, the angel and the monster, but what makes the bad side of the female double bad is agency. According to Gilbert and Gubar, this division in the characters is a reflection of division within the author:

> [T]he mad double is as crucial to the aggressively sane novels of Jane Austen and George Eliot as she is in the more obviously rebellious stories told by Charlotte and Emily Brontë. Both gothic and anti-gothic writers represent themselves as split like Emily Dickinson between the elected nun and the damned witch, or like Mary Shelley between the noble, censorious scientist and the enraged, childish monster. In fact, so important is this female schizophrenia of authorship that . . . it links these nineteenth century writers with such twentieth century descendants as Virginia Woolf (who projects herself into both ladylike Mrs. Dalloway and crazed Septimus Warren Smith), Doris Lessing (who divides herself between sane Martha Hesse and mad Lynda Coldridge), and Sylvia Plath (who sees herself as both a plaster saint and a dangerous "old yellow" monster). (78)

The double of the angel and the monster is particularly popular in Victorian literature, but it can certainly be found today. Fay Weldon's *The Life and Loves of a She-Devil* works both with and against this convention. The She-Devil is Ruth Patchett, a large, ugly woman married to Bobbo, an accountant. Bobbo leaves Ruth for Mary Fisher, the angel, a lovely and

---

10. The quotations are from Elaine Showalter, *A Literature of Their Own*, p. 160 and p. 29.

wealthy writer of romance fiction. Ruth has been a fairly passive person, but after Bobbo leaves, she takes action to get revenge. She commits arson, forgery, fraud, and embezzlement. Through her machinations, Bobbo ends up in prison, Mary Fisher goes bankrupt and then dies of cancer, and Ruth becomes wealthy.

Some of Ruth's agency is directed toward herself—she is her own patient. She undergoes a long series of operations to change her appearance, and by the end of the story she looks just like Mary Fisher. In effect she takes Mary's place. She changes her name to Marlene Hunter, to match the name Mary Fisher; she buys Mary's mansion, and she even writes a romance novel. Once Bobbo is out of prison, a broken man, she takes him in:

> Sometimes I let Bobbo sleep with me. Or I take my lovers in front of him. What agreeable turmoil that causes in the household! Even the dogs sulk. I cause Bobbo as much misery as he ever caused me, and more. I try not to, but somehow it is not a matter of male or female, after all; it never was, merely of power. I have all, and he has none. As I was, so he is now. (240)

Some recent writers of serious fiction have given more-active roles to women—Marge Piercy comes to mind—but serious fiction now generally avoids stories of high transitivity. It is mostly in forms of popular culture such as action movies and comic books that we see the new woman of action.

IV.

The ideal hero of a story of patience is under arrest, as we see at the beginning of Franz Kafka's *The Trial* and Eric Ambler's The *Light of Day*:

> Someone must have traduced Joseph K., for without having done anything wrong, he was arrested one fine morning. (1)

> It came down to this: if I had not been arrested by the Turkish police, I would have been arrested by the Greek police. (9)

The story then consists of the hero's attempts to free himself—and in so doing to become an agent. The narrators of Ambler's stories do achieve a sort of limited freedom and agency at the end, but Joseph K. is killed.

Randle Patrick McMurphy, the hero of Ken Kesey's *One Flew Over the Cuckoo's Nest*, is quite literally a patient, an involuntary inmate of a mental hospital. The story is narrated by another inmate, Chief Broom. Here is Chief Broom's description of McMurphy's arrival on the ward:

> He sounds big. I hear him coming down the hall, and he sounds big in the way he walks, and he sure don't slide; he's got iron on his heels and he rings it on the floor like horseshoes. He shows up in the door and stops and hitches his thumbs in his pockets, boots wide apart, and stands there with the guys looking at him.... (16)

> He's got on work farm pants and shirt, sunned out till they're the color of watered milk. His face and neck and arms are the color of oxblood leather from working long in the fields. He's got a primer-black motorcycle cap stuck in his hair and a leather jacket over one arm, and he's got on boots gray and dusty and heavy enough to kick a man half in two. (17)

Clearly, McMurphy is a man of action; it is not in his nature to be a patient, and the story will work out this contradiction between his nature and the situation in which he finds himself.

The ward is run by Big Nurse, who controls the patients with brutal discipline. Big Nurse's agency is clearly a violation of her proper sexual role:

> Her face is smooth, calculated, and precision-made, like an expensive baby doll, skin like flesh-colored enamel, blend of white and cream and baby-blue eyes, small nose, pink little nostrils—everything working together except the color on her lips and fingernails, and the size of her bosom. A mistake was made somehow in manufacturing, putting those big, womanly breasts on what would of [sic] otherwise been a perfect work, and you can see how bitter she is about it. (11)

The assumption that men should dominate women pervades the story and provides a background for McMurphy's struggle with Big Nurse. For most of the story, the struggle between McMurphy and Big Nurse consists of his attempts to manipulate or break the rules she has established to control the inmates. But at the climax, things become physical: McMurphy tries to strangle Big Nurse, and she takes her revenge by having him lobotomized. Chief Broom cannot bear to see McMurphy in this condition; he smothers him, and then he makes his own escape from the ward.

This story is clearly a version of the Hegelian parable of the master and the slave, as McMurphy and Big Nurse fight to determine who shall be agent and who shall be patient; moreover, as the parable would suggest, it is the patient who gains superiority of self-consciousness. In addition, the shape of this story is a reminder that the word "patient" is etymologically related to the word "passion," and that the passion of Christ is fundamentally a story of patience.[11]

V.

Some stories are concerned neither with what the hero did nor with what happened to the hero, but rather with how the hero felt. Of course any story must have some kind of action, however attenuated—otherwise there will be no story—but in a story of experience, the action is of little importance in itself and serves only as an armature.

Many modern short stories are stories of experience. Some of these are classics; others are simply the effusions of writers who somehow imagine that their feelings will be of general interest. Among the classics are several stories in James Joyce's *Dubliners*. The first story of the collection, "Two Sisters," tells about the death of an old priest. The death occurs offstage, and the only action, such as it is, occurs when the narrator and his aunt visit the old priest's sisters. There is some conversation, which reveals something of the character of the priest. And that is really all that happens.

In "Araby," the narrator tells us that he was in love with a neighborhood girl, and in order to please her he goes to a bazaar, Araby, to buy her a present; but he arrives too late, and most of the booths are closing. As the story ends, something happens, but it is not really an action; it is an experience, as the narrator comes to understand something about himself: "Gazing up into the darkness I saw myself as a creature driven and derided by vanity; and my eyes burned with anguish and anger" (41).

The theory of this narrative mode is stated by one of its best practitioners, Virginia Woolf:

> The mind receives a myriad impressions—trivial, fantastic, evanescent, or engraved with the sharpness of steel. From all sides they come, an incessant shower of innumerable atoms; and as they fall, as they shape themselves into the life of Monday or Tuesday, the accent falls differently from of old; the moment of importance came not here but there; so that, if a writer were a free man and not a slave, if he could write what he chose, not what he must, if he could base his work upon his own feeling and not

---

11. I will have more to say about *One Flew Over the Cuckoo's Nest* in chapter 8.

upon convention, there would be no plot, no comedy, no tragedy, no love interest or catastrophe in the accepted sense. . . . Life is not a series of gig-lamps symmetrically arranged; life is a luminous halo, a semi-transparent envelope surrounding us from the beginning of consciousness to the end. Is it not the task of the novelist to convey this varying, this unknown and uncircumscribed spirit, whatever aberration or complexity it may display, with as little mixture of the alien and external as possible?[12]

Joyce's short stories show that is possible to construct a short narrative with "no plot, no comedy, no tragedy, no love interest or catastrophe." It is harder to write a long narrative on these principles. But Woolf's novel *The Waves* is a nearly pure manifestation of her theory.

The story is written in two distinct styles, which are indicated by typography: ten short sections printed in italic type alternate with longer sections printed in roman type. The italicized sections average a page or so each, though the last is only one short sentence. These sections describe the passage of time during a day. All but the last begin with the position of the sun in the sky. The first, for example, begins:

The sun had not yet risen. The sea was indistinguishable from the sky, except that the sea was slightly creased as if a cloth had wrinkles in it. (5)

And the second begins:

The sun rose higher. Blue waves, green waves swept a quick fan over the beach, circling the spike of sea-holly and leaving shallow pools of light here and there on the sand. (19)

These italicized sections are descriptive, but they do not specify or suggest any particular point of view. There is never a human character interior to any of these descriptions, though there are some human artifacts—a house, tables and chairs, a boat. These are narratives of experience, though the experiencer is absent from the narrative.

The italicized sections divide nine longer sections printed in roman type. These longer sections consist entirely of what is represented as the reported speech of six different characters as they age from infancy to death. There is never any intervention of a narrative voice, except for the formulas "Louis said," or "Rhoda said," and so on, and never any description outside of the reported speech.

12. Virginia Woolf, *The Common Reader 1*, p. 150.

The first of these sections begins:

> "I see a ring," said Bernard, "hanging above me. It quivers and hangs in a loop of light."
> "I see a slab of pale yellow," said Susan, "spreading away until its meets a purple stripe."
> "I hear a sound," Rhoda said, "cheep, chirp; cheep chirp; going up and down."
> "I see a globe," said Neville, "hanging down in a drop against the enormous flanks of some hill."
> "I see a crimson tassel," said Jinny, "twisted with gold threads."
> "I hear something stamping," said Louis. "A great beast's foot is chained. It stamps, and stamps, and stamps." (6)

Though these words are represented as speech, they certainly are not. I suspect they are Woolf's attempt to represent in language the prelinguistic perceptions of infants just learning about the world through sensation.[13] Some of these perceptions are easy to interpret, but the meaning of others I am not sure of. These children do not yet know the names of the world's furniture—they know only their own experiences. Some of the later reported speeches in the novel could be the real words or thoughts of the characters, but I think these first passages suggest that the internal monologues are always the author's interpretation of the characters' perceptions and feelings, their experience.

These initial very short monologues continue only for a page or so. Soon the speeches are a few sentences, and then a few paragraphs:

> "Now they are all gone," said Louis. "I am alone. They have gone into the house for breakfast, and I am left standing by the wall among the flowers. It is very early, before lessons. Flower after flower is specked on the depths of green. The petals are harlequins. Stalks rise from the black hollows beneath. The flowers swim like fish made of light upon the dark, green waters. I hold a stalk in my hand. I am the stalk. My roots go down to the depths of the world. Through the earth dry with brick, and damp earth, through veins of lead and silver. I am all fibre. All tremors shake me, and the weight of the earth is pressed to my ribs. Up here my eyes are green leaves, unseeing. I am a boy in grey flannels with a belt fastened by a brass snake up here. Down there my eyes are the lidless eyes of a stone figure in

---

13. In *The Phantom Table,* Ann Banfield offers an ambitious argument that Woolf's theory of sensation is like (and probably derived from) Bertrand Russell's theory of sensation.

a desert by the Nile. I see women passing with red pitchers to the river; I see camels swaying and men in turbans. I hear tramplings, tremblings, stirrings round me." (8)

For the most part the characters in this story don't do very much, although they experience a great deal. They grow older, they go to school, they leave school, some marry, some have affairs, some have jobs, but the externals of their lives can be only vaguely deduced. A few actual events are reported—in this first section, for example, Jinny kisses Louis—but these events are quite distanced by the narrative technique. Whatever happens is always mediated by, always filtered through, the perceptions of one or another of the speaking characters. There is thus a complete contrast to the italicized sections, which aspire to exist without a perceiving consciousness.

The major event of the story as a whole is the death of another character, Percival, a friend of the speaking characters. This event comes just halfway through the book:

> "He is dead," said Neville. "He fell. His horse tripped. He was thrown. The sails of the world have swung round and caught me on the head. All is over. The lights of the world have gone out. There stands the tree which I cannot pass.
>
> "Oh, to crumple this telegram in my fingers—to let the light of the world flood back—to say this has not happened! But why turn one's head hither and thither? This is the truth. This is the fact. His horse stumbled; he was thrown. The flashing trees and white rails went up in a shower. There was a surge; a drumming in his ears. Then the blow; the world crashed; he breathed heavily. He died where he fell." (101–2)[14]

It is not clear for about a page who has died. It is typical of the narrative style that the death occurs offstage, that the reader sees the death only through the reactions of the principal characters. Percival's death does not matter so much in itself, but rather as it becomes part of the characters' experience.

The final section of the book draws together many of the themes of the story. Here Bernard is the only speaker. He seems to be talking to a chance acquaintance, but the forty-page monologue that follows is not likely to represent real speech.

---

14. This passage is an example of epimone, frequent repetition to dwell on a point, here for vehemence and pathos, as in Judges 5:27: "At her feet he bowed, he fell, he lay down: at her feet he bowed, he fell: where he bowed, there he fell down dead"; or in Spenser, *The Faerie Queene*, I, xi, 54: "So downe he fell, and forth his life did breath . . . So downe he fell, as an huge rockie clift . . . So downe he fell, and like an heaped mountain lay."

There is much to be said about this final section, and about the whole novel—for example, as an account of memory or of the effect of time on character. My concern here, however, is simply with the narration of experience. In this section Bernard offers a sort of summary of Woolf's technique, in a reprise of the very beginning of the story:

> "In the beginning, there was the nursery, with windows opening on to a garden, and beyond that the sea. I saw something brighten—no doubt the brass handle of a cupboard. Then Mrs. Constable raised the sponge above her head, squeezed it, and out shot, right, left, all down the spine, arrows of sensation. And so, as long as we draw breath, for the rest of time, if we knock against a chair, a table, or a woman, we are pierced with arrows of sensation—if we walk in the garden, if we drink this wine." (162)

The narration of experience is an important element in many modern narratives, such as Marcel Proust's *À la recherche du temps perdu,* James Joyce's *Ulysses,* William Faulkner's *The Sound and the Fury* and *As I Lay Dying,* and Jean-Paul Sartre's *Nausea.* None of these, however, is a narrative of pure experience: each is a mixture of narrative modes, but each is mixed in its own way; there is no general recipe.

CHAPTER 8

Dative Subjects
Stevenson, Fitzgerald, Kesey, Robbe-Grillet

The agent, the patient, and the experiencer are the most typical grammatical subjects, in ordinary transitive, intransitive, and passive constructions, and they are also the most typical narrative subjects. In this chapter, I begin the discussion of less typical subject positions, beginning with the dative subject.

The dative case expresses a number of semantic roles, most of which share the feature of being only indirectly involved in the action of the verb. The dative is often used to express a witness to an action or a person who takes an interest in an action. The role of the person interested or the witness is a kind of subjectivity in the wider sense, and as such it can form a kind of narrative subjectivity. Often the witness is primarily a tool of narration, but even such a witness may have a measure of independent existence. In some narratives, the witness is more important, even the hero of the story. In this chapter, I will examine several stories narrated by a witness—Stevenson's *The Master of Ballantrae*, Fitzgerald's *The Great Gatsby*, Kesey's *One Flew Over the Cuckoo's Nest*, and Robbe-Grillet's *Jealousy*—a series in which the witness takes on increasing importance and increasing subjectivity.

I.

In English, as we have seen, most semantic functions are expressed by word order or prepositional phrases rather than by case forms. There is no dative case in English, but the dative is found in many European languages, such as German, Russian, and Latin. The name of the case is taken from the fourth principal part of the Latin verb *do, dare, dedi, datum*, which means "to give." Thus in a Latin sentence of giving, the person to whom something is given, the recipient, is in the dative case, while the giver is nominative and the thing given is accusative, as in "do **tibi** librum" 'I am giving **you** the book' or 'I am giving a book **to you**.'[1]

But the Latin dative is used to express not only the recipient ("do **tibi** librum" 'I am giving **you** the book'), but more generally "a remoter object of the action than is denoted by the accusative. It does not, like the accusative, denote that upon which the action of the verb is directly brought to bear, but that which is less directly affected" (39). Thus the dative is also used to express roles that can be assimilated to the recipient ("monstro **tibi** librum" 'I am showing **you** the book'); the complement of certain verbs ("noceo **tibi**" 'I am injurious **to you**,' that is, 'I am injuring **you**'); possessives ("est **mihi** liber" 'a book is **to me**,' that is, 'I have a book'); the person for whom something is done ("**tibi** me exorno" 'I am decking myself out **for you**'); and so on.

In the Indo-European language family, the recipient role of the dative is probably a secondary development, even though it has become the role that names the case. The core role is probably the dative of interest, which indicates the person who has an interest in what is going on in the clause—as opposed to the agent, the patient, or the experiencer.

Thus, in Latin, the dative case can be used to indicate "the person in whose eyes or in whose judgment the statement of the sentence is true," as in "vir bonus **mihi** videtur" 'he seems **to me** a good man' or '**in my judgment** he seems a good man.' More generally, the dative can be used to introduce the subjectivity of either the first or the second person: "quid **mihi** Celsus agit?" means more or less "how, **please**, does Celsus fare?"; "at **tibi** repente venit ad me Caninius mane" means "but, **lo and behold**, Caninius suddenly came to me in the morning."

English does not have a surface-structure dative case, so the function of the dative of interest is expressed in other ways. We can note, for example, the difference between "Don't give up!" and "Don't give up on me!" In the second phrase, it is clear that the person speaking has an interest in the outcome, and it is partly for the sake of the person speaking that the person being encouraged should not give up. In Latin, the phrase "on me" would show up as the simple pronoun in the dative case, "mihi."

If we take the dative of interest as the core function, most of the other functions fall easily into place. Thus the dative of indirect object could be

---

1. Examples of the Latin dative are from Woodcock, *A New Latin Syntax*. Hereafter, page numbers are cited in the text.

restated in terms of interest: in an act of giving, the thing given is directly affected by the action of the verb; the recipient is less directly affected but still has an interest in the action. The sentence "I am giving you a book" ("do **tibi** librum") might be understood to mean "I am giving a book, and you have an interest in this giving"; the person most obviously interested would be the recipient of the book, so the dative of the recipient is a specialization of the dative of interest.

Likewise with the extended senses of the dative of the recipient: "I am showing you the book" ("monstro **tibi** librum") could mean "I am showing a book, and you have an interest in the showing." The Latin sentence "noceo tibi" means "I am doing an injury and you have an interest in that injury," or "I am doing an injury to you," or "I injure you" (41). The possessive dative can also be interpreted in terms of interest: the sentence "est **mihi** liber," means "there is a book for me" or simply "I have a book"; the sentence "malam **mihi** percussit" means "he struck a cheek and I have an interest in that striking" or simply "he struck my cheek."[2]

In English, the recipient can become the grammatical subject through a passive transformation: "John gave George a book" can become "George was given a book by John." But (as I noted in chapter 6) Latin, Greek, and German, for example, do not allow the recipient to be the subject of a passive verb.[3] The dative of the beneficiary often takes the same form as the dative of the recipient, as in "George told Mary a story," or "George promised Mary a job," or "George bought Mary a book"; or it may use the preposition "for," as in "George washed the dishes for Mary." Some of these will allow a passive transformation in English; others will not: I would accept "Mary was told a story by George" and "Mary was promised a job by George." I would accept "Mary was bought a book by George," but "*Mary was washed the dishes by George" is impossible, although "George washed the dishes for Mary" has the same surface structure as "George bought a book for Mary." I also find "*George washed Mary the dishes" unacceptable, but some beneficiaries do

---

2. The possessive dative is not quite the same as the possessive genitive; as Woodcock (p. 46) says, "The effect of this dative cannot be reproduced in English because it has to be rendered by the possessive case. It differs from the possessive genitive in denoting a warmer interest of the person concerned."

3. Woodcock has a curious note on this point: "In English the direct and the indirect objects, as they are not distinguished by their forms, are apt to be confused. Only the direct accusative object can become the subject of the passive verb, yet it is possible to say in English 'I was given a book.' This, if logically analyzed, is sheer nonsense. The Latin must be *liber mihi datus est*" (p. 44). Here Woodcock is confusing logic with the grammar of Latin; there is nothing illogical about promoting a recipient; it is simply a matter of what the grammar of a particular language will allow.

appear in this form: "The teacher gave George good marks," where George benefits, even though there is no physical transfer of any object, or "George cut Mary some flowers." The first of these beneficiaries I think can become the subject of a passive transformation: "George was given good marks by Mr. Jones." I find "Mary was cut some flowers by George" acceptable, but not everyone would agree with this judgment. A cleft construction, of course, will promote any beneficiary: "It was Mary that George washed the dishes for."

Some of the other datives do not readily become subjects, except through cleft constructions. The function of the dative of interest most often is precisely to indicate the role of someone not directly involved in the action of the verb, someone who is a witness or judge rather than one of the principal characters in the action; it would not ordinarily make much sense to make that person the topic of the clause. Nonetheless, interest is a point of view, a kind of subjectivity, even when it is not the grammatical subject, and this kind of subjectivity of interest is commonly found in narrative.[4]

II.

The Master of Ballantrae, as we have seen in chapter 5, is a story of the Hegelian double, through the conflict between the brothers Henry and James, with the added role of the Freudian third, Alison. These three may be considered the core subjects of the story. In addition, however, we must add the subjectivity of the narrator, Ephraim Mackellar, the family steward. Although in a sense Mackellar is part of the story only in order to tell it, he is nonetheless quite richly characterized, sometimes through the words of others, which he reports even when they are to his disadvantage, and sometimes through his own actions. He quickly proves to be a faithful and competent steward, and he is taken into the confidence of the family. For instance, Henry pays an allowance to a woman seduced and abandoned by James, and on one occasion Mackellar is the emissary and paymaster. When he returns (having been bitten by a dog on his way), he advises Henry to stop the payments because the woman uses the money only for drink. Mackellar takes his master's inter-

---

4. The scholarship on narrative point of view is large; I will discuss only those points relevant for my argument. See, among others, Bal, *Narratology: Introduction to the Theory of Narrative*; Booth, *The Rhetoric of Fiction*; Cohn, *Transparent Minds: Narrative Modes for Presenting Consciousness in Fiction*; and Rimmon-Kenan, *Narrative Fiction: Contemporary Poetics*. For discussion of the minor character as narrator, see Bertil Romberg, *Studies in the Narrative Technique of the First-Person Novel*, pp. 61–63.

ests to heart, and he is willing to speak freely on a painful topic. He is also a rather strict moralist, and he has been repelled by the woman's drunken squalor; but all the same, he is not without pity.

Mackellar is also in Henry's confidence when it is revealed that James is still alive and living in Paris. Henry resolves to send James some money, though the expense will be difficult to bear. Henry consults Mackellar on the best way to raise the money; he proposes to use the mortgage money. Mackellar opposes this decision, but his words make no difference: Henry sends the money anyway.

Occasionally, however, Mackellar's actions do have some effect. For seven years Henry does not tell Alison that he is paying James an allowance. When Alison blames Henry for the financial difficulties the family faces, it is Mackellar who tells her where the money has been going. From this moment, her feelings for her husband begin to soften, though she continues to feel more for the absent James than for her husband. Mackellar gives us his judgment:

> I think there is the devil in women: all these years passed, never a sight of the man, little enough kindness to remember (by all accounts) even while she had him, the notion of his death intervening, his heartless rapacity laid bare to her; that all should not do, and must still keep the best place in her heart for his accursed fellow, is a thing to make a plain man rage. I had never much natural sympathy for the passion of love; but this unreason in my patron's wife disgusted me outright with the whole matter. (68)[5]

Mackellar is a witness, but he is hardly impartial. From the beginning he favors Henry, so the story comes to us from a partisan's perspective. Mackellar is witness and judge at the same time, and his judgments guide those of the reader.

There is some potential disadvantage in giving the narration of a story to a single witness, who can tell only what he has seen or what he is able to learn from others. Stevenson solves this problem by handing things over from time to time to other narrators; thus different voices and different perspectives are introduced. A considerable portion of the tale is told by Francis Burke, a companion of the Master, a thorough scoundrel, but engaging in his way (33–60, 129–32); James tells MacKellar a long inset tale (160–63); and another part of the story Mackellar constructs from several sources (194–206).

---

5. Later on, Mackellar gives Alison a sheaf of documents which show that James was in fact in the pay of the English (pp. 112–15), and with this knowledge Alison's affections finally change.

Late in the story, after James has returned from India, Henry and Alison flee to New York with their children, but they leave Mackellar behind to look after things. James finds out where his brother has fled and follows him, accompanied by Mackellar. This section of the story gives us the chance to see James most clearly through Mackellar's eyes, but we also see Mackellar himself. During their sea voyage to New York, a great storm blows up, and Mackellar hopes that the ship may go down, so that James may be killed. But once he realizes that hoping for his own death and the death of James is hoping for the death of all the crew as well, he repents and prays that God may take just the two of them. The storm then abates, and all are saved.

A little later Mackellar and James are sitting on the poop of the ship, and Mackellar sees that he has the opportunity to push James overboard:

> The words of my own prayer—*I were liker a man if I struck this creature down*—shot at the same time into my memory. I called my energies together, and (the ship then heeling downward toward my enemy) thrust at him swiftly with my foot. It was written I should have the guilt of the attempt without the profit. (164)

Thus once again Mackellar tries to become an actor in the drama, and once again he fails.

Mackellar, like many other witness narrators, is inside the story, but he is not a central character. He tells the story and at times gives his judgments on the other characters and their actions; but he is also a fully realized character, with passion and desire of his own, and he is as fine a stylist as Stevenson himself. He never reaches the center of our interest, but he is more than a tool of the narration.[6]

III.

It would be perverse to argue that Jay Gatsby is not at the center of *The Great Gatsby*. And yet Gatsby is essentially a trivial person whose story on its own hardly deserves the attention of the reader. It is only the judgments of the

---

6. This role of the witness may be tested in various ways. In Vladimir Nabokov's *Pnin*, the reader assumes for most of the book that the narrator is outside the story, only to discover in chapter 6 that the narrator has been inside the story all along; this narrator never becomes a major character, but three times he plays an important role in the hero's life. Even an omniscient narrator firmly outside the story can take on subjectivity, as does the chatty and opinionated narrator of E. M. Forster's *Howards End*.

witness and narrator that justify our interest: through Nick Carraway's narrative we understand and evaluate Gatsby.[7]

Nick tells us quite a lot about himself. We know that he comes from some city in the Middle West, that he was almost engaged to someone there, and that this almost-engagement was one reason he left for New York. We know that his family was prosperous. We know that he attended Yale, that he wrote editorials for the *Yale News*, and that he continues to have some literary ambitions. We know that during the time of the story he is trying to make his way in the bond business, without great success, and we know that he is having some sort of affair with Jordan Baker—a well-known golfer who is suspected of having cheated in a tournament. And we know that at the end of the story he goes back home. This is far more than we ever learn about Stevenson's narrator, Ephaim MacKellar. Clearly, it is important that we should know about Nick.

One of the principal functions of a witness is to provide judgments on the characters and their actions. Nick does indeed offer judgments all along the way; in fact, the book begins with his final judgment:

> When I came back from the East last autumn I felt that I wanted the world to be in uniform and at a sort of moral attention forever; I wanted no more riotous excursions with privileged glimpses into the human heart. Only Gatsby, the man who gives his name to this book, was exempt from my reaction—Gatsby, who represented everything for which I have an unaffected scorn. (2)

Only at the end of the story can the reader can understand something of what Nick means by "riotous excursions with privileged glimpses into the human heart" and perhaps even why he would want "the world to be in uniform and at a sort of moral attention forever"—whatever that exactly means—and why Gatsby somehow remains exempt from Nick's judgment, despite his scorn. The progress of the book is—or ought to be—Nick's moral education.

The geometry of the main plot links three triangles—Gatsby, Daisy, and Tom Buchanan; then Daisy, Tom, and Myrtle Wilson; and then Tom, Myrtle,

---

7. There is extensive critical literature on Nick Carraway's role as witness character; see, for example, Jerome Thale, "The Narrator as Hero"; Peter Liska, "Nick Carraway and the Imagery of Disorder"; Thomas E. Boyle, "Unreliable Narration in *The Great Gatsby*"; James M. Mellard, "Counterpont as Technique in *The Great Gatsby*"; and James Phelan, "Reexamining Reliability: the Multiple Functions of Nick Carraway," in Phelan, *Narrative as Rhetoric*, pp. 105–18. My interest here is not to examine Carraway's function in Gatsby's story, but rather Gatsby's function in Carraway's story.

and George Wilson—to form a capital letter "W." Nick's affair with Jordan Baker sits beside this W without any direct connection. The end of Nick's affair, however, and his subsequent departure from New York are linked to the crisis of the main story. The breakup comes the day after the accident in which Myrtle Wilson is killed, which in turn comes just after Tom's revelation to Daisy that Gatsby's money is tainted, and not long before George Wilson kills Gatsby. These are surely the crucial events of the whole plot, the events that pull together all the characters of the main plot into a tangled web of causation. Nick's breakup with Jordan is somehow connected to these events and comments on them. The reader's judgment of Nick's judgment of Gatsby should be linked to Nick's break with Jordan and his subsequent return to the Midwest. If we are convinced that Nick has good reasons for the breakup and that he is better off afterwards, then we are likely to believe that Nick has grown through his experiences.[8]

After the accident in which Myrtle is killed, Tom, Nick, and Jordan go to Tom's house, and as they approach they can see from the lights that Daisy has come home. Tom invites them in, but Nick declines, even though Jordan adds her own appeal. Nick simply tells us that he wanted to be alone, that he'd had "enough of all of them for one day, and suddenly that included Jordan too" (143). Why that included Jordan he does not say.

The next day, Jordan calls Nick at his office. She tells him that she has left Daisy's house and plans to go to Southampton. Nick thinks that it was probably tactful to leave, but still he is annoyed, and then more than annoyed when Jordan says, "You weren't so nice to me last night" (155). She wants to see him, but he puts her off.

"It's impossible this afternoon. Various—"
We talked like that for a while, and then abruptly we weren't talking any longer. I don't know which of us hung up with a sharp click, but I know I didn't care. I couldn't have talked to her across a tea-table that day if I never talked to her again in this world. (155)

The aposiopesis suggests the vacuity of his excuses. Nick tells how the breakup happened, but he doesn't comment on it much, so the reader is left to do most of the work of interpretation. No doubt Jordan, as part of the riotous world, as a person who is certainly not at moral attention ever, is

8. As Phelan (1996) notes, "By ending his relationship with Jordan, Nick signals the end of his interest in succeeding in New York, the end of his desire to move in the same circles with the Buchanans. Gatsby has no effect on anyone except Nick, and the effect is not exactly heroic" (p. 116).

included in Nick's judgment, and if so the breakup is an essential part of his judgment on the events and the people. We still do not know, however, why Gatsby should be exempt from this judgment.

Toward the end of the book, in the middle of the night after the accident, Nick goes over to Gatsby's house, and it is at this point that Gatsby tells Nick about his past and in particular about his romance with Daisy and with her image. Then Nick and Gatsby have breakfast together, and Nick leaves to go to work.

> We shook hands and I started away. Just before I reached the hedge I remembered something and turned around.
> "They're a rotten crowd," I shouted across the lawn. "You're worth the whole damn bunch put together."
> I've always been glad I said that. It was the only compliment I ever gave him, because I disapproved of him from beginning to end. (154)

One can certainly agree that Tom and Daisy and Jordan are a rotten crowd. It is not clear that Gatsby is any better. Nick claims that "there was something gorgeous about him, some heightened sensitivity to the promises of life . . . a romantic readiness. . . ." But Nick has told us enough about Gatsby to call this judgment into question. Gatsby is certainly a crook, and his crimes are in the service of a shallow ambition. His only virtue is that he loves Daisy, herself part of that rotten crowd. His best quality is a failure of perception.

If there is perception in this story, it belongs, belatedly, to Nick. I do not claim that Nick is the hero of the story—partly because the word "hero" is rather vague, but also because I do not intend to remove Gatsby from the center of the action.[9] The vocabulary presented here allows for a more precise description of roles. Nick is the witness, the dative subject, off to the side of the main events, while Gatsby is clearly the central subject in a complex narrative geometry. Gatsby and Tom are Hegelian opponents, while Daisy is the third in their conflict; Tom and George Wilson are also Hegelian opponents, and Myrtle is the third. The plot works by transferring this second conflict, so that George mistakenly takes Gatsby rather than Tom as his opponent. It is notable, however, that none of these characters learns anything from their various conflicts. If there is any character who gains in perception, it is Nick,

---

9. Jerome Thale, in "The Narrator as Hero," argues that Nick in *The Great Gatsby* and Marlow in *Heart of Darkness* are the real heroes of their stories (p. 70); and according to James Mellard, "*The Great Gatsby* is an initiation story and its most important character is actually its narrator. . . ." ("Counterpoint as Technique in *The Great Gatsby*," p. 853).

the witness, though the moral confusion he displays as narrator after the fact calls any gain into question.

In a sense *The Great Gatsby* is two stories (at least). In one story, Gatsby is at the center, while Nick is the narrator. In another story, Nick is at the center, and Gatsby is the object of Nick's observation and the model for his moral education.[10] Neither story can stand on its own. We are faced, then, with a complex problem of interconnected interpretations: we judge Gatsby by what Nick tells us about him and also by Nick's own judgments; but we also judge Nick and his judgments by our own judgment of Gatsby, as Nick tells us about him and what he does. If Nick approves of Gatsby but we do not, or if Nick's approval of Gatsby seems inconsistent with his claims about his own moral principles, or if we are unable to approve of Nick's behavior, or if we find a disparity between his own behavior and his standards, or if we find that he has not really grown as a result of his witnessing, then we are likely to find that this story, no matter how clever its construction, is morally incoherent.

IV.

At the beginning of Ken Kesey's *One Flew Over the Cuckoo's Nest,* Randle Patrick McMurphy is brought from prison to a ward of a mental hospital. McMurphy is clearly the hero of the story, the center of the action; his antagonist is "Big Nurse" (Nurse Ratched), and the two form a Hegelian double. The witnessing character is Chief Bromden, an inmate of the ward. He has been on the ward for many years, and he pretends to be deaf and mute.[11]

The Chief observes McMurphy, but McMurphy also observes the Chief. He figures out, even on his first day in the ward, that the Chief is not deaf (77). Then later, when the inmates vote on McMurphy's proposal to change the scheduled television time to the afternoon so that they can watch the World Series, McMurphy gets the Chief to raise his hand:

10. According to Phelan (1996), Nick has two functions in the story: as narrator and as character: "part of the significance of Gatsby's quest can be seen by Fitzgerald's audience in how it affects Nick as character.... [I]t makes sense that occasionally Nick's function as narrator will be effaced and his function as character will be foregrounded" (p. 114). I argue that this effacement produces a second story, which places Nick at center and establishes him as the subject of witnessing and judging. This story is in a sense parasitic on Gatsby's story, but without it the narration of Gatsby's story lacks justification.

11. Because everyone believes that the Chief is deaf, he is allowed to witness events that would otherwise be out of bounds for an inmate, most particularly the staff meeting at the beginning of Part 2, pp. 129–37. He is also an extremely unreliable narrator, because of his hallucinations; but these have a kind of superior reliability.

It's too late to stop it now. McMurphy did something to it that first day, put some kind of hex on it with his hand so it won't act like I order it. There's no sense in it, any fool can see; I wouldn't do it on my own. Just by the way the nurse is staring at me with her mouth empty of words I can see I'm in for trouble, but I can't stop it. McMurphy's got hidden wires hooked to it, lifting it slow just to get me out of the fog and into the open where I'm fair game. He's doing it, wires . . .

No. That's not the truth. I lifted it myself. (126)

In the first version, McMurphy is the agent and the Chief is only the patient of McMurphy's agency; in the revised version, the Chief becomes the agent. This moment figures the progression of the plot as a whole, in which the Chief gradually learns to act for himself.

Eventually McMurphy discovers that the Chief can talk. Moreover, although the Chief sees himself as weak and puny, McMurphy sees his true height and strength, though the Chief refuses to believe him. McMurphy offers to make the Chief big and strong again, strong enough to lift the hydrotherapy control panel which McMurphy had failed to lift on a bet. As part of the deal McMurphy offers to pay the Chief's part of the money for the patients' fishing trip (184–88).[12]

The fishing trip is a decisive event—for McMurphy, for the Chief, and for some of the other inmates. The inmates gain a sense of power and independence, but McMurphy, as the Chief sees, is getting weaker (216–18). After the trip Big Nurse convinces the men that McMurphy's motives are entirely mercenary, and even the Chief loses confidence in him. McMurphy has the Chief lift the hydrotherapy control panel when no one else is around to see; then he makes a bet with the others that the Chief can perform this feat of strength, and of course he wins the bet. He offers the Chief five dollars as his share, but the Chief refuses it, and he tells McMurphy why the men have changed in their attitudes.

"You're always . . . *winning* things!"

"Winning things! You damned moose, what are you accusin' me of? All I do is hold up my end of the deal. Now what's so all-fired—"

"We thought it wasn't to be *winning* things. . . ."

[. . .]

---

12. The offer, p. 189; McMurphy's attempt, pp. 108–11; explanation of the control panel, p. 160; the Chief lifts the panel, p. 225; McMurphy wins a bet that the Chief can lift the panel, p. 226.

"Winning, for Christsakes," he said with his eyes closed. "Hoo boy, winning."

The expression "Hoo boy" carries a good deal of complex emotion, and in a sense it marks a turning point. McMurphy does not see himself as simply winning—or one might stay that this dialogue establishes the moment when he begins to reach a new understanding of what winning and losing mean in the context of the hospital and its inmates. As the Chief remarks immediately afterwards, "So I figure what happened in the shower room that afternoon was more my fault than anybody else's" (226–27). In other words, it is this dialogue about winning that brings about the climactic events of the story.

What happens in the shower room is that one of the orderlies tries forcibly to clean one the patients, George, who has an aversion to being touched. McMurphy defends George and gets into a fight with the orderly. When the other orderlies attack McMurphy, the Chief joins in the fight. They are overwhelmed and taken away, eventually for electric shock treatment. But the shock treatment does not have the intended effect; McMurphy and the Chief return to the ward still unsubdued, and their influence among the men on the ward has only been increased.

The final crisis of the story comes when McMurphy sneaks two women into the ward at night—one for himself, and the other for Billy Bibbit, who is something of a mama's boy and whose mother is a friend of Big Nurse. Big Nurse catches Billy with the woman and threatens to tell his mother. Billy kills himself from shame, and McMurphy attacks Big Nurse. He is taken away and returned to the ward after undergoing a lobotomy.

Many of the inmates who are voluntary patients have by now signed themselves out. The Chief, however, is an involuntary patient, so he cannot just leave. The night after McMurphy is brought back to the ward in a vegetative state, the Chief smothers him; then he throws the hydrotherapy control panel through the heavy screen on the window and makes his escape.[13]

The Chief begins this story simply as a witness, as a dative subject. He is particularly well placed to observe, but by his own choice he is entirely passive: he has in effect written himself out of any story. McMurphy, on the other hand, is almost pure agent. In the course of the story, however, McMurphy transfers his agency to the other inmates, and especially to the Chief. Gradually the Chief begins to become an actor in the story; first, he

13. The women on the ward, pp. 246–59; description of Billy, p. 246; Big Nurse discovers Billy with Candy, p. 263; she threatens to tell Billy's mother, p. 264; McMurphy attacks Big Nurse, p. 267; McMurphy is brought back to the ward, p. 269; the Chief smothers him and escapes, pp. 270–72.

admits that he can hear and then that he can talk. He goes along on the fishing trip, and then he joins McMurphy in the fight against the orderlies. By this time he has become McMurphy's partner, and the two undergo shock therapy together. McMurphy's death gives the Chief power and freedom.[14] The Chief's subjectivity has been transformed: he is no longer simply a witness; he is now an agent, the central subject of the story.

V.

Alain Robbe-Grillet's *Jealousy* is an extreme exercise in point of view. The novel takes place in some tropical country, on a banana plantation. The principal characters are the unnamed owner of one plantation, his wife, called A . . . , and the owner of the neighboring plantation, Franck. The plot, such as it is, concerns the unnamed owner's fears that his wife is having an affair with Franck.

The narration of this story is in a way entirely objective—there is a great concentration on objects and a general absence of the usual marks of subjectivity, such as authorial commentary or inside views of the characters' thoughts and feelings. And yet the book is permeated by subjectivity, the dative subjectivity of the witness.[15] The beginning sets the tone:

> Now the shadow of the column—the column which supports the southeast corner of the roof—divides the corresponding corner of the veranda into two equal parts. This veranda is a wide, covered gallery surrounding the house on three sides. Since its width is the same for the central portion as for the sides, the line of shadow cast by the column extends precisely to the corner of the house; but it stops there, for only the veranda flagstones are reached by the sun, which is still too high in the sky. The wooden walls of

---

14. Responsibility for the death of McMurphy is shared: Big Nurse kills his personality through the lobotomy, while the Chief kills only his body. Kesey could have arranged things otherwise, for instance, so that McMurphy died during the operation. But the Chief's action is essential to the transfer of agency from McMurphy; this is part of the Hegelian pattern. Shared responsibility for a death is not uncommon in narrative; we have seen another instance in *A Separate Peace*.

15. The distinction between the subjectivity of the experiencer and the subjectivity of the witness is subtle but crucial. The narrator fights against his emotions; he tries only to see and not to feel, only to witness and not to experience. The pun in the title, which in French can mean either "jealousy" or "Venetian blind," neatly combines these two forms of subjectivity; the tension between the two, and the impossibility of deciding which dominates, are essential to the effect of the novel.

the house—that is, its front and west gable-end—are still protected from the sun by the roof (common to the house proper and the terrace). So at this moment the shadow of the outer edge of the roof coincides exactly with the right angle formed by the terrace and the two vertical surfaces of the corner of the house. (39)

There is nothing odd about beginning a novel with a description: the beginning of Balzac's *Eugénie Grandet,* for example, is a long description of a house in the town of Saumur and its neighborhood; only after several pages do we finally encounter the name of a person, Monsieur Grandet. And yet there is something different about these two descriptions. The houses and the town in Balzac's novel are placed in a human context; Balzac's description is all in terms of human feelings such as melancholy and sadness; even in the desolation there are hypothetical human beings observing each other. The passage from *Jealousy,* by comparison, is cold, objective, obsessive, and there is no human being to see or be seen.[16]

A closer reading, however, shows at least the shadow of an observer. The first word of the novel, "Now," is a shifter; it takes its meaning from the utterance; it means "Now at the time that I am talking or writing." The here-and-now of this initial description is marked in other phrases: "the sun is *still* too high," "so *at this moment* the shadow." These shifters imply a subjective stance even as they conceal it, a person who is in a certain place at a certain time, observing the scene, though this person is not himself visible.

The presence of this subject is again suggested by a phrase a few paragraphs later: "from the far side of the bedroom the eye carries over the balustrade and touches ground only much further away. . . ." (40). Whose eye? The eye of some specific person who is observing this scene?

The second paragraph of the novel introduces a character, A . . . ; she, too, is described with an obsessive objectivity:

Now A . . . has come into the bedroom by the inside door opening onto the central hallway. She does not look at the wide open window through which—from the door—she would see this corner of the terrace. Now she has turned back toward the door to close it behind her. She still has on the light-colored, close-fitting dress with the high collar that she was wearing at lunch. . . . The black curls of her hair shift with a supple movement and brush her shoulders as she turns her head. (39)

---

16. The obsessive quality of the descriptions is perhaps best seen in the descriptions of the banana trees; see, for example, pp. 50–53.

Again the observing subject can be discerned, once again in the shifter "Now," but also in the phrase "this corner of the terrace." Why is it "this" corner of the terrace? Perhaps this corner is the location of the observer? If so, why does A . . . not look toward the observer?

At times the descriptions of people and their actions are reduced to the utterly mechanical, as in this description of Franck eating a meal:

> The right hand picks up the bread and raises it to the mouth, the right hand sets the bread down the white cloth and picks up the knife, the left hand picks up the fork, the fork sinks into the meat, the knife cuts off a piece of meat, the right hand sets down the knife on the cloth, the left hand puts the fork in the right hand, which sinks the fork into the piece of meat, which approaches the mouth, which begins to chew with movements of contraction and extension which are reflected all over the fact, in the cheek-bones, the eyes, the ears, while the right hand again picks up the fork and puts it in the left hand, then picks up the bread, then the knife, then the fork. . . . (88–89)

At other times, however, the subjectivity of the observer is allowed to break through its constraints for brief moments, particularly in adjectives. The description of A . . . quoted above, for example, betrays a more than clinical attention to A . . .'s hair and its supple movement. And little later we read: "The lustrous black hair falls in motionless curls along the line of her back" (42; see also 55, 56, 60, 62, 66–67, 92, 98–99, 123, 135).

Here I must disagree with Roland Barthes's argument that "What Robbe-Grillet is trying to destroy is, in the widest sense of the word, the adjective itself."[17] Barthes opposes in particular Robbe-Grillet's technique which he compares to that of Dutch still-life painting, "in which variety and minuteness of detail are made subservient to a dominant quality that transforms all the materials of vision into a single visceral sensation: *luster,* the sheen of things, for example, is the real subject matter of all those compositions of oysters and glasses and wine and silver so familiar in Dutch painting." But contrary to Barthes's argument, it is the luster of A . . .'s hair which especially captivates the observer, though he may struggle against this feeling. And in these adjectives we can see the subjectivity of the observer.

For the most part the narrator of this story is the unseen point from which everything else is seen. He is an eye, and the eye cannot see itself

---

17. From the essay "Objective Literature: Alain Robbe-Grillet," which is printed with the text in the Grove Press edition, pp. 18 and 19.

except by reflection. Just once, I think, a part of the observer perhaps can be seen—in a photograph, which shows A . . . sitting at a table on the terrace of a seaside cafe: "On the table near a second glass, at the right edge of the picture, are a man's hand and the cuff of a jacket sleeve, cut off by the white vertical margin" (95). Could this be Robbe-Grillet's joke with the reader? Is it the narrator who is cut off by the margin, outside the frame of the photograph?

Still, the presence of this unseen observer can sometimes be deduced or detected by traces he leaves in the text—for example, in the disposition of objects, particularly chairs and plates, or in situations that can be understood only by the presence of an unnamed and unobserved third person (see, for example, 43, 48, 56, 103–4, 126). It is even possible at times to catch the observer in action, if only indirectly:

> This is when she asks if the usual ice cubes will be necessary, declaring that these bottles come out of the refrigerator, though only one of the two has frosted over upon contact with the air.
>
> She calls the boy. No one answers.
>
> "One of us had better go," she says.
>
> But neither she nor Franck moves.
>
> In the pantry, the boy is already taking the ice cubes out of their trays, according to the orders his mistress gave him, he declares. And he adds that he is going to bring them right away, instead of specifying when this order was given. (58–59)

Since neither A . . . nor Franck has moved, it must be the observer who has gone to get ice, to whom the boy is speaking.

Jealousy, and the other works of Robbe-Grillet, have seemed to many critics (and perhaps to Robbe-Grillet himself) to be the triumph of a characterless phenomenology, the highest form of objective narration. Certainly there is a kind of objectivity to the descriptions, and a general absence of what we usually take to be the signs of subjectivity, such as the comments of a narrator or inside views of the characters. But this absence perhaps paradoxically forces the reader into the position of the observer—it forces the reader to see through the observer's eyes and to take on the observer's subjectivity. This subjectivity can be seen in the various traces of the observer's position, such as shifters, in the objects placed to accommodate him, in grammatical structures that require his presence, even in the general absence of adjectives—an absence that only emphasizes those few adjectives which do occur, particularly in the description's of A . . .'s hair; here the observer's passion breaks through, despite his attempts to keep it behind a dam of objectivity.[18] Even the obsessively objective descriptions, such as the description of Franck's eating, can be interpreted as an effort to maintain control, and perhaps to objectify and dehumanize someone he fears. The narrator of this novel is the personification of jealousy—almost entirely etiolated, drained of all presence, reduced merely to the position of a witness, as he looks obsessively through a window-blind; but this position, too, is a form of subjectivity.

---

18. Contrast Bruce Morrisette, "Surfaces and Structures in Robbe-Grillet's Novels," p. 10: "It would be especially simplistic to conclude that Robbe-Grillet's 'realism of presence' only conceals, beneath cunning symbols, signs, analogies, motifs, and correspondences, an even deeper 'depth.'" I am arguing not for a "deeper depth" but only for the presence of a subjectivity in what seems superficially to be an objective narration. Compare Anne Minor, "A Note on Jealousy": "By a kind of enchantment, the reader gradually identifies himself with this gaze [of the observer] and breathlessly follows the slow, tormenting progress of jealousy" (p. 31) Both of these essays, like the essay by Barthes quoted above, are printed in the Grove Press edition of the novel.

CHAPTER 9

Instrumental Subjects
Knowles, Eliot, Davies

The instrument, the thing by or with which something is done, is not a core semantic function. An instrument is most often inanimate—or, if it is animate, its animacy is disregarded—and therefore it seems a poor candidate for subjectivity. Still, in English an instrument can become the subject of a clause, and an instrumental character can take on narrative subjectivity. Instrumental subjectivity occurs whenever an instrumental object is regarded in some degree as autonomous, or whenever a person is regarded as the instrument of another person's action. This chapter begins with the grammatical instrument and then moves to the narrative instrument: objects that have a substantial narrative role, as in Proulx's *Accordion Crimes* or Robbe-Grillet's *In the Labyrinth;* characters who are closely identified with a physical object, as in Eliot's *Silas Marner;* and characters who are used as instruments, as in Davies's *Fifth Business.*

I.

In the sentence "George opened the door with a key," the key is clearly an instrument, and it would be marked as instrument in deep structure. Proto-Indo-European marked the instrumental case in surface structure, as do some of its descendants, such as Sanskrit or Russian. Latin lost the Proto-Indo-European instrumental case, but the instrumental functions have been taken over by the ablative case (without a preposition) in the construction called the *ablative of means:* "**suâ manû** id scripsit" ("**with his own hand** he wrote it," where "suâ manû" is in the ablative case).

English regularly uses a prepositional phrase rather than a case marker to indicate the instrument: "George opened the door **with a key**." But in English, the instrument may also appear as the grammatical subject of a clause: "This key opens the door." If a deep-structure instrument can appear as a grammatical subject, can a physical object appear as a narrative subject? Conversely, can a person appear as the instrument of narrative action?

Agency seems to be structured in a natural hierarchy, in which human beings are higher than animals, and inanimate objects are off the bottom of the chart (Blake 137). "Suppose we have a sentence in which the lexical items are MAN, DOG, HIT and STICK. [The capital letters here indicate that it is the concepts which are in question, not any particular grammatical form of the words.] There is hardly any need for case marking to express the propositional content. In the absence of an indication to the contrary one naturally assumes that MAN will be agent, DOG patient and STICK instrument" (Blake 170).

The words chosen by Blake prove his point because they come with presuppositions. The action of hitting necessarily involves an agent and a patient—someone or something hitting and someone or something being hit—and it may involve an instrument. Moreover, we know that people can use sticks for hitting, but dogs normally can't. Other words have different presuppositions: if we select the words MAN, DOG, HIT, and TAIL, the most obvious resulting sentence will be "The dog hit the man with its tail." If, however, the instrument of hitting is left out, and the words are simply MAN, DOG, and HIT, it is most likely that we would take the man to be the agent and the dog to be the patient: "The man hit the dog" rather than "The dog hit the man," even though a dog can hit a man—with its tail, for example. If a dog is holding a stick in its mouth, it could accidentally hit a man as it walks by. We might then say "The dog hit the man with the stick," but we would not usually say "The stick hit the man by means of the dog."

If there is a hierarchy of agents, there must also be an inverse hierarchy of instruments. The most natural instrument is a physical object (a stick, a hammer, a sword): animals can be seen as instruments ("The farmers here still plow their fields with oxen"), and human instruments are somewhat awkward, but not impossible. And presumably there is a hierarchy of patients as well, though all three categories can fill this role. One could draw a chart of binary oppositions as in figure 1. However, the differences are probably graded rather than binary: a human being can easily be an agent, possibly be a patient, only with difficulty be an instrument, and so on.

Subjectivity, insofar as it is related to agency, is thus usually located in (or somehow connected to) a person, or perhaps one of the higher animals.

	Agent	Patient	Instrument
Human	+	+	−
Animal	+	+	+
Object	−	+	+

Figure 1

The agent, the experiencer, the witness—these functions normally require volition or consciousness or perception. Patients may be divided into two groups: if George hit the ball, the ball is presumably unaware of the blow; but if George hit John, John is both the patient and the experiencer.

An instrument most typically is a thing—a key, a stick, a hammer, a bomb. In some situations, however, a person can be thought of as an instrument. Thus in Latin, a person who is the agent of a passive verb is in the ablative case with the preposition *ab:* "**ab amico** id scriptum est ("it was written **by his friend**"); but the ablative of means without *ab* can be used of a person thought of as the instrument of another person's action: "**armatis hominibus** expulsi sunt fabri de area nostra" ("The workmen were driven from my building-site **by means of armed men**," Cic. *Att.* 4, 3, 2). As Woodcock comments (32), "Here the real author of the deed was Clodius, and the armed men were his hired tools."

A person thought of as an instrument to some extent becomes a thing and takes on what might be called *instrumental subjectivity;* since instruments generally lack volition or perception, a person regarded as an instrument thereby also lacks these qualities—or at least those qualities become irrelevant. On the other hand, an object regarded as a subject to some extent assumes volition and perception.

II.

The analysis of instrumental subjectivity in narrative is part of a larger discussion of narrative objects. A narrative object can be a prop, a symbol, a structural device, the object of the subject's desire, or a desiring subject in itself. Some authors make do with only meager furnishings. Jane Austen has very little interest in props; she can write page after page without sitting her characters down on chairs or putting anything in their hands. The opening chapter of *Pride and Prejudice* mentions not a single object. It is easy to imagine that the same scene written by Balzac would be full of things. Ordinarily

Austen mentions an object only if it contributes directly to the social or psychological point she wants to make. At the beginning of the second chapter of *Pride and Prejudice,* Lizzie is trimming a hat, and her father says to her, "I hope Mr Bingley will like it Lizzy." The hat is called into existence only so that Mr. Bennet can tease his daughter; once it has performed its function, it disappears from the narrative universe.

Symbolic objects are as old as our literary tradition: in the first book of the *Iliad,* the scepter that Achilles dashes to the ground at the end of his argument with Agamemnon is symbolic of proper political relationships; in Book Twenty-Three of the *Odyssey,* the olive-tree bed is symbolic of the marriage of Odysseus and Penelope.[1] Following Roland Barthes, we may distinguish symbolic objects, which signify, from objects which do not signify but only refer. But then, according to Barthes, these insignificant objects become significant—they signify reality:

> [J]ust when these details are reputed to *denote* the real directly, all that they do ... is to signify it; [they] finally say nothing but this: *we are the real*; it is the category of "the real" (and not its contingent contents) which is then signified; in other words, the very absence of the signified, to the advantage of the referent alone, becomes the very signifier of realism: the *reality effect* is produced.[2]

Styles might then be arranged in a kind of continuum, ranging from Austen, whose novels are barely furnished; to Balzac, whose novels are virtual department stores; to Dickens, whose characters are objectified while objects take on consciousness; to Robbe-Grillet, whose objects have almost replaced the people.

A narrative object can be a structural device. Annie Proulx's *Accordion Crimes* announces itself as novel, but formally it is a series of stories, arranged chronologically, each concerning a different person or group of people. The only link among these stories is a little green accordion. In the first story the accordion is constructed (and the first section of the first story has the appropriate subtitle "The instrument"); in the last story it is destroyed. As a note at the beginning of the novel explains, "The green accordion travels from hand

---

1. See Jasper Griffin, "Significant Objects," in *Homer on Life and Death.*
2. "The Reality Effect," in *The Rustle of Language,* 148. See also Willa Cather, "The Novel Démeublé" (pp. 43–51): "The novel, for a long time, has been overfurnished. The property-man has been so busy on its pages, the importance of material objects and their vivid presentation have been so stressed, that we take it for granted whoever can observe, and can write the English language, can write a novel. Often the latter qualification is considered unnecessary."

to hand over a hundred-year period, plays the music of many different ethnic groups" (17). This device allows Proulx to cover a lot of time and territory; it allows her to investigate a wide variety of social and ethnic groups, all part of America as Proulx sees it, all linked together, if only by the little accordion; otherwise, these groups seem almost without connection, a collection rather than a unity. If this narrative is a novel, its only continuing character is an instrument.

Don DeLillo's *Underworld* is a large, complex, and sprawling novel; one of the devices holding the story together is a baseball, the famous lost baseball which Bobby Thomson hit for a homerun at the Polo Grounds in New York, when the Giants beat the Dodgers to win the pennant on October 3, 1951. Nick Shay, the principal character of the novel, eventually seeks out and buys this baseball. Most of the other characters in the novel have some connection to Nick, or to the baseball, or to both, though the connections may be indirect. But the baseball shows up only from time to time during the story: sometimes it is the subject of an episode; sometimes it is mentioned only in passing. It is both a linking device and a symbol of certain aspects of the postwar American world. DeLillo's baseball is structurally less important than Proulx's accordion, which is the primary structural element linking her otherwise independent stories, but Proulx's use of the linking object also seems more contrived.

An object (or a person thought of as an object) may be the object of desire, the goal of a quest. The Golden Fleece is merely the excuse for some adventures, and it isn't very interesting in itself. The Holy Grail, however, has great intrinsic value. Though the origin of the Grail stories is obscure, by the time the stories we have were composed, it is the vessel used in the Last Supper or the vessel that caught the blood of Christ as he was crucified, or else these two vessels are one and the same. In one of many versions of the story, *The Quest of the Holy Grail*, it has the power to provide an endless supply of food, serving each person's desire; it can heal wounds and prolong life.[3] A theme repeated throughout the story is the doctrine of transubstantiation, according to which the communion wafer and wine are the body and blood of Christ—in fact, not merely as a symbol. At one point Bors explains that he cannot see the body of Christ in the wafer because his eyes are only mortal (180), but the final vision of the Grail provides a vision of Christ himself in the bread (275).

There are many symbolic objects in *The Quest of the Holy Grail*; these

---

3. *The Quest of the Holy Grail*, translated by P. M. Matarasso. There are many theories about the origin of the Grail stories, some scholarly, some fantastic, some both. A plausible account is given in Roger Sherman Loomis, *The Grail: From Celtic Myth to Christian Symbol*.

are explained in the text, rather than being left for the readers to interpret idiosyncratically.[4] The idea that the world is a cosmic order, a complex network of significant objects, persisted through the Middle Ages and beyond. The significance of an object was at least in principle public rather than private, either shared as part of the cultural understanding or capable of explanation. The scientific view of the world withdrew intrinsic significance from objects, which could now be fully specified and understood through location, dimension, and velocity. Poets and storytellers, however, retained the idea that objects have meaning, though this meaning was now private, available to the reader only through a kind of sympathetic guesswork.

J. R. R. Tolkien's *The Lord of the Rings* in a way attempts to return to an earlier understanding of the meaning and power of an object. The story takes the form of an anti-quest: the goal is not to find the Ring, but to get rid of it. The Ring is by no means a passive object within its own story; it has power and agency and desire, beyond even the power it gives to the person wearing it, and in a way it owns its owner. It is certainly a character in the story, one of the central characters, and it takes on a kind of subjectivity.

Alain Robbe-Grillet's *In the Labyrinth* has also some of the character of an anti-quest: the nameless wounded soldier who is the principal character in the story is attempting to deliver a box, roughly the size and shape of shoebox, covered with brown paper and tied with white string. The soldier doesn't know what is in the box, and he makes no effort to find out; when other characters ask what is in the box, he simply says he doesn't know. Nor does he know the person who is supposed to receive the box, or even exactly where they were supposed to meet. At the end of the story the soldier dies, and the doctor who cared for him takes the box. He opens it and finds letters and a few other objects:

> At first glance the letters contain no secret of any kind and are of no general or personal importance. They are ordinary letters, the kind a country girl sends every week to her fiancé, giving news of the farm or the neighbors, regularly repeating the same conventional formulas about separation and return. The box also contains an old gold watch, of no particular value, with a tarnished gilded-brass chain; there is no name engraved inside the lid over the watch face; there is also a ring, a signet ring made of silver or nickel alloy, the kind workers often make for themselves in factories, with "H.M." engraved on it; finally, a dagger-bayonet of the current

---

4. See, for example, the vision of the hand, bridle, and candle (p. 165), which is then interpreted by a holy man on pp. 173–74. See E. M. W. Tillyard's *The Elizabethan World Picture* for a discussion of the system of symbolic objects in medieval and Renaissance thought.

model. . . . The box is not a shoe box, it is a biscuit box of the same dimensions, but made out of tin. (268)

It is not easy to know what to make of all this. In a traditional story, the mystery of the contents of the box would keep the reader in suspense, until a final revelation of meaning. But the reader of Robbe-Grillet's fiction perhaps has learned that there is no suspense and no meaning; perhaps the banality of the contents of the box is indeed symbolic—of the banality of meaning in the story and the absence of meaning in the modern view of the world. This is the reality of Robbe-Grillet's reality effect.

III.

Magic objects abound in fairy tales, but they are by no means absent in modern fiction.[5] In John Cheever's story "The Enormous Radio," Jim and Irene Westcott buy a new radio:

> The radio was delivered at the kitchen door [. . .], and with the assistance of her maid and the handyman Irene uncrated it and brought it into the living room. [. . .] She was confounded by the number of dials and switches on the instrument panel, and she studied them thoroughly before she put the plug into a wall socket and turned the radio on. The dials flooded with a malevolent green light, and in the distance she heard the music of a piano quintet. The quintet was in the distance for only an instant; it bore down upon her with a speed greater than light and filled the apartment with the noise of music amplified so mightily that it knocked a china ornament from a table to the floor. She rushed to the instrument and reduced the volume. The violent forces that were snared in the ugly gumwood cabinet made her uneasy. (38)

Clearly, this is no ordinary instrument. Jim and Irene find that it allows them to hear the conversations of other people in their apartment building. Irene

---

5. The idea that objects can have a sort of agency is not limited to fairy tales and other fictions, but can also be found in modern technology studies. Langdon Winner, for example, notes that "technologies are not merely aids to human activity, but also powerful forces acting to reshape that activity and its meaning" (*The Whale and the Reactor,* p. 6). There are a number of books devoted to the story of a particular object or kind of object; see, for example, Henry Petroski's *The Pencil* and Witold Rybczynski's *One Good Turn: A Natural History of the Screwdriver and the Screw.*

is shocked and disturbed to find that the lives of their neighbors are full of violence and despair, but by the end of the story, the reader finds that Jim and Irene are no better than their neighbors. The story does for us what the radio did for Jim and Irene.

The magic of a magical object is not simply its extraordinary powers but also its independent agency, its autonomy, its will.[6] In Gabriel Garcia Marquez' *One Hundred Years of Solitude*, there is a profusion of things, most of which seem to have a life and a meaning beyond their practical function in the story. At the very start of the book, the gypsy Melquíades says, "Things have a life of their own. It's simply a matter of waking up their souls" (11). To pick just one example out of many, when José Arcadio is mysteriously murdered, his blood takes it upon itself to notify his mother:

> As soon as José Arcadio closed the bedroom door the sound of a pistol shot echoed through the house. A trickle of blood came out under the door, crossed the living room, went out into the street, continued on in a straight line across the uneven terraces, went down steps and climbed over curbs, passed along the Street of the Turks, turned a corner to the right and another to the left, made a right angle at the Buendía house, went in under the closed door, crossed through the parlor, hugging the walls so as not to stain the rugs, went on to the other living room, made a wide curve to avoid the dining-room table, went along the porch with the begonias, and passed without being seen under Amaranta's chair as she gave an arithmetic lesson to Aureliano José, and went through the pantry and came out in the kitchen, where Ursula was getting ready to crack thirty-six eggs to make bread. (129–39)

In this narrative universe, the town of Moncado, objects have power and meaning, as they did for the medieval and Renaissance mind; but whereas the meanings of medieval objects were public, widely shared, or at least clearly explicable, the objects in Moncado do not give up their secrets easily.

---

6. As John Dillon and Tania Gergel note in *The Greek Sophists*, "in Athenian law an inanimate object could be prosecuted for murder, as being liable to pollution." According to Plutarch (Pericles, ch. 36 = 80A10), when an athlete was accidentally killed by the throw of a javelin, Pericles and Protagoras spent an entire day debating whether the javelin or the person who threw the javelin was responsible. A similar debate is the topic of Antiphon's second Tetralogy. And an old Athenian ritual, the Bouphonia, is based on the idea that an object can be a responsible agent. In this ritual, a group of oxen are led around an altar on which sacrificial grain has been placed. Eventually one of the oxen eats some of the grain, whereupon it is killed by a priest who then runs away. A trial is held; the participants claim that they don't know the person who killed the ox and ran away; they each deny responsibility; and finally the knife is found guilty and thrown into the sea.

IV.

Realistic fiction will not allow magical objects—or, conversely, we exclude from the category of the realistic a fiction that includes magical objects. But even in realistic fiction an object can have a certain power. At the beginning of *A Separate Peace*, the narrator, Gene, returns after some fifteen years to the Devon School, to revisit the scene of the events that will take up the body of the story. He begins by visiting the First Academy Building, and particularly its marble staircase:

> In through swinging doors I reached a marble foyer, and stopped at the foot of a long white marble flight of stairs. Although they were old stairs, the worn moons in the middle of each step were not very deep. The marble must be unusually hard. That seemed very likely, only too likely, although with all my thought about these stairs this exceptional hardness had not occurred to me. It was surprising that I had overlooked that, that crucial fact. (8)

Gene does not explain, but these are the stairs where Phineas fell at the end of the story. Next, Gene visits a grove of trees by the riverbank:

> Moving through the soaked, coarse grass I began to examine each one closely, and finally identified the tree I was looking for by means of certain small scars rising along its trunk, and by a limb extending over the river, and another thinner limb growing near it. This was the tree, and it seemed to me standing there to resemble those men, the giants of your childhood, whom you encounter years later and find that they are not merely smaller in relation to your growth, but that they are absolutely smaller, shrunken by age. In this double demotion the old giants have become pigmies while you were looking the other way.
>
> The tree was not only stripped by the cold season, it seemed weary from age, enfeebled, dry. I was thankful, very thankful that I had seen it. (11)

Again Gene does not explain, but this is the tree from which Phineas fell.

This tree in fact provides the transition, the hinge, between the brief prologue and the events of the story, fifteen years earlier. A few sentences after the passage just quoted, the description of the tree as it seems to Gene the narrator, the main story begins, with a description of the tree as it seemed to Gene the character: "The tree was tremendous, an irate, steely black steeple beside the river. I was damned if I'd climb it. The hell with it. No one but Phineas could think up such a crazy idea" (11-12). This tree is not magical, but it is not simply an inert object, either. Here in its first appearance it is irate, and a few pages later Gene admits that the tree "flooded me with a sensation of alarm all the way to my tingling fingers" (14). After Phineas and Gene jump, Phineas dares Leper: "The tree is waiting" (16). Then, after the fall, when Gene visits Finny in the infirmary, he seems to take out his anger on the tree:

"What happened there at the tree? That goddam tree, I'm going to cut down that tree. Who cares who can jump out of it. What happened, what happened? How did you fall, how could you fall off like that." (77)

Of course is he taking out his own feelings of guilt by attacking the tree; an object can take on subjectivity by projection.

No one goes to the tree again after Finny's accident, but the tree is mentioned from time to time. At the end of the summer, as Gene is on his way back to school, he visits the convalescing Finny at home, where he confesses his guilt, though Finny rejects his confession (83). Then another boy, Brinker Hadley, hints that he knows what happened at the tree (109-10); and when Gene visits Leper, who has deserted from the army, Leper accuses him directly of pushing Finny out of the tree (180). And finally, Brinker puts Gene on trial at a sort of kangaroo court. "Have you ever thought," Brinker asks Finny, "that you didn't just fall out of that tree?" Finny answers, "It's very funny, [. . .] but ever since then I've had a feeling that the tree did it by itself. It's an impression I've had. Almost as though the tree shook me out by itself" (211).

This is the climactic appearance of the tree, but it is not the last. The kangaroo court brings Leper in to tell what he saw when Finny fell, but I think he adds nothing particularly important about the tree (217-19). The point of the kangaroo court, of course, is to find Gene guilty; but before the verdict can be reached, Finny rushes out of the room and falls down the marble stairway—the same stairway that Gene visits when he returns to the school fifteen years later.

Of course, Finny has known all along that Gene caused him to fall from the tree, as we see clearly in their last conversation, after Finny's second fall: "It was just some kind of blind impulse you had in the tree there," he says to Gene; "you didn't know what you were doing. Was that it?" And then, "Something just seized you. It wasn't anything you really felt against me, it wasn't some kind of hate you've felt all along. It wasn't anything personal"

(239). Here the Hegelian conflict that organizes the story is clearly stated, if only in the negative. Finny can't accept the idea that Gene might have deliberately caused him to fall, so at first he refuses to hear Gene's confession, and then he projects the causation onto the tree itself.

The tree in *A Separate Peace* is not magical; it does not really have any power or agency of its own. This is, after all, a realistic novel, and magical objects are not welcome. The tree's agency is only a projection of Gene's agency. Whenever a narrative object takes on subjectivity, perhaps this subjectivity is only a projection. But perhaps this is a very modern way of looking at the world. Perhaps only a superficial kind of realism would deny that objects have souls waiting to be awakened.

V.

A fictional character may take on some of the quality of an instrumental object by identification. The principal character of Graham Greene's *A Gun for Sale* is a pathetic loser, a nobody, a weakling; to compensate for his feelings of inferiority, he becomes a hired gun. He is hardly a person, little more than the weapon he uses, as one of the other characters realizes: "she was astonished at the smallness of his wrists; his hands had no more strength or substance than a delicate boy's. The whole of his strength lay in the mechanical instrument at his feet" (133).[7]

In Conrad's *The Secret Agent,* the Professor knows that he will never be arrested, because he knows that the police know that he always carries with him a supply of the explosives he manufactures; in effect he has made himself into a bomb: "I walk always with my right hand closed around the indiarubber ball which I have in my trouser pocket. The pressing of this ball actuates a detonator inside the flask I carry in my pocket" (91). In our time we have seen that many people are willing to turn themselves into bombs.

In *A Gun for Sale* and *The Secret Agent* people turn into objects, but in George Eliot's *Silas Marner* the process is reversed, as a person comes to symbolize an object. Marner has hoarded a pile of gold, which he treats almost as if it were alive:

---

7. The book was published in the United States as *This Gun for Hire;* this title clearly identifies the character with his characteristic instrument. The chief character is also identified by his "hare-lip"—a term used by the narrator twice on the opening page of the novel. Here we see a person reduced by metonymy to a single part of his body. Something of the opposite effect is found in Nicolai Gogol's story "The Nose," in which Major Kovalyov's nose escapes and leads an independent existence.

> He began to think [the pile of coins] was conscious of him . . . , and he would on no account have exchanged those coins, which had become his familiars, for other coins with unknown faces. He handled them, he counted them, till their form and colour were like the satisfaction of a thirst to him; but it was only in the night, when his work was done, that he drew them out to enjoy their companionship. (68)

But his money is stolen from him, and without it he becomes a broken man. Then one evening, a little orphan girl finds her way to his cottage. His fire has burned low and his eyesight is bad, so at first he doesn't see her; when he does see her, he does not know what she is:

> Turning towards the hearth, where the two logs had fallen apart, and sent forth only a red uncertain glimmer, he seated himself on his fireside chair, and was stooping to push his logs together, when, to his blurred vision, it seemed as if there were gold on the floor in front of the hearth. Gold!—his own gold—brought back to him as mysteriously as it had been taken away! He felt his heart begin to beat violently, and for a few moments he was unable to stretch out his hand and grasp the restored treasure. The heap of gold seemed to flow and get larger beneath his agitated gaze. He leaned forward at last, and stretched forth his hand; but instead of hard coin with the familiar resisting outline, his fingers encountered soft warm curls. (167)

Marner regards this child as equivalent to his lost money—"Thought and feeling were so confused within him that if he had tried to give them utterance, he could only have said that the child was come instead of the gold—that the gold had turned into the child" (180). In Marner's mind, the child has become so closely identified with the gold that it is difficult to draw a line between the person and the thing. Marner adopts the child and names her Eppie. She takes the place of his gold, but through her Marner becomes humanized and takes his place in the society of the village. Eppie proves to be more valuable than gold.

VI.

People become instruments when they are used by other people. In many stories, the minor characters are often little more than tools used by the author or by one of the major characters to achieve a particular point in the plot. In Euripides' play *Hippolytus,* for example, Phaedra is ashamed to reveal that she is in love with her stepson, so she uses her nurse to make the revelation for her. She gives only riddling answers to the nurse's questions about the cause of her distress, though the riddles are very easy to read. When the nurse finally says directly that Phaedra must be in love with Hippolytus, Phaedra says, "You have spoken, not I!" According to Martin Mueller:

> The nurse thus appears to be the initiator of the action, but she is in reality the instrument of Phaedra's desire, while Phaedra, although the hidden beneficiary of this action, retains the power to disavow both the nurse's means and her ends as alien from her own intentions. Whereas on the surface the mistress suffers the servant to take over, this reversal of roles is in reality the mistress' device for evading the responsibility for an evil act secretly desired. (49–50)

Mueller's discussion of psychology employs terminology which could just as well refer to the roles of grammar: action, instrument, and beneficiary. Or one can say that grammar is also psychology.

Phaedra's nurse is a minor character, but an instrumental character can be at the center of the story. The title of Robertson Davies's novel *Fifth Business* refers to a particular sort of instrumental character: as Liesl, one of the characters in the story, explains the traditional roles in opera to the narrator, Dunstan Ramsay:

> "[Y]ou must have a prima dona [sic]—always a soprano, always the heroine, often a fool; and a tenor who always plays the lover to her; and then you must have a contralto, who is a rival to the soprano, or a sorceress or something; and a basso, who is the villain or the rival or whatever threatens the tenor.
>
> "So far, so good. But you cannot make a plot work without another man, and he is usually a baritone, and he is called in the profession Fifth Business, because he is the odd man out, the person who has no opposite of the other sex. And you must have Fifth Business because he is the one who knows the secret of the hero's birth, or comes to the assistance of the heroine when she thinks all is lost, or keeps the hermitess in her cell, or may even be the cause of somebody's death if that is part of the plot." (261)[8]

---

8. Davies uses a similar explanation of the term as the epigraph to the novel; he credits this citation to Tho. Overskou, *Den Danske Skueplads,* but without bibliographic information. See also pp. 10, 305, and 307–8; this last passage, at the very end of the story, suggests which characters in the novel have played which roles.

Ramsay, the narrator, calls himself Fifth Business, and he is called Fifth Business by Liesl as well, because he is instrumental to the major events of the story: he knows the secret of the hero's birth, and indirectly he is the cause of somebody's death as well.

When the story begins, in the early years of the twentieth century, Dunstan is a young boy growing up in a rural Ontario town. One winter day another boy, Percy Staunton, throws a snowball at him, but the snowball misses Dunstan and instead hits Mary Dempster, a young wife just six months pregnant. She falls down from the blow, and as a result of the shock she gives birth prematurely. The experience leaves her mentally unbalanced, and she becomes an outcast in the town. Her child, Paul, is ostracized, and at the age of ten he runs away to join a circus; under the name Magnus Eisengrim he becomes a famous stage magician. Percy, meanwhile, makes a fortune in sugar beets.

The plot is full of events, which I will not summarize. It is enough to say that one evening at the end of the novel, Dunstan brings Percy Staunton and Paul Dempster together; the next morning Percy is found drowned in his car in Lake Ontario, with a small stone in his mouth. The stone was the core of the snowball which hit Mary Dempster—Dunstan has kept it ever since, but Paul has stolen it from him.[9] Although the point is never made directly, the reader can deduce that Percy killed himself while hypnotized by Paul; the narrator goes to some trouble to explain that the subject (object?) of hypnosis cannot be forced to act out of character.

The outline of the plot, then, runs from the birth of Paul, caused by Percy, to the death of Percy, caused by Paul; Dunstan plays a role in both, but his role is incidental. He is Fifth Business, while Percy and Paul are the stars. "This is one of the cruelties of the theatre of life," Ramsay says; "we all think of ourselves as stars and rarely recognize it when we are indeed mere supporting characters or even supernumeraries" (18). And yet the whole thrust of this novel is that even a Fifth Business has a story worth telling, that even an instrumental character can become a subject.

---

9. The stone is the physical instrument of Paul's birth and (in a sense) of Percy's death, while Dunstan is the personal instrument. The story needs the stone because the snowball has long melted by the time of Percy's death. But the stone also explains why the snowball hit Mary Dempster so hard.

CHAPTER 10

Locative Subjects
Mahfouz, Lem, Forster

The instrumental and the locative are to some extent distinguished by scale: both are material, but the prototypical instrument is small enough to fit in the hand while the prototypical location is big enough to live in. Although the locative case is not one of the core functions of the sentence, it can nonetheless be promoted to the subject position of an English clause, and thus it may become the topic of the discourse. Some sentences, of course, do not express a locative function, but every story presumably takes place somewhere, and that scene can take on a kind of subjectivity.[1] Many stories begin with the description of the scene; this scene may be simply the place where events unfold, or perhaps the only place where these particular events could unfold. The scene may become a microcosm, and in some stories the location can become a participant in the action. In this chapter I discuss three modes of locative subjectivity: a location can be personified (as in Naguib Mahfouz' *Midac Alley*), a person can be localized (as in Rabelais's account of the world in Pantagruel's mouth), and a person and a place can be identified (as in Forster's *Howards End*)—though the boundaries of these modes are not firm. The locative, like the instrumental, must be included in a complete theory of the subject.

    1. For a recent summary of work on space in narrative, see David Herman, *Story Logic*, chapter 7, pp. 263–99. Herman makes a claim, with which I am in full agreement, that "spatial reference plays a crucial, not an optional or derivative role, in stories" (p. 264). Herman does not, however, discuss the subjectivity of locations, which is the topic of the present chapter.

161

I.

Locatives in English are usually expressed in a prepositional phrase, but English grammar allows a locative semantic function to be expressed as the subject of a clause. Thus we can say either "It's cold in the Yukon," with the locative in a prepositional phrase, or "The Yukon is cold," with the locative as subject.[2] A cleft construction can also promote the locative: "It's in the Yukon that it's cold" or "The Yukon is where it's cold." And we can simply move the prepositional phrase of location to the front of the clause: "In the Yukon it's cold." This prepositional phrase is not the grammatical subject, but because it begins the sentence it sets the tone of the sentence. "It's cold in the Yukon" directs our attention first to the cold, whereas "In the Yukon it's cold" directs our attention first to the Yukon.[3]

If a locative prepositional phrase begins a sentence, it takes on a certain emphasis. In the terms of M. A. K. Halliday's functional grammar, it is the theme of the sentence. In English, according to Halliday, the theme always begins the sentence. The beginning of a sentence is the beginning of the flow of information, the "point of departure of the message."[4] Consider again our initial examples:

The Yukon is cold.
It's cold in the Yukon.
In the Yukon it's cold.
The Yukon is where it's cold.
It's in the Yukon that it's cold.

Each of these has a slightly different tone, a slightly different emphasis and flow of information, but the exact tone of each phrase may become clear only in context. Different contexts will accept different forms more readily, but the rules of inclusion are not ironclad. The nuances are real and they deserve

---

2. But the sentence "Frank is cold" cannot be transformed to "It's cold in Frank": Frank is experiencer, not locative.

3. Compare also "This house hasn't been lived in for twenty years" or "This bed hasn't been slept in tonight" where the locative object of a preposition has been raised to the subject position. See G. David Morley, *Syntax in Functional Linguistics*, pp. 194–96.

4. "The Theme is the element which is the point of departure of the message; it is that with which the clause is concerned. The remainder of the message, the part in which the Theme is developed, is called . . . the Rheme" (Halliday, *An Introduction to Functional Grammar*, p. 38). It is not clear, however, that the point of departure of a message is invariably "that with which the clause is concerned."

attention, but there is some danger in making a simple equation of form and meaning without considering the context.

A story, like a sentence, may begin with a locative, as in William Faulkner's novel *The Hamlet*:[5]

> Frenchman's Bend was a section of rich river-bottom country lying twenty miles southeast of Jefferson. Hill-cradled and remote, definite yet without boundaries, straddling into two counties and owning allegiance to neither, it had been the original grant and site of a tremendous pre–Civil War plantation, the ruins of which—the gutted shell of an enormous house with its fallen stables and slave quarters and overgrown gardens and brick terraces and promenades—were still known as the Old Frenchman's place, although the original boundaries now existed only on old faded records in the Chancery Clerk's office in the county courthouse in Jefferson, and even some of the once-fertile fields had long since reverted to the cane-and-cypress jungle from which their first master had hewed them. (3)

The locative in the first sentence, in Halliday's system, is the theme; it is the subject of its sentence, and it continues to be the topic of the paragraph. Setting is certainly important in Faulkner's fiction, but I would not claim that this setting takes on much narrative subjectivity.

Dickens's *Bleak House* begins with the single word "London," which is then elaborated in the following sentences and sentence fragments, which serve almost as stage properties in a play. The atmospheric description of this beginning surely carries over to influence our reading of the rest of the story; it is thematic, but again, I think not truly a subject in the story.

Initial locatives can be expressed in various grammatical forms: the subject of a sentence, as in *The Hamlet*; a fragment, as in *Bleak House*; or as the object in a prepositional phrase, as in Willa Cather's *Lucy Gayheart*: "In Haverford on the Platte the townspeople still talk of Lucy Gayheart." This locative construction sets the location of the story, or at least the location of the beginning of the story, but this location is neither the grammatical subject of the sentence nor the narrative subject of the novel.[6] The grammatical subject is "the townspeople," but the narrative subject is certainly Lucy Gay-

---

5. This novel also takes its title from a location, as many novels do; it would be easy to multiply examples: a few are mentioned in this chapter.
6. But location has meaning in this story. Haverford is a town of limited vision, but at the same time it offers some sense of family and community. Lucy rejects family and community for the larger world of art and love in the big city. When these fail, she goes back home, but too late to recover what she has lost.

heart, placed last in the sentence for emphasis. And, of course, the title of the book prepares the reader to think that Lucy will be the heroine of the story.[7]

Temporal phrases are usually considered locatives, and these also can be expressed in a prepositional phrase. As features of narrative, time and space should be differentiated, though they are certainly often connected to each other. Many narratives begin with a double locative—a locative of time and a locative of space—and also perhaps the notation of a person or an event, as we see in the beginning paragraphs of Henry James's *The American,* Willa Cather's *Shadows on the Rock,* and Thomas Pynchon's *V:*

> On a brilliant day in May, in the year 1868, a gentleman was reclining at his ease on the great circular divan which at that period occupied the centre of the Salon Carré, in the Museum of the Louvre. (5)

> One afternoon late in October in the year 1697, Euclide Auclair, the philosopher apothecary of Quebec, stood on the top of Cap Diament gazing down the broad, empty river far beneath him. (3)

> Christmas Eve, 1955, Benny Profane, wearing black levis, suede jacket, sneakers and big cowboy hat, happened to pass through Norfolk, Virginia. (1)

In all these openings, the place is important, but the place is only what it is at a certain moment: Paris in 1868, Quebec in 1697, Norfolk in 1955. At another time, each of these would be a different place.[8]

All of these locatives are important in making the world of the story, but just as the initial position in a sentence is not necessarily the grammatical subject, neither is the initial position in a story the narrative subject. Something more is needed to turn setting into subjectivity.

---

7. Henry James's "Daisy Miller: A Study" also begins with a double prepositional phrase, and then the sentence ends with a more specific location: "In the little town of Vevey, in Switzerland, there is a particularly comfortable hotel." The narrative subject, Daisy Miller, does not appear for several pages.

8. Compare here Bakhtin's "chronotope," which expresses "the intrinsic connectedness of temporal and spatial relationships." According to Bakhtin, "In the literary artistic chronotope, spatial and temporal indicators are fused into one carefully thought-out, concrete whole. Time, as it were, thickens, takes on flesh, becomes artistically visible; likewise, space becomes charged and responsive to the movements of time, plot, and history" ("Forms of Time and of the Chronotope in the Novel," in *The Dialogic Imagination,* p. 84). Bakhtin does not discuss the subjectivity of space and location.

II.

The setting of a story can be a little world of its own, a world that seems to create the people and the events of the story. The setting in such a story tends to take on a personality, and the people and the events tend to become identified with the setting. Mahfouz' *Midaq Alley* begins with a locative description:

> Many things combine to show that Midaq Alley is one of the gems of times gone by and that it once shone forth like a flashing star in the history of Cairo. Which Cairo do I mean? That of the Fatimids, the Mamlukes or the Sultans? Only God and the archeologists know the answer to that, but in any case, the alley is certainly an ancient relic and a precious one. . . .
> Although Midaq Alley lives in almost complete isolation from all surrounding activity, it clamors with a distinctive and personal life of its own. Fundamentally and basically, its roots connect with life as a whole and yet, at the same time, it retains a number of the secrets of a world now past.
> The sun began to set and Midaq Alley was veiled in the brown hues of the glow. The darkness was all the greater because it was enclosed like a trap between three walls. (1)

This novel consists of the interlaced stories of a number of the people who live in the alley, the people who are trapped there, like the darkness. The business of the novel is to show the complex interconnections among the various denizens of the alley. By the end, one character has remarried; a second has been arrested for stealing the gold from the mouths of corpses; a third has been killed in a fight over the fourth, who has become a prostitute.

Although the plot is about the lives and fortunes of the characters, the alley itself takes on a certain personality, which is constructed in several ways. For example, the alley shares with the characters a position in the narrative structure. Many of the chapters begin with the name and actions of a particular character: "Mr. Kirsha, the coffeehouse owner, was occupied with an important matter . . ." (chapter 6, p. 38). But several of the chapters begin with the name of the alley and a notation of what is going on there at the time: "In the early morning Midaq Alley is dreary and cold" (chapter 4, p. 25; see also chapter 5, p. 33; chapter 19, p. 127; chapter 27, p. 193; and chapter 35, p. 242). This formal equivalence of people and place amounts to a structural personification of the Alley.

Furthermore, through metonymy the alley often stands for the people who live there. Thus Mrs. Kirsha is angry with her husband, who has taken a young man as his lover; nonetheless, "she was really proud of him, proud of his masculinity, proud of his position in the alley and of the influence he had over his associates" (65). She tells another character, Radwan Hussainy, "Today I am controlling my anger, but if I see there is no hope of reforming him, then I will send fire raging through the whole alley and the fuel for it will be his filthy body" (79). Mr. Hussainy summons Kirsha and tries to reason with him, without success: "Scowling and muttering to himself, Kirsha left the flat, cursing people in general and particularly Midaq Alley and Radwan Hussainy" (85). In the first and second of these passages, it is possible to take the alley just as the name of the place where the characters live, but in the third it is part of a parallel structure of increasing definiteness: people in general, Midaq Alley—standing for its residents—and then the individual Radwan Hussainy. This personal understanding of the name of the alley then can be read back into the first two passages, and to other similar passages throughout the story.

And finally, the end of the book completes the personification of the alley which was suggested at the beginning:

> The morning light filled the alley. . . . The alley was turning another of the pages of its monotonous life. . . .
>
> The early morning, then, found the alley enjoying its quiet and peaceful life as usual. . . .
>
> This crisis, too, like all the others, finally subsided and the alley returned to its usual state of indifference and forgetfulness. It continued, as was its custom, to weep in the morning when there was material for tear, and resound with laughter in the evening. . . .
>
> Then the interest of the alley was suddenly aroused when a butcher and his family came to occupy Booshy's flat. . . . (242–45)

Here the alley takes its place in grammatical structures usually reserved for animate nouns: it turns the page of its life, it enjoys its quiet and peaceful life, it weeps, and its interest is aroused. By the end, one has a feeling that the people come and go, live and die, but the alley continues to live.[9]

III.

The settings of Gothic stories often take on a kind of brooding and ominous

---

9. For another example of a street as a microcosm, see Gloria Naylor's *The Women of Brewster Place*.

personality. Mervyn Peake's Gothic novel *Titus Groan* takes place (except for a minor subplot) inside the walls of the castle Gormenghast, and the story begins with a description of the castle.[10] It is a remarkable edifice, almost a world in itself, and it is cut off from the rest of the world by natural barriers on all directions. Its size can only be imagined, and its plan is impossible to reconstruct. There is at least a hint in the story that this castle takes on some subjectivity. Now and again it is personified—particularly in the final chapter, which ends with a description of the castle. Moreover, the castle is identified with its master, Sepulchrave Groan, the seventy-sixth Earl of Gormenghast:

> How could he *love* this place? He was a part of it. He could not imagine a world outside it; and the idea of loving Gormenghast would have shocked him. To have asked him of his feelings for his hereditary home would be like asking a man what his feelings were towards his own hand or his own throat. (42)

But overall, the hints of subjectivity are never developed, and this fantastic construction is finally only decoration for a plot in which it plays no essential role.

The setting of Shirley Jackson's *The Haunting of Hill House* is takes on a somewhat greater subjectivity. The story begins with an ominous description:

> No live organism can continue for long to exist sanely under conditions of absolute reality; even larks and katydids are supposed, by some, to dream. Hill House, not sane, stood by itself against its hills, holding darkness within; it had stood so for eighty years and might stand for eighty more. Within, walls continued upright, bricks met neatly, floors were firm, and doors were sensibly shut; silence lay steadily against the wood and stone of Hill House, and whatever walked there, walked alone. (3)

Insanity surely implies subjectivity, even for a house.

As the story begins, Dr. John Montague, a psychic researcher, has gathered a small group of volunteers to stay with him in the house to investigate—and to endure—whatever may happen, whatever the house may do.

---

10. Gaston Bachelard's *The Poetics of Space* is a valuable document for the student of location in literature; he is most interested in the house as a location of intimacy, however, and consequently has little discussion of haunted houses or other Gothic structures. Nor does he discuss at any length the subjectivity of space.

By cinematic standards, the events are not all that spooky, but they certainly disturb the investigators, one of whom kills herself at the end of the story.

The house itself is persistently personified: the narrator says that "the face of Hill House seemed awake, with a watchfulness from the bland windows and a touch of glee in the eyebrows of a cornice" (34); Dr. Montague says that the house "watches every move you make" (85); and when graffiti naming her is found on the walls, Eleanor comes to believe that the house knows her name (146). The final paragraph repeats, almost word for word, the description of the house in the first chapter; by this time the reader has experienced the events that justify the personification.

Larger places of habitation can also take on subjectivity.[11] The title of Jane Smiley's *A Thousand Acres* directs our attention to a large tract of land, a family farm in the American Midwest, first settled in 1890. This land has been worked and fundamentally changed by the people who have lived on it, but now it dominates the people. At the beginning of the novel, the owner of the farm, Laurence Cook, has decided to retire and to divide the land among his three daughters, Ginny (who narrates the story), Rose, and Caroline. Caroline thinks the plan is foolish, and she is written out of the deal: echoes of *King Lear* are obvious throughout the story.

Laurence gradually comes to distrust and hate his two older daughters, and eventually he and Caroline sue to regain possession, without success. The fight over the land brings to the surface long-suppressed conflicts in the family. By the end of the book several of the characters have died and all the survivors hate each other.

From time to time the people in the story personify the land; as Ginny says to her husband Ty, "You were on Caroline's side! You talked with her about me!" and he replies, "I was on the side of the farm, that was all" (341)—as if the land could have an interest. Moreover, the land is identified with human characters, particularly with the patriarch, Laurence:

> Perhaps there is a distance that is the optimum distance for seeing one's father, farther than across the supper table or across the room, somewhere in the middle distance: he is dwarfed by trees or the sweep of a hill, but his features are still visible, his body language still distinct. Well, that is a

---

11. One of the most famous instances in English literature, of course, is the heath in Thomas Hardy's *The Return of the Native*. According to Avron Fleishman, "Landscape is not satisfied to act in *The Return of the Native* as background, with human subjects in the foreground.... Instead, Egdon Heath becomes one of the principal agents of the action, a protagonist in the classical sense of the dramatic actor, and probably the most memorable figure to emerge from the events" (Fleishman, "The Buried Giant of Egdon Heath," p. 100; see also Lance St John Butler, p. 33).

distance I never found. He was never dwarfed by the landscape—the fields, the buildings, the white pine windbreak were as much my father as if he had grown them and shed them like a husk. (20)

Eventually Ginny and Rose win the suit and keep possession of the land, but one disaster after another occurs, and finally the farms go bankrupt and are sold by auction to an agribusiness corporation. Ginny has moved to the city where she works as a waitress, but she knows that she will never lose the land:

> [A]lthough the farm and all its burdens and gifts are scattered, my inheritance is with me, sitting in my chair. Lodged in my every cell, along with the DNA, are molecules of topsoil and atrazine and paraquat and anhydrous ammonia and diesel fuel and plant dust. . . . (369)

The relationship between the land and the people is a complex interaction. One aspect of this interaction is most clearly seen through Jess, a local boy who left thirteen years before to join the army, and then deserted and went to Canada. At the beginning of the story he comes back home, just at the time when Laurence is dividing his land among his daughters. Jess has developed an interest in organic farming, and although by the end of the story he has moved back to Vancouver, some of his influence remains:

> When I am reminded of Jess, I think of the loop of poison we drank from, the water running down through the soil, into the drainage wells, into the lightless mysterious underground chemical sea, then being drawn up, cold and appetizing, from the drinking well into Rose's faucet, my faucet. I am reminded of Jess when I drive in the country, and see the anhydrous trucks in the distance, or the herbicide incorporators, or the farmers plowing their fields in the fall, or hills that are ringed with black earth and crowned with soil so pale that the corn only stands in it, as in gravel, because there are no nutrients to draw from it. (370)

So, at the end of the story, the land itself has become one of the victims, along with the people who have lived there.

IV.

According to Jared Diamond, "History followed different courses for different peoples because of differences among people's environments, not because of biological differences among peoples themselves."[12] If a different geography does in fact determine a different culture, then authors interested in inventing different cultures may want to invent different worlds.

Almost by definition, stories of invented worlds belong to the genres of fantasy or science fiction—though perhaps the greatest of all invented worlds, the world of *The Divine Comedy*, fits rather uneasily in those categories. No doubt Dante believed that his world was not invented at all but was the very map of what is most real. But most inventors of worlds have been content with a more private cartography.

A story may begin in our world and move to the invented world. Points of entry are various: strange doors, holes in the ground, mirrors, tornadoes, shipwrecks, trances, spaceships, time machines. In addition there may be a guide: a rabbit, a raven, Virgil, or a wondrous maiden. But some other worlds exist simply on their own, with no relationship to ours: to open the door you simply open the book.

The inventor of a world may legislate a different nature, even the supernatural. Distinctions can be drawn here: a world may allow strange things to happen; a world may be somehow strange in itself; a world may strangely take part in the action as an independent agent and subject. The differences are subtle but nonetheless real and important. There may be aliens on Mars, but Mars itself, however strange it may be, does nothing by itself; it is simply where the aliens live.[13] The principal setting of Larry Niven's *Ringworld* is a gigantic ring circling a sun at about ninety million miles. The engineers of this world took the whole of the planetary mass of a solar system and molded it into a single ring with a truly enormous surface, room for countless cultures and countless stories. But as remarkable as the ring is, it doesn't actually do anything itself—it only provides a huge arena in which the actors can play their parts.

Philip Jose Farmer has specialized in the invention of strange worlds. The most famous of his creations is Riverworld—a gigantic river valley that twists and turns back in endless meanders. All human beings who have ever lived are reborn on the banks of this river. There is room here for as many stories as one wants to tell—or to hear—but the basic plot throughout the Riverworld series is the drive to find out who has created this world and for what purpose. In another series by Farmer, the World of Tiers series, the

---

12. Jared M. Diamond, *Guns, Gems, and Steel: The Fates of Human Societies*, p. 25.
13. See, for example, Edgar Rice Burroughs, *John Carter of Mars*, and many more in the series; C. S. Lewis, *Out of the Silent Planet*; Stanley G. Weinbaum, *A Martian Odyssey*; Ray Bradbury, *The Martian Chronicles*; Robert Heinlein, *Red Planet*; Philip K. Dick, *The Martian Time-Slip*; and many others.

major characters have the ability to create what are called "pocket universes," worlds with strange and dangerous characteristics.

The hero of Farmer's *The Stone God Awakens* is a twentieth-century physicist, Ulysses Singing Bear, who has been petrified by one of his experiments. After millions of years in stasis, he wakes in a world drastically changed from our own. There are no human beings left, but a variety of other species have developed consciousness. In his petrified form he has been worshiped by a race of catlike humanoids, and when he wakes, he becomes their leader.

The continent on which they live is largely covered by an enormous tree, called Wurutana. Wurutana is a world in itself, a complete ecological system hosting many different species of plants and animals. It has developed consciousness, and it controls the races that live on it. Ulysses forms an uneasy coalition of the races that are not controlled by Wurutana, and they fight a major battle against some of the tree's races. He manages to establish communication with the tree, which offers a deal to Ulysses and his followers: they can live on the tree as long as they agree not to develop science or civilization. Ulysses rejects the deal and attacks the tree itself. At the end of the book the contest is a standoff. In the final sentences of the book, Ulysses asks himself, "If the mind of flesh can meet with another mind of flesh, why not with a vegetable mind? Who knows?" (190). Thus the story leads to a Hegelian confrontation between Humanity, represented by Ulysses, and Nature, represented by the great tree Wurutana, with at least the prospect of some kind of gain in consciousness through the confrontation.

The Hegelian conflict of Humanity and Nature is presented perhaps even more starkly in Stanislaw Lem's novel *Solaris*. The hero of the story, Kris Kelvin, joins a small research team already living on the planet Solaris. The planet is primarily ocean, with only a few small rocky islands, on one of which the research station has been established.

Previous research has determined that the ocean is organic, in effect a single giant cell. Moreover, it is somehow capable of directing the orbit of the planet itself. Previous teams have discovered that the ocean is in the habit of forming from its own material enormous constructions; some of these, which have been termed "mimoids," reproduce the shapes of human artifacts or even the shapes of human beings.[14] These phenomena have led some scientists to conclude that the ocean is conscious and rational, but all attempts to communicate with it have failed.

When Kelvin arrives, he finds the research station in complete disarray.

14. Lem's descriptions of these structures are quite amazing; see the passages beginning on p. 88 and p. 122.

Of the three resident scientists, one has committed suicide and the other two seem to be insane, victims of hallucinations. These hallucinations, however, are not mere phantasms; they are as fully physical as any living person. Soon Kelvin himself has a visitor—the revenant of his dead wife, Rheya, who had killed herself years ago after he left her. Evidently, the ocean has created these bodily forms after examining the minds of the scientists. Perhaps it is doing experiments on human beings.

The ontology of these forms is difficult to determine. They are created by the ocean, perhaps made from its own material, and yet they derive from the minds of the human beings at the research station. In a sense they are the peculiar synthetic offspring of the confrontation of these two forms of life. They cannot be killed—or, rather, if killed, they simply re-appear a short while later. Their blood, as examined by Kelvin, is exactly like human blood, down to the molecular level; but below that, there are no atoms to be found: Kelvin speculates that they are actually made of nothing.

Kelvin's visitor has a measure of confused self-awareness. At first she thinks that she is the original Rheya; when she realizes that she is only a creation of the ocean, she falls into despair and tries to kill herself—without success. Much of the plot of the story concerns Kelvin's complex relationship with this revenant Rheya. Kelvin falls in love with his visitor, but she cannot bear her ontological ambiguity, and so, finally, with the help of the other scientists, she manages to kill herself once and for all.

In a sense this revenant Rheya represents the ocean; but in another sense she represents a part of Kelvin that he does not want to acknowledge:

> [T]here may be thoughts, intentions, and cruel hopes in my mind of which I know nothing, because I am a murderer unawares. Man has gone out to explore other worlds and other civilizations without having explored his own labyrinth of dark passages and secret chambers, and without finding what lies behind doorways that he himself has sealed. (165)

At the end of the story, Kelvin decides that he must stay on Solaris:

> That liquid giant had been the death of hundreds of men. The entire human race had tried in vain to establish even the most tenuous link with it, and it bore my weight without noticing me any more than it would notice a speck of dust. I did not believe that it could respond to the tragedy of two human beings. Yet its activities did have a purpose. . . . True, I was not absolutely certain, but leaving would mean giving up a chance, perhaps an infinitesimal one, perhaps only imaginary. . . . Must I go on living here then, among

the objects we both had touched, in the air she had breathed? In the name of what? In the hope of her return? I hoped for nothing. And yet I lived in expectation. Since she had gone, that was all that remained. I did not know what achievements, what mockery, even what tortures still awaited me. I knew nothing, and I persisted in the faith that the time of cruel miracles was not past. (211)

What is it that he is waiting for? A re-creation of the original Rheya? The new Rheya as an independent being in herself? A manifestation of his own memories and desires? Something created by the ocean? Or some aspect of the ocean itself? All of these, however, are manifestations of the same fundamental Hegelian confrontation, in one form or another. This story, then, poses two questions: First, would it be possible for humanity to confront and communicate with a fundamentally alien consciousness? And second, is it possible for humanity to confront and communicate with itself? These two questions finally can be seen as identical.

V.

Just as place can be personified, so can a person be localized. This seems to be the least productive of the modes of locative subjectivity, but stories exist which manifest it in three ways at least: a gigantic person can be home for people of normal size; a person of normal size can be home for tiny organisms living on the body; or miniaturized people can enter the world inside a person of normal size.

The narrator of the second book of François Rabelais's great fantasy takes refuge from a storm in the mouth of the giant Pantagruel. There he finds meadows, forests, and cities. On the top of one of Pantagruel's teeth he finds tennis courts, galleries, meadows, and summer houses in the Italian fashion. He lives in Pantagruel's mouth for several months, but then returns to the outside world.[15]

In Isaac Asimov's *Fantastic Voyage*, a prominent scientist is in danger of dying from an inoperable blood clot, but through the wonders of modern science fiction, a team of people is miniaturized so that they can enter the patient's bloodstream to perform the operation from inside. On their voyage

---

15. See Eric Auerbach's *Mimesis*, chapter 11, "The World in Pantagruel's Mouth"; also in M. M. Bakhtin's essay "Forms of Time," the section "The Rabelaisian Chronotope," pp. 167–206, in *The Dialogic Imagination*; and in Bakhtin's *Rabelais and His World*, chapter 5, "The Grotesque Image of the Body and Its Sources," pp. 303–436.

they have various adventures inside the scientist's body, as they battle against various dangers, including the patient's immune system.[16]

In *The Dream Life of Balso Snell,* Nathaniel West (or, rather, his character Maloney the Areopagite) briefly tells the story of Saint Puce, a flea who was born in the armpit of Christ.[17] This little fantasy is worth quoting at some length:

> "O happy, happy childhood! Playing in the curled brown silk, sheltered from all harm by Christ's arm. Eating the sweet flesh of our Savior; drinking His blood; bathing in His sweat; partaking, oh how fully! of His Godhead. . . .
>
> ". . . The music of our Lord's skin sliding over his flesh!—more exact than the fugues of Bach. The pattern of His veins!—more intricate than the Maze at Cnossos. The odors of His Body!—more fragrant than the Temple of Solomon. The temperature of His flesh!—more pleasant than the Roman baths to the young Puce. And finally, the taste of His blood! In this wine all pleasure, all excitement, was magnified, until with ecstasy Saint Puce's small body roared like a furnace.
>
> "In his prime, Saint Puce wandered far from his birthplace, that hair-silk pocketbook, the armpit of our Lord. He roamed the forest of God's chest and crossed the hill of His abdomen. He measured and sounded that fathomless well, the Navel of our Lord. He explored and charted every crevasse, ridge, and cavern of Christ's body. From notes taken during his travels he later wrote his great work, *A Geography of Our Lord.*" (116)

No doubt West intended to be irreverent, but perhaps in a certain theological systems there would be something appropriate in making Christ into a location as well as a person: a pantheist might well claim that god is the world and the world is god, and so in a sense we all live in and on the body of god.

VI.

We have already seen several instances of the identification of a person and a place; for example, Sepulchrave Groan was identified with the castle Gormenghast in *Titus Groan,* and Laurence Cook was identified with his farm in

---

16. Asimov's novel is based on the movie of the same title written by Jerome Bixby, David Duncan, Harry Kleiner, and Otto Klement and directed by Richard Fleischer.

17. "Puce" is French for "flea," so "Saint Puce" really "Saint Flea." For an interesting discussion of microscopic organisms that inhabit the human body, see Theodore Rosebury, *Life on Man.*

A Thousand Acres. These were momentary identifications, however. In E. M. Forster's *Howards End* the identification of a person and a place is persistent and crucial to the theme of the story.

While traveling on the continent, Mr. and Mrs. Wilcox have met two young unmarried sisters, Helen and Margaret Schlegel. They have invited the sisters to visit them at their home, Howards End (which, in fact, is owned by Mrs. Wilcox); Margaret, however, has to stay in London to take care of her brother Tibby, who is ill, so Helen goes by herself. The story begins with a few letters Helen writes to Margaret from Howards End, in which she describes the house and the family, particularly Mrs. Wilcox, a rather saintly figure who seems to float above all merely human concerns.

Then in her third letter Helen announces that she and Paul, the younger son of the family, have suddenly fallen in love. Margaret feels that she should go to Howards End to see what is going on, but she is still tending her brother, so she sends her rather officious Aunt Juley. Domestic comedy ensues; Helen and Paul have fallen out of love as suddenly as they fell into it. Aunt Juley puts her foot in her mouth, and nearly everyone is left feeling uncomfortable—except for Mrs. Wilcox:

> She approached just as Helen's letter had described her, trailing noiselessly over the lawn, and there was actually a wisp of hay in her hands. She seemed to belong not to the young people and their motor, but to the house, and to the tree that overshadowed it. (22)

Already we see the identification of Mrs. Wilcox and Howards End.

For some time after this contretemps, the Schlegels and the Wilcoxes have nothing to do with each other, but they are thrown together when the Wilcoxes rent a flat just opposite the Schlegels' home in London. Margaret and Mrs. Wilcox become friends, and one day Mrs. Wilcox invites Margaret to come with her to see Howards End, but Margaret declines.

Shortly thereafter, Mrs, Wilcox dies, and, as we find out later, Margaret had been very attentive to her in her last illness. The Wilcoxes discover that Mrs. Wilcox has left a note asking them to give Howards End to Margaret. The family confer and decide to ignore Mrs. Wilcox's instruction. As the narrator notes, for the other Wilcoxes, Howards End was just a house: "they could not know that for her it had been a spirit, for which she sought a spiritual heir" (94).

Mr. Wilcox now begins to seek out Margaret's company, and eventually he proposes to her. Margaret accepts, to the surprise of Helen, and perhaps the reader as well; so Margaret is about to become Mrs. Wilcox.

Mr. Wilcox and Margaret now have to decide where they will live once they are married. Howards End has been let, so it is unavailable, but Mr. Wilcox has another house at Oniton Grange, and Margaret assumes that they will live there. But Howards End is for the moment empty, and Mr. Wilcox takes Margaret to see it. When they arrive, Mr. Wilcox realizes he has forgotten the key; while he is off looking for it, Margaret finds that the door is open and she goes inside. She hears something, a reverberation: "it was the heart of the house beating, faintly at first, then loudly, martially" (188). Margaret flings open the door to the stairs and finds an old woman, Mrs. Avery, who momentarily mistakes her for the former Mrs. Wilcox.

The plot at this point becomes rather complicated. In short, Margaret and Helen—especially Helen—have taken up a young man of a lower class with intellectual and artistic ambitions, Leonard Bast. Then it comes out that some ten years before, Bast's wife had been Mr. Wilcox's mistress. Mr. Wilcox offers to release Margaret from their engagement, but she refuses. Meanwhile, the Basts disappear.

The lease on the Schlegels' house in London has run out, and the landlord has refused to renew. In any case the family is now broken up: Margaret is about to be married, Helen has suddenly left for the continent, and Tibby is at Oxford. So their furniture is packed up and sent to Howards End. Margaret and Mr. Wilcox marry quietly, spend their honeymoon at Innsbruck, and then move into his London house for the time being.

Howards End has been left in the care of Mrs. Avery. Margaret visits the house and finds that that everything has been unpacked and the house has been furnished. She tells Mrs. Avery that this was not what they had wanted, that a mistake has been made, and Mrs. Avery replies, "Mrs Wilcox, it has been mistake upon mistake for fifty years. The house is Mrs Wilcox's, and she would not desire it to stand empty any longer" (253). Margaret has become the double of the first Mrs. Wilcox, and Margaret even wonders for a moment if Mrs. Avery is so confused as to not know the difference.

Helen returns to England but refuses to see anyone in the family. Margaret tricks her into coming to Howards End, and when Helen arrives, the mystery is solved: she is pregnant. Helen declares that she will go back to the continent, but she convinces Margaret to stay over night with her at Howards End, now completely furnished with their belongings. Mr. Wilcox is at the house of his son Charles, in the village nearby, and Margaret goes to ask his permission. He refuses on moral grounds to let Helen stay at the house. Margaret reminds him of his affair with Mrs. Bast and charges him with hypocrisy. Finally she returns to the house against his will, and their marriage seems to be in danger. Meanwhile Charles finds out from Tibby that Helen's likely seducer is Leonard Bast.

The crisis of the story depends on a coincidence. Bast, who has been reduced to poverty, has caught sight of Margaret in London. He follows her to Howards End, and he arrives just as Charles also arrives; Charles attacks him and he dies, perhaps of heart failure. Charles is tried and sentenced to a term in prison for manslaughter. Mr. Wilcox is broken by the verdict, and Margaret takes him to Howards End to recover.

In the last chapter, Margaret and Mr. Wilcox and Helen and Helen's baby are all living together happily at Howards End. In this chapter Mr. Wilcox calls a conclave of his family in which he declares that he intends to leave Howards End to Margaret. His silly daughter-in-law Dolly says, "It does seem curious that Mrs Wilcox should have left Margaret Howards End, and yet she gets it after all," and thus Margaret finds out that she was Mrs. Wilcox's intended heir. This is almost the very end of the book; the last two paragraphs are simply an idyllic cadence, as Helen runs in with her baby and the neighbor's boy to say that the big meadow has been cut.

Howards End is certainly the center around which the story is organized. Mrs. Wilcox is frequently identified with the house, and then Margaret as her double is identified with it as well. Moreover, the house is not simply a place: it is a living being that determines the action, even against the will of the human characters in the story.

VII.

Cartesian subjectivity resides in the single subject, though a certain courtesy will perhaps extend subjectivity to other people. Hegelian subjectivity needs two centers of consciousness, each of which impels the other to self-consciousness. Freud's subject lives in a family, whereas Mead's self is one part of a society of selves, all defined by their mutual interrelations. Subjectivity, as I have defined it in the introduction, is a role played by a self. One might then expect that subjectivity is restricted to what we might call *persons,* since things are not possessed of selves. But the evidence of this chapter, on locative subjectivity, and of the previous chapter, on instrumental subjectivity, suggests that the boundary between a person and a thing, a person and a place, is not so firm.

Our experience of life is consistent with less-than-firm boundaries between persons and things. At times we feel that we have been used, that we are only the instrument of another person's action, a tool in someone's hand. At times we feel that some object thrown in our path has a will of its own and refuses to act as it should. And at times we feel that some object has become identified with a person, so that the object alone will stand in for that person.

Likewise, we can feel that a person and a place have become identified, or that a place has a personality of its own. I suppose it is less common to think of a person as a location, though for the organisms living on us we are just as much home as the earth is home to us; but even this situation shows up in narrative, as we have seen. A complete account of the subject and the self must include these modes of subjectivity, as eccentric as they may seem. The scientific and rationalist view of the world would reduce instruments to mere matter and location to points in a grid, but our experience tells us otherwise. The animistic world may have been banished from our official philosophies, but it continues to find expression in narrative.

CONCLUSION

Narrative and the Self
Hartley, Sartre, Ishiguro

In this study I have been concerned with the self and with narrative: the self in narrative and narratives of the self. In previous chapters I have described a set of modes of subjectivity—versions of the self—as they are found in narratives. I have argued that there are various ways of conceiving the self: the Cartesian self; the Hegelian self; the Freudian self; the self as agent, as patient, as experiencer, as witness; and even the self as instrument or as location.[1] I have further argued that these various modes of subjectivity find their representation in narratives—sometimes in narratives written by philosophers, but more often and often more interestingly in narratives written by storytellers. In order to understand the self, we should look to these stories, and in order to understand these stories, we should think about the self.

The study of narrative demands a concept of the self richer than the nearly ubiquitous binary division of the self and the other, or the subject and the object. This dichotomous model has its uses in particular situations, but it does not provide a generally adequate account of the self. We must always ask: What kind of self? What kind of other?

---

1. But this list is hardly exhaustive. The locative case can also express location in time, and time can become a subject in novels of a year (such as *The Return of the Native*) or of a day (such as *Ulysses*). The abessive case, the case of lack, as in the form "money-less," marks the subjectivity of quest stories. The translative case, which marks the end point of a state of change, might correspond to stories of transformation (such as *The Golden Ass*). The vocative case may be the case of interpellation, the subjectivity of the audience (as in *The Fall*). Modes of subjectivity may also be suggested by titles, such as *The Clown, The Rogue, The Confidence Man*, or even *The Man Without Qualities*.

I have organized the discussion of the narrative self around certain theoretical and philosophic models, but I do not believe that narratives are imperfect imitations of ideal theoretical forms. One might say instead that theoretical and philosophic models are imperfect abstractions of lived experience. Narrative, of course, is not lived experience, but rather a selection and ordering of the overwhelming abundance of life according to some plan for some purpose. Each selection and ordering amounts to a theory, though in the telling, the theory is usually better left implicit. Narrative thus sits between and mediates theory and experience, and it draws its particular strength from its participation in both. A narrative will use an implicit model to make sense of life, and it will show what it might feel like to live within some model.

So much I take to be a general claim about narrative. In the terms of this study, each narrative I have examined says: Here is what one particular way of being a self feels like. Here is the experience of one particular kind of subjectivity. *Notes from Underground* tells us what it might feel like to live as a Cartesian self, and so does *The Talented Mr. Ripley*, in a rather different way. *A Farewell to Arms* presents one possible life according to the Hegelian model, and *A Separate Peace* presents another. Moreover, all of these narratives taken together provide a complex vision of possible subjectivities, a theory of theories of the self.

This concluding chapter extends the discussion in two directions. The first section of the chapter presents an analysis of L. P. Hartley's *The Go-Between*, which displays many modes of the self in a single story. Whereas each of the earlier chapters has concentrated on one dominant form of subjectivity, here I want to show the complex interactions among several different modes. This discussion of multiple subjectivities then leads into the second section, which is concerned with the nature of the self and the subject. This question again finds itself represented in narrative, in Ishiguro's fable of the butler in *The Remains of the Day* and in Sartre's fable of the waiter in *Being and Nothingness*.

I.

L. P. Hartley's *The Go-Between* is the story of a romantic triangle. It is also the story of a young boy observing a romantic triangle. And it is also the story of an old man remembering himself as a young boy observing a romantic triangle. The narrative moves from the outside in and then back out, though the boundaries of the narrative layers are not entirely firm.

The novel begins with a brief prologue, set in 1952. The narrator, Leo Colston, now in his sixties, has come across a diary he kept in the year 1900, when he was twelve and thirteen. He has suppressed many of his memories of that time in his life, but in unlocking the diary he unlocks the memories, and Leo's narrative of these recovered memories forms the long central section of the novel.

The diary itself is an important object in the story. Not only does it play a role in some of the events of the story, but it also provides an important set of symbols. The diary is decorated with the signs of the zodiac, and several of these become identified with characters in the story, as we will see below.

The old Leo who finds the diary and thereby remembers himself is sharply divided from the young Leo he remembers. As we saw in chapter 1, almost any self-reflexive memoir, fictional or nonfictional, will show some division of the self. In some reflexive narratives this division is small and unimportant, but in this novel the division is both extreme and an essential point of the story. There is, of course, a large temporal gap—over fifty years—between the two Leos, but more fundamentally the young Leo has been partly hidden from the old Leo, until he opens the diary and recovers his past. If memory is a part of what makes a self, then Leo's loss of memory is a loss of self.

The older Leo is very aware of this division. In the prologue he imagines a dialogue between himself in the present and the self he is now remembering:

> If my twelve-year-old self, of whom I had grown rather fond, thinking about him, were to reproach me: "Why have you grown up such a dull dog, when I gave you such a good start? Why have you spent your time in dusty libraries, cataloguing other people's books instead of writing your own? . . ."
>
> I should have an answer ready. "Well, it was you who let me down, and I will tell you how. You flew too near the sun, and you were scorched. This cindery creature is what you made me." (31–32)

This dialogue, which continues for about a page, clearly shows the division and even the conflict between Leo's two selves. This difference is maintained throughout the novel, as the old Leo in his narration often notes that he now understands what had been mysterious to him when he was a boy. Only at the end of the novel is there a sense that Leo's two selves have finally come together into a single person as he regains the memories of the summer of 1900.

Still in the prologue, before the long central section of the novel, Leo tells us about his troubles in boarding school in the months just before the main story begins. Leo was a late-comer to school; his father, a bank manager, had wanted to educate him at home, but (as we learn in chapter 1) after his father died he was sent to school by his socially ambitious mother. We can easily imagine the complex feelings Leo has to deal with: the pain of his father's recent death, the fear that he is of a lower class than most of his schoolmates, his insecurity as a late arrival to the school. It's no wonder that he has to struggle to find his place.

This problem comes to a head when some of the other boys steal his diary—the same diary he will find in 1952—and read his rather pretentious entries. They ridicule and torment him, and in revenge he writes a formal curse in his diary. The boys also read this and torment him even more. But the next night the ringleaders, Jenkins and Strode, are badly injured when they fall off a roof. Leo gets a reputation for magical powers, which he himself more than half believes. He also gets an invitation to stay the summer with one of his schoolmates, Marcus Maudsley, at Brandham Hall, an estate near Norfolk. The events of Leo's summer at Brandham Hall form the central section of the novel, in twenty-three numbered chapters.

The preliminary story in the prologue introduces questions about Leo's social self. The social self, as G. H. Mead has told us, is defined by its relation to other selves, as the role of a player on an athletic team is defined by the roles of the other players. Every boarding school is a miniature society, and each boy has to find his place in that society. When we first see Leo, he is the object of torment and ridicule, a patient, but he becomes an agent through the seeming success of his curse. These questions of Leo's agency and his position in society are then developed in the central section of the novel.[2]

At Brandham Hall, Leo is a middle-class boy thrust among the upper classes, and the problem of his social self becomes if anything more acute. His friend Marcus has to give him instructions in proper behavior. Leo has brought only heavy clothing, but the weather has become very hot. He wonders if he should wear his cricket clothes, but Marcus firmly tells him that "only cads wear their school clothes in the holidays. It isn't done" (55). Marcus continues with his advice: "You oughtn't really to be wearing the school band round your hat, but I didn't say anything. And, Leo, you mustn't come down to breakfast in your slippers. It's the sort of thing bank clerks do." (55). This comment cuts Leo: "I winced at the reference to bank clerks, and remembered that on Sunday my father had always come down to breakfast

2. In the epilogue, Leo explicitly marks the connection between the events at school and the events at Brandham Hall: "A certain set of circumstances had arisen and it was for me to deal with them, just as at school I had had to deal with the persecution of Jenkins and Strode. Then I had succeeded. . . . This time I had failed. . ." (p. 307).

in his slippers. But it had been a shot in the dark; I had never told Marcus of my father's lowly social status" (55–56). And the lesson continues. Marcus explains that when Leo undresses for the night he must not leave his clothes neatly on a chair. "You must leave them lying wherever they happen to fall—the servants will pick them up—that's what they're for" (56).[3]

Leo's clothing becomes a topic of discussion, and the teasing comments and sarcasm remind Leo of the persecution he suffered at school (56–57). Marcus's older sister Marian, however, offers to take Leo to the nearby town to buy him a summer suit. Once he is dressed properly, he feels less out of place. Because the suit is Lincoln green, Leo gets the nickname Robin Hood; he delighted by the name, and he imagines himself "roaming the greenwood with Maid Marian" (64). Marian's good deed is the beginning of Leo's special relationship with her.

The climax of this strand of the story comes just halfway through the novel, in a cricket match between the Hall and the nearby village. Leo's ambiguous status at the Hall is reflected by his place on the team—he is the twelfth player, available to field if someone is injured but not available to be a batsman—on the team but not of it. As fate, and the laws of narrative, would have it, one of the players for the Hall is injured late in the game; Leo takes his place on the field and makes the crucial catch. According to Mead's athletic model of the social self, he has found his place, his role, his self.

In addition to these three narrative layers—Leo in 1952, Leo in 1900 at school, and Leo in 1900 at Brandham Hall—there is another, inner layer: a romantic triangle, which Leo witnesses, without fully understanding. The three points of the triangle are Marian; Lord Trimingham, the ninth Viscount Trimingham, whom Marian is supposed to marry (though the engagement is supposed to be secret); and Ted Burgess, a local farmer, with whom Marian is having an affair. This triangle is marked by class tensions, since Burgess is barely acknowledged by the high society of Marian's family and friends.

The romantic triangle in this novel can be compared to triangles in other narratives, such as *The Master of Ballantrae, The Age of Innocence,* and *A Room with a View,* which we have examined in chapter 5, "Freudian Thirds." We can imagine that this romantic intrigue could have been the primary focus of interest—in another and rather different novel. The story could have been told from the perspective of any of the three characters involved.

---

3. Nor does Marcus give instructions to Leo only here: see his comments on the eating of porridge (p. 78) and on wearing a made-up tie (p. 291). These instructions can be compared to Herbert Pocket's lessons to Pip in *Great Expectations;* in each instance a lower-class boy is furnishing a new self.

Marian could easily have been the central character, and she does receive much attention in the story. Or the story could have centered on Ted and Trimingham as Hegelian rivals. They are perhaps not a strong double, but they are certainly a contrasting pair: Trimingham is an aristocrat, while Ted is a working farmer; Ted is handsome, while Trimingham has been badly disfigured in the Boer War. Several times Leo makes an explicit comparison between the two, as in his description of the banquet after the cricket match:

> Wearing a lounge suit and a high starched collar [Ted] looked even less like himself than he did in [cricket] flannels. The more clothes he put on, the less he looked like himself. Whereas Lord Trimingham's clothes always seemed part of him, Ted's fine feathers made him look like a yokel. (169)

But none of these characters is at the center of the novel as we have it. The romantic triangle is only a component in another story.

Leo is the witness to the romantic triangle, and thus he can be compared to McKellar in *The Master of Ballantrae* and to Nick in *The Great Gatsby*. But the treatment of the witness is different in each of these three novels. McKellar is clearly a subordinate character, though he has enough personality to give him at least a certain individuality, and he also functions to some extent as a guide to the reader's judgments. No one could say, however, that *The Master of Ballantrae* is McKellar's story. Nick, as I have argued in chapter 8, has a more prominent role in *The Great Gatsby*, and he can be seen as an important center of subjectivity, if still subordinated to Gatsby, who is clearly the hero. Leo is a witness, but the story he witnesses takes its meaning and importance from him; this story belongs to Leo and to no one else.

But Leo is not simply the witness to this romantic intrigue: he plays a role in it, as messenger, as go-between. He is an instrumental character. He makes himself useful to others partly in an effort to find his place in the society of Brandham Hall, and the other characters are happy to use him for their own ends.[4] The first message he carries is from Trimingham to Marian (89; see also 117, 145, and elsewhere), but mostly he carries messages back and forth between Marian and Ted. His role as messenger is often mentioned by other characters. Trimingham gives him the nickname Mercury, since Mercury was the messenger to the gods (110 and elsewhere). Ted, rather more prosai-

---

4. In the epilogue, Marian admits to Leo, "you were our instrument—we couldn't have carried on without you" (p. 324).

cally, calls Leo the postman (134 and elsewhere).[5] Leo's role as a messenger is inherent in his character.[6]

If Leo is the messenger of the gods, then the other principal characters are the gods themselves. Here the symbolism of the Zodiac becomes operative: Trimingham is the Archer, Ted is the Water-Carrier, and Marian, of course, is the Virgin. Or she should be.

Even as Leo delivers messages for these gods, he does not understand what is going on; sex is a great and terrible mystery to him. A psychoanalytic interpretation of this story is easy, and not out of place.[7] Leo seems to be working through oedipal conflicts: His father has died, and for the moment he is free of his mother's somewhat smothering influence. He is clearly in love with Marian, Robin Hood to her Maid Marian, but in some ways Marian also stands in for his mother. Both Ted and Trimingham stand in paternal relation to him; they are split versions of the father figure. Leo has elevated Trimingham too high for rivalry, but he does feel that Ted is his rival:

> I liked Ted Burgess in a reluctant, half-admiring, half-hating way. . . . He was, I felt, what a man ought to be, what I should like to be when I grew up. At the same time I was jealous of him, jealous of his power over Marian, little as I understood its nature, jealous of whatever it was he had that I had not. He came between me and my image of her. In my thoughts I wanted to humiliate him, and sometimes did. But I also identified with him, so that I could not think of his discomfiture without pain, I could not hurt him without hurting myself. (182)

It is not an incidental detail that when Leo wins the cricket match, it is Ted's ball that he catches.[8] Thus Leo is Ted's Hegelian rival for Marian's affections, and thus there is a second and more important triangle.

Although Leo does not understand what is going on, he nonetheless feels the sexual tension that pervades the story. He knows that Marian's affair with

---

5. In a stroke of irony, just before the cricket match begins, Trimingham tells Ted that he should use Leo to run errands for him—"he's a nailer at that"—and Ted replies, "I'm sure he's a useful young gentleman" (pp. 150–51).

6. In the Author's Introduction added to the book in 1962, Hartley notes that "Leo was a natural go-between, it was his function in life. . . . His only life was in the lives of other people: cut off from them, he withered" (p. 11).

7. For psychoanalytic interpretations, see Peter Bien and Alan Radley.

8. Leo also out-sings Ted at the banquet after the cricket match. This little victory also plays its part in the rivalry Leo feels, but it is only a supplement to the victory in the cricket match, which would have been sufficient on its own.

Ted is wrong, and once he finds out that Marian is engaged to marry Trimingham (at the end of chapter 13, just before the passage quoted above), he tries unsuccessfully to get out of his role as messenger. He also begins to feel that he is simply being used.

Finally Leo decides to put a stop to the affair. At school he had managed to solve his problem through a magic spell, and now he resorts to the same method. The key to his spell is a large belladonna plant, which is growing in one of the sheds on the estate, evidently unnoticed except by Leo. This plant is first introduced in chapter 2, rather portentously, and then left almost without mention until chapter 21, when Leo goes late at night, all alone and in secret, to gather parts of it for his magic spell.[9] The plant has become a symbolic object; it is probably a metaphor for the poisonous nature of uncontrolled passion, and of course the name of the plant, "beautiful woman," relates it to Marian. When Leo goes to gather part of the plant for his spell, he finds that it has taken on a kind of autonomy:

> I was almost on top of the outhouses before I saw the thick blur of the deadly nightshade. It was like a lady standing in her doorway looking out for someone. I was prepared to dread it, but not prepared for the tumult of emotions it aroused in me. In some way it wanted me, I felt, just as I wanted it; and the fancy took me that it wanted me as an ingredient, and would have me. The spell was not waiting to be born in my bedroom, as I meant it should be, but here in this roofless shed, and I was not preparing it for the deadly nightshade, but the deadly nightshade was preparing it for me. (281)

In his panic he tears up the plant. He then returns to his room and casts the spell. In a sense the spell is successful, but with consequences he does not intend.

The next day is Leo's thirteenth birthday, and the Maudsleys have planned a party for him. Marian, however, is unaccountably absent. In fact she is meeting Ted, as arranged in the last message Ted gave to Leo.[10] The party goes on, but the tension caused by Miriam's absence grows. By this time Mrs. Maudsley has figured out that something is going on and that Leo has played a role in it:

---

9. The introduction of the belladonna plant and its symbolic function are in my opinion the most contrived and least successful aspects of the story.

10. In fact Leo has deliberately falsified this message; he tells Marian that Ted said six, instead of their usual time of six-thirty. I believe that Hartley means that this confusion of time leads to Marian's absence from the party, so in a sense Leo brings about the disaster that follows; in the epilogue the older Leo says that the falsification had fatal consequences—so in a way the disaster was Leo's fault.

> [A]ll at once Mrs Maudsley pushed her chair back and stood up. Her elbows were sticking out, her body was bent and trembling, and her face unrecognizable.
> "No," she said. "We won't wait. I'm going to look for her. Leo, you know where she is; you shall show me the way." (304)

But in fact Mrs. Maudsley leads the way, to the shed where the belladonna had grown. There they find Ted and Marian.

> [I]t was then that we saw them, together on the ground, the Virgin and the Water-Carrier, two bodies moving like one. I think I was more mystified than horrified; it was Mrs Maudsley's repeated screams that frightened me, and a shadow on the wall that opened and closed like an umbrella.
> I remember very little more, but somehow it got through to me, while I was still at Brandham Hall, that Ted Burgess had gone home and shot himself. (305)

The Epilogue, which immediately follows, first recounts the aftermath of this disaster. Leo suffers a breakdown; even after he begins to recover, he refuses to talk about what had happened or to hear anything about it. Eventually he returns to school, but he and Marcus are no longer friends. He feels responsible for what had happened: "The spell had worked: I couldn't deny that. It had broken off the relationship between Ted and Marian. . . . But it had recoiled on me. In destroying the belladonna I had also destroyed Ted, and perhaps destroyed myself" (307).

His life thereafter became blighted; he retreated into a world of facts: "Indeed, the life of facts proved no bad substitute for the facts of life" (309). He constructed a life for himself without others.

When the older Leo found the diary, he also found an unaddressed and unopened letter, Marian's last letter to Ted, which the young Leo had never had the chance to deliver. He opens it now, and he learns that whatever else happened, Marian was not simply using him, and he was not simply the instrument of her desires. He was useful to her, but her affection for him was independent of his usefulness.

The older Leo returns to Brandham Hall, and he finds that Marian is still alive, living in the village nearby. He discovers that she did indeed marry Trimingham; she then had a child seven months later in February of 1901, so the child must be Ted's. Trimingham died in 1910. Marian's son died in 1944, in the war, so the current Viscount Trimingham is Marian's and Ted's grandson; he lives in a part of Brandham Hall. Some of this information Leo gathers from memorial markers in the church; some from the current Viscount, whom he meets accidentally; and some from Marian herself, whom he visits. But the current Trimingham seems to be ashamed of his scandalous origin, and he rarely sees his grandmother.

Leo goes to see Marian, and from her he learns the aftermath of the events of fifty years before. He also learns that Marian's grandson has hesitated to marry the girl he loves: "He feels . . . that he's under some sort of spell or curse, and that he'd hand it on" (323). (Marian, of course, does not know about Leo's curse, but the reader does; here the author is speaking through her to the reader.) Marian then gives Leo one final message to deliver: he is to tell her grandson the story of her love with Ted; he is to tell him that there was nothing to be ashamed of and that "there's no spell or curse except an unloving heart" (325). Leo hesitates, but finally he decides to deliver this last message, and in his so doing, the reader is to feel that he has successfully reunited the two parts of his self.

I do not pretend that my account exhausts the complexities of this very carefully constructed narrative; there are many touches of art to be discovered in reading and rereading. My purpose, however, is not so much a complete reading of the novel, but rather a demonstration of the various modes of subjectivity it deploys.

This story is a Cartesian narrative, the story of a divided self observing itself and finally to some extent overcoming the division. It also contains two Freudian triangles: one of Ted and Marian and Trimingham, and another of Ted and Marian and the young Leo himself. It is the story of Leo's attempt and failure to find an adequate social self—through his successful curse at school, then through his catch in the cricket game, but then through the disaster in which he played the role of go-between and the blight that came over his life afterwards. The belladonna plant takes on at least a momentary subjectivity as a symbol of this disaster. Leo is, of course, the witness to the events, and he is also an instrument, but a witness and an instrument at the center of the story.

In this novel there is no single and perhaps no dominant mode of subjectivity, no single idea of what it means to be a self. The self in Hartley's world is one thing at one time and another thing at another time, and even two or more things simultaneously. Analysis is necessary in order to show these various modes and their interactions and combinations, but it is also to some extent artificial, as it pretends to disentangle and discriminate what is flowing and fused. How is it possible to pin down the self if it is so various and so mutable? Is there really a self at all? These questions, raised by my reading of *The Go-Between,* should be kept in mind as we consider the portrayal of the self in Kazuo Ishiguro's *The Remains of the Day* and in Jean-Paul Sartre's *Being and Nothingness*.

II.

The narrator of Ishiguro's *The Remains of the Day*, Stevens, is a butler and the son of a butler. He believes that his father was a great butler, and he takes some trouble to explain exactly what he means. After narrating a couple of instances in which his father behaved in an exemplary manner, he sums it all up in the idea of "dignity":

> And now let me posit this: "dignity" has to do crucially with a butler's ability not to abandon the professional being he inhabits. Lesser butlers will abandon their professional being for the private one at the least provocation. For such persons, being a butler is like playing some pantomime role; a small push, a slight stumble, and the façade will drop off to reveal the actor underneath. The great butlers are great by the ability to inhabit their professional role and inhabit it to the utmost; they will not be shaken out by external events, however surprising, alarming, or vexing. They wear their professionalism as a decent gentleman wears his suit: he will not allow ruffians or circumstance [to] tear it off him in the public gaze; he will discard it when, and only when, he wills to do so, and this will invariably be when he is entirely alone. It is, as I say, a matter of "dignity." (42–43)

Here dignity and professionalism consist in handing oneself entirely over to a role. And yet there is something of the self that is not identical to the role, just as there is something underneath the clothing one wears. In public one will never go naked, but underneath the clothing there is a naked body, which will be revealed only in private; there is also a naked self underneath the role one plays. So the self is at once entirely subsumed in the role, and yet essentially different from it.[11]

This passage is in some ways similar to another passage, this one not from a novel, but from Sartre's *Being and Nothingness*. Whereas Ishiguro inserts a little passage of philosophy in the midst of his narrative, Sartre inserts a little passage of narrative in the midst of his philosophy:

---

11. This view of the self should, of course, be attributed to Stevens, the character, rather than to Ishiguro, the novelist. Indeed, much of the novel is a critique of this view, expressed particularly through the housekeeper, Miss Kenton; see, for example, p. 154: "Why, Mr. Stevens, why, why, why, do you always have to *pretend*?"

> Let us consider this waiter in the café. His movement is quick and forward, a little too precise, a little too rapid. He bends forward a little too eagerly; his voice, his eyes express an interest a little too solicitous for the order of the customer. Finally there he returns, trying to imitate in his walk the inflexible stiffness of some kind of automaton while carrying his tray with the recklessness of a tight-rope walker by putting it in a perpetually unstable, perpetually broken equilibrium which he perpetually reestablishes by a light movement of the arm and hand. All his behavior seems to us a game. He applies himself to chaining his movements as if they were mechanisms, the one regulating the other; his gestures and even his voice seem to be mechanisms; he gives himself the quickness and pitiless rapidity of things. He is playing, he is assuming himself. But what is he playing? He is playing at being a waiter in a café. (59)

Sartre, like Ishiguro, places great importance on the relationship between the social role and the self, and, like Ishiguro, he ultimately distinguishes the self from the social role it plays. Sartre's idea of the self and Ishiguro's are more than a little similar, and yet there is also a difference—a difference in dignity. Sartre's waiter is always in excess of his role, and this excess constitutes a violation of dignity; through this undignified excess we see the person as distinct from the role. Could Sartre have told the same story about a waiter who did *not* move a little too quickly, who is *not* a little too solicitous, who does *not* imitate an automaton? The great butler certainly would not be in such a state of excess. He does not want to call attention to the difference between his role and his self. Ishiguro seems to draw this contrast quite specifically:

> It is sometimes said that butlers only truly exist in England. Other countries, whatever title is actually used, have only manservants. I tend to believe this is true. Continentals are unable to be butlers because they are as a breed incapable of the emotional restraint which only the English race are capable of.... If I may return to my earlier metaphor—you will excuse my putting it so coarsely—they are like a man who will, at the slightest provocation, tear off his suit and shirt and run about screaming. In a word, "dignity" is beyond such persons. (43)

There are two ways to call attention to the condition of being clothed and to the difference between being clothed and being naked. One way is to take off your clothes, but the other is to wear clothing that obviously does not fit, and to call attention to the bad fit. This is the way of Sartre's waiter. For Sartre, bad fit leads to bad faith (*mauvaise foi*).

These passages call into question the relation between the self and its roles. When the social clothing is removed, what then remains? What was left of my grandfather when he put away all his twenty different business cards? What is the naked self?

Richard Lanham distinguishes two fundamental attitudes toward the self, one of which he labels "serious" and the other "rhetorical." According to the serious attitude, "[e]very man possesses a central self, an irreducible identity" (1). But "[r]hetorical man is an actor; his reality public, dramatic. His sense of identity, his self, depends on the reassurance of daily histrionic reenactment" (4). Lanham's two representative figures are Plato and Ovid: "all serious poets finally, like Plato, posit a referential mystic center and all rhetorical stylists try, like Ovid, to avoid one" (36).[12]

Alasdair MacIntyre draws something of the same contrast between Sartre, who "depicted the self as entirely distinct from any particular social role," and Erving Goffman, who "liquidated the self into its role playing, arguing that the self is no more than 'a 'peg' on which the clothes of the role are hung" (30–31).[13] But, as MacIntyre points out, these two apparently opposed positions are not really so different. If Goffman's roles are hung on a peg, that peg is presumably the self; on the other hand, Sartre's self turns out to consist of negation, "not a substance but a set of perpetually open possibilities" (31).

The analysis presented in this study is in no way intended to suggest that there is no self. My argument tends in another direction. The primary subjectivities I have described can be exchanged, but the narrated self must always wear one or another; there is no place in narrative for the naked self. As soon as the self enters language, as soon as it is spoken of, it necessarily takes on some kind of subjectivity, which will inevitably be expressed in some kind of semantic role. According to MacIntyre, "in Goffman's anecdotal descriptions of the social world there is still discernable that ghostly 'I,' the psychological peg to whom Goffman denies substantial selfhood" (31). But this self may not be a nominative "I"—it may be an accusative "me," or (in Latin) a dative "mihi," or (in Proto-Indo-European) an instrumental or a locative.

Language by its nature imposes these roles. Synchronically, we learn these semantic roles when we learn language; diachronically, human speakers have

---

12. Achilles and Odysseus are another representative pair: Achilles is the stable self who then changes his mind; Odysseus is the mutable self who retains a fixed goal.

13. According to Goffman, the self is a "performed character," a "dramatic effect"; what matters is not its essential truth, but "whether it will be credited or discredited"; the person and the body "merely provide the peg on which something of collaborative manufacture will be hung for a time" (pp. 252–53). What Goffman calls the *self* I call the *subject*, and what he calls the *peg* may be what I think of as the *self*.

built these roles into language in order to say what seems most important about the roles of the self.

But language does not exhaust reality; the self in language or the self in narrative is not the only self there is. One can express oneself, for example, in music, and this musical self, I expect, would not be bound by deep-structure semantic roles—though it might be bound by other roles, roles that belong to music rather than to language. I feel, though I cannot prove it, that the self is more than its linguistic subjectivities. Take these away, and there is still some mystic residue, some self before we talk, and after. But whatever the self is outside of language, we have no way to talk about it.

No doubt my grandfather had a self when he was by himself, but whenever he presented that self to someone else, he had a business card in hand, a story to tell, a role to play. Whenever we tell stories, we place ourselves and others in various roles; we choose and deal out cards—cards labeled "agent," "patient," "witness," "instrument," and so on—from the deck language provides. These cards are roles of semantic deep structure, and they are the self in its subjectivity. The stories we tell select and combine these roles as elements in the geometry of plots, and these plots, in all the configurations and complications devised by storytellers, become in turn ways of understanding the roles of the self, the modes of subjectivity.

BIBLIOGRAPHY

Ambler, Eric. 1972 [1962]. *The Light of Day*. Glasgow: Fontana.
Anderson, Roger. 1986. *Dostoevsky: Myths of Duality*. Gainesville: University Press of Florida. 40n11.
Anderson, William S. 1997. *Ovid's Metamorphoses, Books 1–5*. With Introduction and Commentary. Norman: Oklahoma University Press.
Aristotle. 1961. *Poetics*. Translated by S. H. Butcher; Introduction by Francis Fergusson. New York: Hill and Wang.
Asimov, Isaac. 1966. *Fantastic Voyage*. New York: Bantam Books.
Atwood, Margaret. 1973. *The Edible Woman*. Toronto: McClelland and Stewart.
Auerbach, Eric. 1953. *Mimesis: The Representation of Reality in Western Literature*. Translated by Willard Trask. Garden City, NY: Doubleday Anchor Books.
Austen, Jane. 1985 [1813]. *Pride and Prejudice*. London: Penguin Books.
Austin, J. L. 1975 [1955]. *How to Do Things with Words*. Cambridge: Harvard University Press.
Bach, Emmon and Robert T. Harms, eds. 1968. *Universals in Linguistic Theory*. New York: Holt, Rinehart & Winston.
Bachelard, Gaston. 1994 [1958]. *The Poetics of Space*. Translated by Maria Jolas. Boston: Beacon Press.
Bakhtin, Mikhail. 1981. *The Dialogic Imagination*. Translated by Michael Holquist and Caryl Emerson. Austin: University of Texas Press.
———. 1984a. *Problems of Dostoevski's Poetics*. Edited and translated by Caryl Emerson. Minneapolis: University of Minnesota Press.
———. 1984b. *Rabelais and His World*. Translated by Hélène Iswolsky. Bloomington: Indiana University Press.
Bal, Mieke. 1985. *Narratology: Introduction to the Theory of Narrative*. Translated by Christine van Boheemen. Toronto: University of Toronto Press.
Balzac, Honoré de. 1972 [1833]. *Eugénie Grandet*. Paris: Le Livre de Poche.
———. 1976 [1833]. *Eugénie Grandet*. Translated by M. A. Crawford. Harmondsworth: Penguin.

———. 2000. *The Phantom Table: Woolf, Fry, and Epistemology of Modernism.* Cambridge: Cambridge University Press.
Barthes, Roland. 1965. "Objective Literature: Alain Robbe-Grillet." In Robbe-Grillet 1965. 11–25.
Basie, William. 1985. *Good Morning Blues.* As told to Albert Murray. New York: Random House.
Beck, L. J. 1965. *The Metaphysics of Descartes: A Study of the Meditations.* Oxford: Clarendon Press.
Bell, Millicent. 1987. "Pseudoautobiography and Personal Metaphor." In Bloom 1987a. New York: Chelsea House Publishers.
Bellow, Saul. 1944. *Dangling Man.* New York: Vanguard Press.
Bennett, Tony and Janet Woollacott. 1987. *Bond and Beyond: The Political Career of a Popular Hero.* Houndsmills, Basingstoke, Hampshire: Macmillan Education.
Benveniste, Émile. 1971. *Problems in General Linguistics.* Coral Gables, Fla.: University of Miami Press.
Bien, Peter. 1963. *L. P. Hartley.* University Park: Pennsylvania State University Press.
Blake, Barry J. 2001. *Case.* Second Edition. Cambridge: Cambridge University Press.
Bloom, Harold, ed. 1987a. *Ernest Hemingway's* A Farewell to Arms. New York: Chelsea House Publishers.
———, ed. 1987b. *Thomas Hardy's* The Return of the Native. New York: Chelsea House Publishers.
Booth, Wayne. 1961. *The Rhetoric of Fiction.* Chicago: The University of Chicago Press.
Boyle, Thomas E. 1969. "Unreliable Narration in *The Great Gatsby.*" *The Bulletin of the Rocky Mountain Modern Language Association* 23, no. 1: 21–26.
Bremond, C. 1981. "La logique des possibles narratifs." In *L'analyse structurale du récit.* Paris. 66–82. (a reprint of *Communications* 8 [1966]: 60–69).
Brenner, Gerry. 1983. *Concealments in Hemingway's Works.* Columbus: The Ohio State University Press.
Brontë, Emily. 1984 [1847]. *Wuthering Heights.* Harmondsworth: Penguin Books.
Bryant, Hallman Bell. 1990. *A Separate Peace: The War Within.* Boston: Twayne Publishers.
Burke, Kenneth. 1969. *A Grammar of Motives.* Berkeley: University of California Press.
Butler, Judith. 1999. *Gender Trouble: Feminism and the Subversion of Identity.* New York: Routledge.
Butler, Lance St John. 1978. *Thomas Hardy.* Cambridge: Cambridge University Press.
Cather, Willa. 1971 [1931]. *Shadows on the Rock.* New York: Vintage Books (Random House).
———. 1935. *Lucy Gayheart.* Toronto: The Ryerson Press.
———. 1936. *Not Under Forty.* New York: Alfred A. Knopf.
Caton, Hiram. 1973. *The Origin of Subjectivity: An Essay on Descartes.* New Haven: Yale University Press.
Chariton. 1995. *Callirhoe.* Edited and translated by G. P. Gould. Cambridge: Harvard University Press.
Cheever, John. 1977. *Falconer.* New York: Alfred A. Knopf.
———. 1980. *The Stories of John Cheever.* New York: Ballantine.

Chamisso, Adalbert von. 1929 [1813]. *Peter Schlemihl*. Philadelphia: D. MacKay.
Chomsky, Noam. 1957. *Syntactic Structures*. The Hague: Mouton and Co.
———. 1995. *The Minimalist Program*. Cambridge: The MIT Press.
Cohn, Dorrit. 1978. *Transparent Minds: Narrative Modes for Presenting Consciousness in Fiction*. Princeton: Princeton University Press.
Collins, Wilkie. 1980. *The Woman in White*. Oxford: Oxford University Press.
Comrie, Bernard. 1989. *Language Universals and Linguistic Typology*. Second Edition. Chicago: University of Chicago Press.
Conrad, Joseph. 1974 [1900]. *Lord Jim*. Harmondsworth: Penguin.
———. 1984 [1907]. *The Secret Agent*. Harmondsworth: Penguin.
Croft, William. 1994. "The Semantics of Subjecthood." In Yaguello 1994.
Davies, Robertson. 1970. *Fifth Business*. New York: Viking Press.
DeLillo, Don. 1997. *Underworld*. New York: Simon and Schuster.
Descartes, René. 1956. *Discourse on Method*. Translated and with an Introduction by Laurence J. Lafleur. Indianapolis: The Library of Liberal Arts, Bobbs-Merrill.
———. 1976. *Discours de la méthode*. Cinquième edition: texte et commentair par Étienne Gilson. Paris: Libraire Philosophique J. Vrin.
Diamond, Jared M. 1997. *Guns, Gems, and Steel: The Fates of Human Societies*. New York: Norton.
Dickens, Charles. 1966 [1837–39]. *Oliver Twist*. Harmondsworth: Penguin.
———. 1932 [1852–53]. *Bleak House*. London: J. M. Dent and Sons.
———. 1981 [1859]. *A Tale of Two Cities*. New York: Bantam Books.
Diderot, Denis. 1986. *Jacques the Fatalist and his Master*. Translated by Michael Henry; Introduction and Notes by Martin Hall. London: Penguin Books.
Dillon, John and Tania Gergel. 2003. *The Greek Sophists*. London: Penguin.
Dixon, R. M. W., ed. 1987. *Studies in Ergativity*. North-Holland: Amsterdam.
———. 1994. *Ergativity*. Cambridge: Cambridge University Press.
Donaldson, Scott, ed. 1990. *New Essays on* A Farewell to Arms. Cambridge: Cambridge University Press.
Dostoyevsky, Fyodor. 1961. *Notes from Underground, White Nights, The Dream of a Ridiculous Man, and selections from The House of the Dead*. Translated and with an Afterword by Andrew R. MacAndrew. New York: New American Library.
Doyle, Arthur Conan, Sir. 1956. *The Complete Sherlock Holmes*. New York: Doubleday.
Dumas, Alexandre. 1952 [1844]. *The Three Musketeers*. Translated by Lord Sudley. Harmondsworth: Penguin.
Eco, Umberto. 1979. *A Theory of Semiotics*. Bloomington: University of Indiana Press.
———. 1984. *The Role of the Reader: Explorations in the Semiotics of Texts*. Indianapolis: University of Indiana Press.
Eliot, George. 1985 [1861]. *Silas Marner*. London: Penguin.
Eliot, Thomas Stearns. 1935. *Murder in the Cathedral*. New York: Harcourt, Brace and World.
Farmer, Philip Jose. 1970. *The Stone God Awakens*. New York: Ace Books.
Faulkner, William. 1956. *The Hamlet*. New York: Vintage Books.
Fenollosa, Ernest. 1936. *The Chinese Written Character as a Medium for Poetry*. Edited by Ezra Pound. San Francisco: City Lights.

Fetterley, Judith. 1978. *The Resisting Reader: A Feminist Approach to American Fiction.* Bloomington: Indiana University Press.

Fillmore, Charles J. 1968. "The Case for Case." In Bach and Harms 1968.

———. 1971. "Some Problems for Case Grammar." *Working Papers in Linguistics* 10: 245–65. Columbus: The Ohio State University Department of Linguistics.

Fitzgerald, F. Scott. 1953 [1925]. *The Great Gatsby.* New York: Charles Scribner's Sons.

Fleishman, Avron. 1987. "The Buried Giant of Egdon Heath." In Bloom 1987b. New York: Chelsea House Publishers.

Fleming, Ian. 1963. *On Her Majesty's Secret Service.* London: Book Club.

Forster, E. M. 1966 [1908]. *A Room with A View.* Harmondsworth: Penguin Books.

———. 1968 [1910]. *Howards End.* Harmondsworth: Penguin.

Fothergill, Robert A. 1974. *Private Chronicles: A Study of English Diaries.* London: Oxford University Press.

Frank, Anne. 1995. *The Diary of a Young Girl.* The Definitive Edition. Edited by Otto H. Frank and Mirjam Pressler; translated by Susan Massotty. New York: Doubleday.

Frank, Joseph. "Nihilism and *Notes from Underground.*" In *Modern Critical Views: Fyodor Dostoevsky.* Edited by Harold Bloom. New York: Chelsea House, 1988. 35–58.

Freud, Sigmund. 1946 [1913]. *Totem and Taboo.* Translated by A. A. Brill. New York: Vintage Books.

———. 1965. *The Interpretation of Dreams.* New York: Avon Books.

———. 2002. *Civilization and Its Discontents.* Translated by David McLintock. London: Penguin Books.

Friedman, Thomas L. 1990. *From Beirut to Jerusalem.* New York: Anchor Books.

George, Andrew, trans. 1999. *The Epic of Gilgamesh: A New Translation.* London: Penguin Books.

Gilbert, Sandra M. and Susan Gubar. 1984. *The Madwoman in the Attic: The Woman Writer and the Nineteenth-Century Literary Imagination.* New Haven: Yale University Press.

Goffman, Erving. 1959. *The Presentation of Self in Everyday Life.* Garden City, NY: Doubleday and Company.

Gogol, Nicolai. 1965. *The Overcoat and Other Tales of Good and Evil.* Translated by David Magarshack. New York: W. W. Norton & Company.

Golding, William. 1956. *Pincher Martin.* London: Faber and Faber.

Graves, Robert. 1971 [1934]. *I, Claudius.* Harmondsworth: Penguin.

Greene, Graham. 1956. *The Quiet American.* New York: The Viking Press.

———. 1974 [1936]. *A Gun for Sale.* London: Penguin Books.

Greimas, A. J. 1984. *Structural Semantics: An Attempt at a Method.* Translated by Daniele McDowell, Ronald Schleifer, and Alan Velie. Lincoln: University of Nebraska Press.

Griffin, Jasper. 1980. *Homer on Life and Death.* Oxford: Clarendon Press.

Halliday, M. A. K. 1985. *An Introduction to Functional Grammar.* London: Edward Arnold.

Hardy, Thomas. 1974 [1878]. *The Return of the Native.* London: Macmillan.

Hartley, L. P. 2002 [1953]. *The Go-Between.* New York: New York Review Books.

Hassan, Andrew. 1993. *Writing Reality: A Study of Modern British Diary Fiction.* Westport, Conn.: Greenwood Press.

Hawkins, John A. 1986. *A Comparative Typology of English and German*. London: Croom Helm.
Hegel, G. F. 1967 [1807]. *The Phenomenology of Mind*. Translated by J. B. Baillie. New York: Harper & Row.
———. 1979 [1807]. *Phenomenology of Spirit*. Translated by A. V. Miller. Oxford: Oxford University Press.
Heminway, Ernest. 1997 [1929]. *A Farewell to Arms*. New York: Charles Scribner's Sons.
———. 1940. *For Whom the Bell Tolls*. New York: Charles Scribner's Sons.
Heinlein, Robert. 1956. *Double Star*. New York: Signet Books.
———. 1959. "All You Zombies." In *The Unpleasant Profession of Jonathan Hoag*. New York: Berkley Books.
Herdman, John. 1991. *The Double in Nineteenth-Century Fiction*. New York: St. Martin's Press.
Herman, David. 2002. *Story Logic: Problems and Possibilities of Narrative*. Lincoln: University of Nebraska Press.
Highsmith, Patricia. 1983 [1955]. *The Talented Mr. Ripley*. New York: Random House.
Hope, Anthony. 1994 [1894]. *The Prisoner of Zenda*. London: Dent.
Horrocks, Geoffrey. 1987. *Generative Grammar*. London: Longman.
Ishiguro, Kazuo. 1989. *The Remains of the Day*. Toronto: Key Porter Books.
Jackson, Robert Louis. 1981. *The Art of Dostoevsky: Deliriums and Nocturnes*. Princeton: Princeton University Press.
Jackson, Shirley. 1986 [1959]. *The Haunting of Hill House*. Harmondsworth: Penguin.
Jakobson, Roman. 1957. *Shifters, Verbal Categories, and the Russian Verb*. Russian Language Project, Department of Slavic Languages and Literatures, Harvard University.
———. 1987. *Language in Literature*. Cambridge: Harvard University Press.
James, Alice. 1964. *The Diary of Alice James*. Edited and with an Introduction by Leon Edel. London: Penguin.
James, Henry. 1963 [1877]. *The American*. New York: New American Library (Signet).
———. 1975 [1880]. *Washington Square*. Harmondsworth: Penguin.
———. 1962. "Daisy Miller: A Study." In *The Turn of the Screw and Other Short Novels*. Toronto: New American Library (Signet).
James, William. 1892. *Psychology, Briefer Course*. London: Macmillan.
Jefferson, Thomas. n.d. *The Autobiography of Thomas Jefferson*. With an Introductory Essay by Dumas Malone. New York: Capricorn Books.
Jones, Edward. 1978. *L. P. Hartley*. Boston: Twayne Publishers.
Joyce, James. 1924. *Dubliners*. New York: The Modern Library.
———. 1971. *Ulysses*. Harmondsworth: Penguin.
Judovitz, Dalia. 1988. *Subjectivity and Representation in Descartes: The Origins of Modernity*. Cambridge: Cambridge University Press.
Kafalenos, Emma. 2006. *Narrative Causalities*. Columbus: The Ohio State University Press.
Kafka, Franz. 1968. *The Trial*. Translated by Willa and Edwin Muir. New York: Schocken Books.
Kelly, Amy. 1950. *Eleanor of Aquitaine and the Four Kings*. Cambridge: Harvard University Press.

Kemmer, Suzanne. 1993. *The Middle Voice*. Amsterdam: John Benjamins Publishing Company.
———. 1995. "Emphatic and Reflexive -self: Expectations, Viewpoint, and Subjectivity." In Stein and Wright 1995.
Keppler, C. F. 1972. *The Literature of the Second Self*. Tucson: University of Arizona Press.
Kesey, Ken. 1962. *One Flew Over the Cuckoo's Nest*. New York: Signet Books.
Knowles, John. 1959. *A Separate Peace*. New York: Dell Publishing Company.
Kosman, L. Aryeh. 1986. "The Naive Narrator: Meditation in Descartes's Meditations." In Rorty 1986.
Lacan, Jacques. 1968. *The Language of the Self: The Function of Language in Psychoanalysis*. Translated by Anthony Wilden. New York: Dell.
———. 1977. *Écrits: A Selection*. Translated by Alan Sheridan. New York: W. W. Norton.
Lanham, Richard. *The Motives of Eloquence: Literary Rhetoric in the Renaissance*. New Haven: Yale University Press.
Lasnik, Howard, with Marcela Deplante and Arthur Stepanov. 2000. *Syntactic Structures Revisited: Contemporary Lectures on Classic Transformational Theory*. Cambridge: The MIT Press.
le Carré, John. 1964a [1961]. *Call for the Dead*. Harmondsworth: Penguin Books.
———. 1964b [1962]. *A Murder of Quality*. Harmondsworth: Penguin Books.
Lem, Stanislaw. 1971 [1961]. *Solaris*. Translated from the French by Joanna Kilmartin and Steve Cox. New York: Berkley Books.
Levin, Richard. 1979. *New Readings vs. Old Plays: Recent Trends in the Reinterpretation of English Renaissance Drama*. Chicago: University of Chicago Press.
Lévi-Strauss, Claude. 1969 [1949]. *The Elementary Structures of Kinship*. Boston: Beacon Press.
Lewis, Robert W., Jr. 1965. *Hemingway on Love*. Austin: University of Texas Press.
Liska, Peter. 1967. "Nick Carraway and the Imagery of Disorder." *Twentieth Century Literature* 13, no. 1: 18–28.
Llinás, Roldolfo R. 2001. *I of the Vortex: From Neurons to Self*. Cambridge: The MIT Press.
Longacre, R. E. 1976. *An Anatomy of Speech Notions*. Lisse, The Netherlands: The Peter de Ridder Press.
Loomis, Roger Sherman. 1963. *The Grail: From Celtic Myth to Christian Symbol*. Cardiff: University of Wales Press.
MacIntyre, Alasdair. 1981. *After Virtue: A Study in Moral Theory*. Notre Dame: University of Notre Dame Press.
Mahfouz, Naguib. 1975. *Midaq Alley*. Translated by Trevor Le Gassick. London: Heineman.
Mann, Thomas. 1955. *The Confessions of Felix Krull, Confidence Man*. Translated from the German by Denver Lindley. London: Secker and Warburg.
Manning, Christopher D. 1996. *Ergativity: Argument Structure and Grammatical Relations*. Stanford, Calif.: Center for the Study of Language and Information.
Márquez, Gabriel García. 1971 [1967]. *One Hundred Years of Solitude*. New York: Avon Books.

Martinsen, Deborah. 2006. "Of Shame and Human Bondage." In *Dostoevsky on the Threshold of Other Worlds: Essays in Honour of Malcolm V. Jones*. Edited by Sarah Young and Lesley Milne. Ilkeston: Bramcote Press. 40n11.
Matarasso, Pauline M. 1969. *The Quest of the Holy Grail*. Harmondworth: Penguin.
Mead, George Herbert. 1962 [1934]. *Mind, Self and Society from the Standpoint of a Social Behaviorist*. Edited and with an Introduction by Charles W. Morris. Chicago: University of Chicago Press.
Meares, Russell. 2000. *Intimacy and Alienation: Memory, Trauma, and Personal Being*. London: Brunner-Routledge.
Melehy, Hassan. 1997. *Writing Cogito: Montaigne, Descartes, and the Institution of the Modern Subject*. Albany: State University of New York Press.
Mellard, James M. 1966. "Counterpoint as Technique in *The Great Gatsby*." *The English Journal* 55, no. 7: 853–59.
———. 1967. "Counterpoint and 'Double Vision' in *A Separate Peace*." *Studies in Short Fiction* 4, no. 2 (Winter): 127–34.
Mengeling, Marvin E. 1969. "A Separate Peace: Meaning and Myth." *The English Journal* 58, no, 9: 1322–29.
Minor, Anne. 1965. "A Note on Jealousy." In Robbe-Grillet 1965. 27–31.
Moan, Margaret A. 1973. "Setting and Structure: An Approach to Hartley's *The Go-Between*." *Critique* 15, no. 2: 27–36.
Montaigne, Michel de. 1987. *Essays*. Translated by M. A. Screech. London: Penguin.
Morley, G. David. 2000. *Syntax in Functional Grammar: An Introduction to Lexicogrammar in Systemic Linguistics*. London: Continuum.
Morrisette, Bruce. 1965. "Surfaces and Structures in Robbe-Grillet's Novels." In Robbe-Grillet 1965. 1–10.
Mueller, Martin. 1980. *Children of Oedipus and Other Essays on the Imitation of Greek Tragedy 1550–1800*. Toronto: University of Toronto Press.
Mulkeen, Anne. 1974. *Wild Thyme, Winter Lightning: The Symbolic Novels of L. P. Hartley*. London: Hamish Hamilton.
Nabokov, Vladimir. 1963. *Pnin*. New York: Atheneum.
Nagy, Gregory. 1979. *The Best of the Achaeans: Concepts of the Hero in Archaic Greek Poetry*. Baltimore: Johns Hopkins University Press.
Naylor, Gloria. 1983. *The Women of Brewster Place*. Harmondsworth: Penguin.
O'Neill, John, ed. 1996. *Hegel's Dialectic of Desire and Recognition: Texts and Commentary*. Albany: State University of New York Press.
Orczy, Baroness. 1997. *The Scarlet Pimpernel*. New York: Puffin Books.
Palmer, F. R. 1994. *Grammatical Roles and Relations*. Cambridge: Cambridge University Press.
Pavel, Thomas. 1985. *The Poetics of Plot: The Case of English Renaissance Drama*. Minneapolis.
Peake, Mervyn. 1964. *Titus Groan*. New York: Reynal and Hitchcock.
Petroski, Henry. 1992. *The Pencil*. New York: Random House.
Phelan, James. 1989. *Reading People, Reading Plots: Character, Progression, and the Interpretation of Narrative*. Chicago: University of Chicago Press.
———. 1990. "Distance, Voice, and Temporal Perspective in Frederic Henry's Narra-

tion: Success, Problems, and Paradox." In Donaldson 1990. Cambridge: Cambridge University Press.

———. 1996. *Narrative as Rhetoric: Technique, Audiences, Ethics, Ideology.* Columbus: The Ohio State University Press.

Plutarch. 1960. *The Rise and Fall of Athens: Nine Greek Lives.* Translated and with an Introduction by Ian Scott-Kilvert. London: Penguin.

Poe, Edgar Allan. 1944. *Tales of Edgar Allan Poe.* New York: Random House.

Propp, Vladimir. 1968 [1928]. *The Morphology of the Folktale.* Austin: University of Texas Press.

Proulx, E. Annie. 1996. *Accordion Crimes.* New York: Simon and Schuster.

Proust, Marcel. 1970a. *The Captive.* Translated by C. K. Scott Moncrieff. New York: Vintage Books (Random House).

———. 1970b. *Swan's Way.* Translated by C. K. Scott Moncrieff. New York: Vintage Books (Random House).

Pynchon, Thomas. 1964. *V.* New York: Bantam Books.

Rabinowitz, Peter. 1998. *Before Reading.* Columbus: The Ohio State University Press.

Radley. Alan. 1987. "Psychological Realism in L. P. Hartley's *The Go-Between.*" *Literature and Psychology* 33, no. 2: 1–10.

Rank, Otto. 1979. *The Double.* New York: New American Library.

Ridder, Frederick. 1973. *The Dialectic of Selfhood in Montaigne.* Stanford: Stanford University Press.

Rimmon-Kenan, Shlomith. 1983. *Narrative Fiction: Contemporary Poetics.* London: Methuen.

Robbe-Grillet. 1965. *Two Novels:* Jealousy *and* In the Labyrinth. New York: Grove Press.

Romberg, Bertil. 1962. *Studies in the Narrative Technique of the First-Person Novel.* Stockholm: Almquist and Wiksell.Rorty, Amélie Oksenberg, ed. 1986. *Essays on Descartes' Meditations.* Berkeley: University of California Press.

Rosebury, Theodore. 1969. *Life on Man.* New York: Viking Books.

Roy, Arundhati. 1997. *The God of Small Things.* Toronto: Vintage Canada.

Rybcznski, Witold. 2002. *One Good Turn: A Natural History of the Screwdriver and the Screw.* New York: HarperCollins.

Sartre, Jean Paul. 1956. *Being and Nothingness.* Translated by Hazel Barnes. New York: Philosophical Library.

———. 1964. *Nausea.* Translated from the French by Lloyd Alexander; Introduction by Hayden Carruth. New York: New Directions.

Schneider, Daniel. 1987. "The Novel as Pure Poetry." In Bloom 1987a. New York: Chelsea House Publishers.

Scholes, Robert. 1974. *Structuralism in Literature: An Introduction.* New Haven: Yale University Press.

Shakespeare, William. 1998. *Twelfth Night.* New York: Signet.

———. 2002. *The Comedy of Errors.* New York: Signet.

Showalter, Elaine. 1977. *A Literature of Their Own: British Women Novelists from Brontë to Lessing.* Princeton: Princeton University Press.

Singer, Peter. 1983. *Hegel.* Oxford: Oxford University Press.

Smiley, Jane. 1991. *A Thousand Acres.* New York: Fawcett Columbine (Ballantine).

Smyth, Herbert Weir. 1920. *Greek Grammar.* Cambridge: Harvard University Press.
Spanier, Sandra Whipple. 1987. "Catherine Berkley and the Hemingway Code: Ritual and Survival in *A Farewell to Arms.*" In Bloom 1987a. New York: Chelsea House Publishers.
———. 1990. "Hemingway's Unknown Soldier: Catherine Barkley, the Critics, and the Great War." In Donaldson 1990. Cambridge: Cambridge University Press.
Starobinski, Jean. 1985. *Montaigne in Motion.* Translated by Arthur Goldhammer. Chicago: University of Chicago Press.
Stein, Dieter and Susan Wright, eds. 1995. *Subjectivity and Subjectivisation: Linguistic Perspectives.* Cambridge: Cambridge University Press.
Stevenson, Robert Louis. 1996 [1889]. *The Master of Ballantrae.* London: Penguin Books.
Stolorow, Robert D., Bernard Brandchaft, and George E. Atwood. 1987. *Psychoanalytic Treatment: An Intersubjective Approach.* Hillsdale, N.J.: The Analytic Press.
Stoyanov, Yuri. 1994. *The Hidden Tradition in Europe.* London: Arkana.
Taylor, Charles. 1975. *Hegel.* Cambridge: Cambridge University Press.
Thale, Jerome. 1957. "The Narrator as Hero." *Twentieth Century Literature* 3, no. 2: 69–73.
Tillyard, E. M. W. 1963 [1943]. *The Elizabethan World Picture.* Harmondsworth: Penguin.
Tolkien, J. R. R. 1968. *The Lord of the Rings.* London: George Allen & Unwin.
Toulmin, Steven. 1990. *Cosmopolis: The Hidden Agenda of Modernity.* New York: The Free Press.
Twain, Mark [Samuel Clemens]. 1986. *Pudd'nhead Wilson.* Harmondsworth: Penguin Books.
Tymms, Ralph. 1949. *Doubles in Literary Psychology.* Cambridge: Bowes and Bowes.
Van Nortwick, Thomas. 1992. *Somewhere I Have Never Travelled: The Second Self and the Hero's Journey in Ancient Epic.* Oxford: Oxford University Press.
Ward, Donald. 1968. *The Divine Twins: An Indo-European Myth in Germanic Tradition.* Berkeley: University of California Press.
Wasiolek, Edward. 1971. *Dostoevsky: The Major Fiction.* Cambridge: MIT Press.
Weldon, Fay. 1983. *The Life and Loves of a She-Devil.* London: Hodder and Stoughton.
West, Nathaniel. 1965 [1931]. *A Cool Million and the Dream Life of Balso Snell.* New York: Avon Books.
Wharton, Edith. 1968 [1920]. *The Age of Innocence.* New York: Charles Scribner's Sons.
Wiley, Norbert. 1994. *The Semiotic Self.* Chicago: University of Chicago Press.
Winkler, John J. 1985. *Auctor et Actor: A Narratological Reading of Apuleius' Golden Ass.* Berkeley: University of California Press.
Winner, Langdon. 1986. *The Whale and the Reactor: A Search for Limits in an Age of High Technology.* Chicago: University of Chicago Press.
Woodcock, E. C. 1987. *A New Latin Syntax.* Bristol: Bristol Classical Press.
Woolf, Virginia. 1984 [1925]. *The Common Reader 1.* Edited and with an Introduction by Andrew McNellie. London: The Hogarth Press.
———. 1977 [1931]. *The Waves.* London: Granada Publishing.
Yaguello, Marina, ed. 1994. *Subjecthood and Subjectivity: The Status of the Subject in Linguistic Theory.* London: Institut français du Royaume-Uni.

# INDEX

Accordion Crimes (Proulx), 147, 150–51
agency. *See* agent
agent/agent subjectivity, 2, 3, 4, 6n9, 7, 17, 52, 60, 61, 97–102, 105, 107–12, 114, 115–20, 123–24, 130–31, 140–42, 148–49, 154n6, 168n11, 170, 179, 182, 192
Age of Innocence, The (Wharton), 91, 92, 183
À la recherche du temps perdu (Proust), 17, 53, 129
"All You Zombies" (Heinlein), 39n10
Ambler, Eric (*Light of Day, The*), 123
American, The (James), 164
Anderson, Roger, 40n11
Anderson, William S., 24n15
Apuleius (*The Golden Ass*), 23n13, 85n1
Aristophanes/Aristophanic self, 4, 44, 54–57, 61, 62, 64, 67, 71, 75, 77, 80, 81, 92
Aristotle (*Poetics*), 5
As I Lay Dying (Faulkner), 129
Asimov, Isaac, 173, 174n16. *See also Fantastic Voyage*
Aspects of the Novel (Forster), 5n2
Auerbach, Eric, 173n15
Austen, Jane, 64, 65, 78–79, 94, 122, 149–50. *See also Pride and Prejudice*

Austin, J. L., 21n10, 21n11

Bachelard, Gaston, 167
Baillie, J. B., 45n1
Bakhtin, Mikhail, 40, 164. *See also Dialogic Imagination, The; Problems of Dostoevski's Poetics; Rabelais and His World*
Bal, Mieke, 133n4
Balzac, Honoré de, 91, 143, 149, 150. *See also Eugénie Grandet*
Banfield, Ann, 127n13
Barthes, Roland, 144, 146n18, 150
Beck, L. J., 14n1
Being and Nothingness (Sartre), 180, 189–91
Bell, Millicent, 58n10
Bellow, Saul, 38, 39. *See also Dangling Man*
Bennett, Tony, 120n8
Benveniste, Émile, 19–21, 24, 28
Bien, Peter, 185n7
Blake, Barry, 104n12, 106–7, 108n15, 148
Bleak House (Dickens), 163
Bolinger, Dwight, 10
Booth, Wayne, 21–22, 133n4

203

Boyle, Thomas E., 136n7
Bremond, Claude, 5–6
Brenner, Gerry, 58n10
Brontë, Emily, 57, 122. See also *Wuthering Heights*
Brothers Menaechmi, The (Plautus), 53, 67
Bryant, Hallman Bell, 75n6
Burke, Kenneth, 6n9
Butler, Judith, 21n10
Butler, Lance St John, 168n11

Call for the Dead (le Carré), 52, 56, 60, 70, 117–18, 120
Cartesian self/subject, 3, 4, 7, 13–15, 18, 20, 26, 27, 28, 34, 36, 37, 39, 40, 43–47, 56, 80, 93, 94, 97, 117, 179, 180, 188
Case Grammar, 4, 10, 105, 107n14, 115
Cather, Willa, 150n2, 163–64. See also *Lucy Gayheart*; *Shadows on the Rock*
Caton, Hiram, 14n1
Chamisso, Adalbert von. See *Peter Schlemihl*
Chariton of Aphrodisieus, 19
Cheever, John, 153. See also "Enormous Radio, The"
Chomsky, Noam, 10, 111–12
Cicero, 31
Civilization and Its Discontents (Freud), 54–56
Claudian, 31
cleft construction, 113–14, 133, 162
cogito, 14, 16, 20, 24, 44, 117
Cohn, Dorrit, 133n4; and Rimmon-Kenan, 133n4
Collins, Wilkie, 121. See also *Woman in White, The*
Comedy of Errors (Shakespeare), 53, 65, 67
Common Reader, The (Woolf), 125–26
Comrie, Bernard, 100, 101n9
Confessions of Felix Krull, The (Mann), 34, 92

Conrad, Joseph, 19, 157. See also *Heart of Darkness*; *Lord Jim*; *Secret Agent, The*

"Daisy Miller: A Study" (James), 164
Dangling Man (Bellow), 38, 39
dative case, 4, 16, 23, 103–9, 113, 130–33, 191
dative subject, 130, 138, 141, 142
Davies, Robertson, 147, 159–60. See also *Fifth Business*
deep structure, 9, 94, 107, 109–11, 113–14, 147, 148, 192
DeLillo, Don, 151. See also *Underworld*
Descartes, René, 3, 4, 9, 13–17, 20, 24, 26, 28, 29, 39n10, 45, 46, 47, 92, 117. See also cogito; *Discourse on Method*
Dialogic Imagination, The (Bakhtin), 164, 173
Diamond, Jared, 169–70
Diary of Alice James (James, Alice), 38n7, 39
Diary of a Young Girl, The (Frank), 38, 39–40
Dickens, Charles, 65, 150, 163. See also *Bleak House*; *Great Expectations*; *Oliver Twist*; *Tale of Two Cities, A*
Diderot, Denis, 53. See also *Jacques the Fatalist and His Master*
Dillon, John, 154n6
Discourse on Method (*Discours de la méthode*), 13–16, 28n1
Dixon, R. M. W., 101n9
Dostoevsky, Fyodor, 27, 40, 44, 92. See also *Notes from Underground*
Double Star (Heinlein), 80–84, 89, 92
doubles: and doubled doubles, 4, 18n6, 47, 52, 54, 55, 56n8, 64–79, 80, 81, 83, 84, 88–92, 122, 133, 139, 176, 177, 184; types of, 65
Doyle, Sir Arthur Conan. See "Final Problem, The"
Dream Life of Balso Snell, The (West), 174

Dubliners (Joyce), 125–26
dyadic subject, 44–63, 65, 67, 71, 75, 76, 91, 92. *See also* doubles

Eco, Umberto, 20n9
Edel, Leon, 38n7
Eliot, George, 122, 147, 157. See also *Silas Marner*
Eliot, T. S., 116
"Enormous Radio, The" (Cheever), 153–54
Epic of Gilgamesh, The, 44, 55–57, 59–62, 75
ergative-absolutive, 100–101, 106, 117. *See also* nominative-accusative
Eugénie Grandet (Balzac), 91, 143
Euripides, 49, 67, 81, 158
experiencer, 4, 99–102, 108, 109, 110, 114, 115–19, 126, 130, 131, 142n15, 149, 162n2, 179

Fantastic Voyage (Asimov), 173–74
Farewell to Arms, A (Hemingway), 44, 56–63, 64, 75, 78, 92, 180
Farmer, Philip Jose, 170–71. See also *Stone God Awakens, The*
Faulkner, William, 129, 163. See also *As I Lay Dying; Hamlet, The; Sound and the Fury, The*
Fenollosa, Ernest, 115
Fetterley, Judith, 60–62
Fifth Business (Davies), 147
Fillmore, Charles, 10, 107–8, 110
"Final Problem, The" (Doyle), 65, 70, 71
Fitzgerald, F. Scott, 7, 130, 139n10. See also *Great Gatsby, The*
Fleishman, Avron, 168
Fleming, Ian, 119–20
For Whom the Bell Tolls (Hemingway), 19
Forster, E. M., 5, 80, 89, 121, 135n6, 161, 210. See also *Aspects of the Novel; Howards End; Room with a View, A*

Fothergill, Robert, 37n6
Frank, Anne, 38, 39–40. See also *Diary of a Young Girl, The*
Frank, Joseph, 40n11
Freud, Sigmund, 3, 4, 14, 54–55, 80–92, 97, 133, 177, 179, 183, 188. See also *Civilization and Its Discontents; On the Interpretation of Dreams; Totem and Taboo*
Freudian self/third/subject, 4, 18n6, 80, 84, 89, 91, 92, 97, 133, 179, 183, 188
Friedman, Thomas L., 116
Frost, Robert, 8

George, Andrew, 55
Gergel, Tania, 154n6
Gilbert, Sandra, 121–22
Gilson, Étienne, 28n1
Givon, Talmy, 10
Go-Between, The (Hartley), 7, 9, 180–89
Goffman, Erving, 191
Gogol, Nicolai, 157
Golding, William, 39n10
Graves, Robert, 19
Great Expectations (Dickens), 183n3
Great Gatsby, The (Fitzgerald), 7, 130, 135–39, 184
Greene, Graham, 88n3, 157. See also *Gun for Sale, A*
Greimas, A. J., 6
Griffin, Jasper, 150n1
Gubar, Susan, 121–22
Gun For Sale, A (Greene), 157

Halliday, M. A. K., 10, 162, 163
Hamlet, The (Faulkner), 163
Hardy, Thomas, 168. See also *Return of the Native, The*
Hartley, L. P. (*The Go-Between*), 7, 9, 179, 180, 185n6, 186n10, 188
Hassan, Andrew, 37n6
Haunting of Hill House, The (Jackson), 167–68

Heart of Darkness (Conrad), 138
Hegel, Georg W. F., 3, 4, 14, 34, 43–51, 54, 71, 89, 92, 117
Hegelian self/subject, 4, 7, 18n6, 44–49, 51–53, 55–57, 59–62, 64, 67, 69–71, 75–77, 80, 88n3, 89, 91–94, 97, 117, 124, 133, 138, 139, 142n14, 157, 171, 173, 177, 179, 180, 184, 185. *See also* dyadic self; double; Master and Slave, dialectic of
Heinlein, Robert, 39n10, 80, 81, 84, 92, 170. *See also* "All You Zombies"; *Double Star*
Hemingway, Ernest, 19, 44, 56–63. *See also Farewell to Arms, A; For Whom the Bell Tolls*
Herdman, John, 64n1
Herman, David (*Story Logic*), 6n8, 97n1, 161n1
Highsmith, Patricia, 27, 34–37, 74n5, 92. *See also Talented Mr. Ripley, The*
Hippodameia, 8, 84
Hippolytus, 8, 81, 158–59
Homer. *See Iliad, Odyssey*
Hope, Anthony. *See Prisoner of Zenda, The*
Howards End (Forster), 135n6, 161, 175–77

Iliad (Homer), 23, 66, 120, 150
instrument/instrumental subject, 4, 34, 50, 147, 149, 157–60, 177, 178, 179, 184, 187, 188, 191, 192
instrumental case, 104, 106, 108, 109, 110, 111, 114, 119, 147, 148, 149, 161, 191
In the Labyrinth (Robbe-Grillet), 147, 152–53
Ishiguro, Kazuo, 38n7, 179, 180, 189–190. *See also Remains of the Day, The*
Itys, 8

Jackson, Shirley, 167. *See also Haunting of Hill House, The*
Jackson, Robert Louis, 40n11
Jacques the Fatalist and His Master (Diderot), 53
Jakobson, Roman, 8n11, 9, 20
James, Alice, 38n7, 39. *See also Diary of Alice James*
James, Henry, 5, 15, 85, 121, 164. *See also American, The*; "Daisy Miller"; *Washington Square*
James, William, 15, 44
Jealousy (Robbe-Grillet), 130, 142–46
Joyce, James, 85n2, 125–26, 129. *See also Dubliners; Ulysses*
Judovitz, Dalia, 14n1

Kafalenos, Emma, 5–7
Kafka, Franz, 123
Kelly, Amy, 18
Kemmer, Suzanne, 16n4, 17n5, 102n10
Keppler, C. F., 64n1, 67
Kesey, Ken. *See One Flew Over the Cuckoo's Nest*
King Lear (Shakespeare), 168
Knowles, John, 64, 71–76, 147. *See also Separate Peace, A*
Kosman, L. Aryeh, 14n1

Labov, William, 10
Lanham, Richard, 191
Lasnik, Howard, 112n17
Lattimore, Richmond, 23n14
le Carré, John, 52, 56, 60, 70, 115, 117–18, 120. *See also Call for the Dead; Murder of Quality, A*
Lem, Stanislaw, 171. *See also Solaris*
Levin, Richard, 8n13
Lévi-Strauss, Claude, 89n4
Lewis, Robert W., 58, 60n12
Life and Loves of a She-Devil (Weldon), 122–23
Liska, Peter, 136n7

Llinás, Roldolfo R., 2n1
locative case, 104, 106, 108–11, 114, 161–65, 179n1, 191
locative subject, 4, 161, 165–178
Longacre, Ronald, 10, 107, 108, 112n18
Loomis, Roger Sherman, 151n3
Lord Jim (Conrad), 19
Lord of the Rings, The (Tolkien), 64, 77–78, 121, 152
Lucretius, 31
Lucy Gayheart (Cather), 163–64

MacIntyre, Alasdair, 191
Mahfouz, Naguib, 161, 165. See also *Midac Alley*
Mann, Thomas, 34. See also *Confessions of Felix Krull, The*
Manning, Christopher, 101n8
Marquez, Gabriel Garcia, 154. See also *One Hundred Years of Solitude*
Martinsen, Deborah, 40n11
Master and Slave: dialectic of, 4, 34, 43, 44–51, 52–54, 58, 70, 77, 124
Master of Ballantrae, The (Stevenson), 9, 65, 68, 80, 86–92, 130, 133–35, 183, 184
Mead, George Herbert, 3, 4, 92–94, 97, 177, 182, 183. See also social self
Medea, 49, 62n15
Melehy, Hassan, 14n1, 28n1
Mellard, James M., 75n7, 136n7, 138n9
Mengeling, Marvin E., 75n7
Metamorphoses (Ovid), 24–26
Midac Alley (Mahfouz), 165–66
Miller, A. V., 45n1
Minor, Anne, 146n18
Montaigne, Michel de, 4, 27–34, 37, 39, 40, 41, 44, 46, 92
Morley, G. David, 162
Morphology of the Folktale, The (Propp), 5
Morrisette, Bruce, 146n18
Mueller, Martin, 159
Murder of Quality, A (le Carré), 120

Narcissus, 13, 24–26
narrative geometry, 7, 44, 57, 71, 75, 76, 78, 79, 80, 83, 84, 85, 90, 91, 92, 136, 138, 192
Nausea (Sartre), 9, 38n7, 39n9, 92, 129
Naylor, Gloria, 166. See also *Women of Brewster Place, The*
nominative-accusative, 100–101, 103, 117. *See also* ergative-absolutive
Notes from Underground (Dostoevsky), 27, 40–43, 44, 53, 92, 180

Odyssey (Homer), 150
Oedipus, 8, 81
Oionomaos, 8, 84
Oliver Twist (Dickens), 65, 68, 78n8
On the Interpretation of Dreams (Freud), 81
One Flew Over the Cuckoo's Nest (Kesey), 115, 123–25, 130, 139–42
One Hundred Years of Solitude (Marquez), 154
O'Neill, John, 45n1
Orczy, Baroness. See *Scarlet Pimpernel, The*
Orestes, 8
Ovid, 13, 24–26, 191

patient/patient subjectivity, 3, 4, 17, 97–102, 107–12, 114, 115–19, 121, 123–25, 130, 131, 140, 148, 149, 179, 182, 192
Pavel, Thomas, 5–6
Peake, Mervyn, 167. See also *Titus Groan*
Pelops, 8, 84
Peter Schlemihl (Chamisso), 65, 66–67
Petroski, Henry, 153n5
Phelan, James, 7n11, 61, 136n7, 137n8, 139n10
Phenomenology of Spirit (Hegel), 44–51
Pike, Kenneth, 10
Plato, 3, 4, 14, 44, 54, 71, 75–77, 91–94, 191

Plautus, 53, 67. See also *Brothers Menaechmi, The*
Poe, Edgar Alan. *See* "William Wilson"
Pride and Prejudice (Austen), 64, 65, 78–79, 149–50
Prisoner of Zenda, The (Hope), 65, 68
Problems of Dostoevski's Poetics (Bakhtin), 40
Procne, 8
Propp, Vladimir, 5–6
Proulx, Annie, 147, 150–51. See also *Accordion Crimes*
Proust, Marcel, 17, 53, 129. See also *À la recherche du temps perdu*
Pudd'nhead Wilson (Twain), 65, 67, 69–70
Pynchon, Thomas, 164. See also *V*

Quest of the Holy Grail, The, 151–52

Rabelais, François, 161, 173
Rabelais and His World (Bakhtin), 173
Rabinowitz, 22n12
Radley, Alan, 185n7
Rank, Otto, 64n1
reflexive pronoun, 13, 15, 16, 17, 18, 25
reflexive self, 3, 4, 9, 13, 25–26, 27, 29, 30, 37–40, 47, 92, 181. See also Cartesian self
Remains of the Day, The (Ishiguro), 38n7, 180, 189–90
Return of the Native, The (Hardy), 168, 179
Ridder, Frederick, 28n1
Rimmon-Kenan, Shlomith, 6n8, 133n4
Robbe-Grillet, Alain, 130, 142, 144–46, 147, 150, 152–53. See also *In the Labyrinth; Jealousy*
Romberg, Bertil, 133n4
Room with a View, A (Forster), 80, 89–92, 121, 183
Rosebury, Theodore, 174n17
Roy, Arundhati, 68

Rybczynski, Witold, 153n5

Sartre, Jean-Paul, 9, 38–39, 92, 129, 179, 180, 189–91. See also *Being and Nothingness; Nausea*
Saussure, Ferdinand de, 9
Scarlet Pimpernel, The (Orczy), 65, 66
Schneider, Daniel, 57n9
Scholes, Robert, 6n8, 8n11
Secret Agent, The (Conrad), 157
self. *See* agent, Aristophanic self, Cartesian self, dative subject, dyadic subject, experiencer, Freudian self, Hegelian self, instrumental subject, locative subject, patient, Platonic self, reflexive self, social self, witness
Separate Peace, A (Knowles), 64, 71–76, 78, 92, 142n14, 155–57, 180
Shadows on the Rock (Cather), 164
Shakespeare, William, 53, 65, 67, 68. See also *Comedy of Errors; Twelfth Night; King Lear*
shifters, 20, 21n10, 143, 145
Showalter, Elaine (*A Literature of Their Own*), 121–22
Silas Marner (Eliot), 147, 157–58
Singer, Peter, 45n1
Smiley, Jane, 168. See also *Thousand Acres, A*
Smyrna, 8
Smyth, Herbert Weir, 105, 118n
social self, 4, 78, 92–93, 97, 182, 183, 188
Solaris (Lem), 171–73
Sophocles, 81
Sound and the Fury, The (Faulkner), 129
Spanier, Sandra Whipple, 58
Starobinski, Jean, 28n1
Stevenson, Robert Louis, 9, 47, 65, 68, 80, 86, 88, 92, 130–36. See also *Master of Ballantrae, The; Strange Case of Dr. Jekyll and Mr. Hyde, The*
Stone God Awakens, The (Farmer), 171
Stoyanov, Yuri, 67n3

Strange Case of Dr. Jekyll and Mr. Hyde, The, 47, 65–66, 71
structuralism, 9
subject, 2; defined, 3; grammatical, 2; narrative, 2, 3; logical, 2–3; opposition with "object," 1; psychological, 2, 3; roles of, 3. *See also* agent; Aristophanic self; Cartesian self; dative subject; double; dyadic subject; experiencer; Freudian self; Hegelian self; instrumental subject; locative subject; patient, Platonic self; reflexive self; social self; witness
subjectivity. *See* subject
Symposium (Plato), 4, 44, 54, 71

Tale of Two Cities, A (Dickens), 66
Talented Mr. Ripley, The (Highsmith), 27, 34–37, 74n5, 92, 180
Taylor, Charles, 45n1
Tereus, 8
Thale, Jerome, 136n7, 138n9
"Those Incredible Twins" (Twain), 65, 67, 69
Thousand Acres, A (Smiley), 168–69, 175
Tillyard, E. M. W., 152n4
Titus Groan (Peake), 167, 174
Tolkien, J. R. R., 77, 152. *See also The Lord of the Rings*
Totem and Taboo (Freud), 85, 88
Toulmin, Steven, 28n1
Twain, Mark (Samuel Clemens), 65, 67, 69. *See also Pudd'nhead Wilson;* "Those Incredible Twins"
Twelfth Night (Shakespeare), 65, 68

Tymms, Ralph, 64n1

Ulysses (Joyce), 129
Underworld (DeLillo), 151

V (Pynchon), 164
Van Nortwick, 56

Ward, Donald, 67n2
Washington Square (Henry James), 15, 85n2
Wasiolek, Edward, 40n11
Waves, The (Woolf), 115, 126–29
Weldon, Fay, 115, 122–23. *See also Life and Loves of a She-Devil*
West, Nathaniel, 174. *See also Dream Life of Balso Snell, The*
Wharton, Edith, 80, 91, 92, 121. *See also Age of Innocence, The*
Wiley, Nobert, 46n3, 93n6
"William Wilson" (Poe), 65, 68–69, 72
Winkler, John, 23n1
Winner, Langdon, 153n5
witness, 4, 130, 133–36, 138–39, 141–42, 146
Women of Brewster Place, The (Naylor), 166
Woodcock, E. C., 131n1, 132n2, 132n3, 149
Woolf, Virginia, 115, 122, 125, 126–27, 129. *See also Common Reader, The; Waves, The*
Woollacott, Janet, 120n8
Wuthering Heights (Brontë), 70, 71

THEORY AND INTERPRETATION OF NARRATIVE
James Phelan and Peter J. Rabinowitz, Series Editors

Because the series editors believe that the most significant work in narrative studies today contributes both to our knowledge of specific narratives and to our understanding of narrative in general, studies in the series typically offer interpretations of individual narratives and address significant theoretical issues underlying those interpretations. The series does not privilege one critical perspective but is open to work from any strong theoretical position.

Imagining Minds: The Neuro-Aesthetics of Austen, Eliot, and Hardy
    Kay Young

Postclassical Narratology: Approaches and Analyses
    Edited by Jan Alber and Monika Fludernik

Techniques for Living: Fiction and Theory in the Work of Christine Brooke-Rose
    Karen R. Lawrence

Towards the Ethics of Form in Fiction: Narratives of Cultural Remission
    Leona Toker

Tabloid, Inc.: Crimes, Newspapers, Narratives
    V. Penelope Pelizzon and Nancy M. West

Narrative Means, Lyric Ends: Temporality in the Nineteenth-Century British Long Poem
    Monique R. Morgan

Understanding Nationalism: On Narrative, Cognitive Science, and Identity
    Patrick Colm Hogan

Joseph Conrad: Voice, Sequence, History, Genre
    Edited by Jakob Lothe, Jeremy Hawthorn, James Phelan

The Rhetoric of Fictionality: Narrative Theory and the Idea of Fiction
    Richard Walsh

Experiencing Fiction: Judgments, Progressions, and the Rhetorical Theory of Narrative
    James Phelan

Unnatural Voices: Extreme Narration in Modern and Contemporary Fiction
    Brian Richardson

Narrative Causalities
    Emma Kafalenos

Why We Read Fiction: Theory of Mind and the Novel
   Lisa Zunshine

I Know That You Know That I Know: Narrating Subjects from Moll Flanders *to* Marnie
   George Butte

Bloodscripts: Writing the Violent Subject
   Elana Gomel

Surprised by Shame: Dostoevsky's Liars and Narrative Exposure
   Deborah A. Martinsen

Having a Good Cry: Effeminate Feelings and Pop-Culture Forms
   Robyn R. Warhol

Politics, Persuasion, and Pragmatism: A Rhetoric of Feminist Utopian Fiction
   Ellen Peel

Telling Tales: Gender and Narrative Form in Victorian Literature and Culture
   Elizabeth Langland

Narrative Dynamics: Essays on Time, Plot, Closure, and Frames
   Edited by Brian Richardson

Breaking the Frame: Metalepsis and the Construction of the Subject
   Debra Malina

Invisible Author: Last Essays
   Christine Brooke-Rose

Ordinary Pleasures: Couples, Conversation, and Comedy
   Kay Young

Narratologies: New Perspectives on Narrative Analysis
   Edited by David Herman

Before Reading: Narrative Conventions and the Politics of Interpretation
   Peter J. Rabinowitz

Matters of Fact: Reading Nonfiction over the Edge
   Daniel W. Lehman

The Progress of Romance: Literary Historiography and the Gothic Novel
   David H. Richter

A Glance Beyond Doubt: Narration, Representation, Subjectivity
   Shlomith Rimmon-Kenan

Narrative as Rhetoric: Technique, Audiences, Ethics, Ideology
   James Phelan

Misreading Jane Eyre: *A Postformalist Paradigm*
  Jerome Beaty

Psychological Politics of the American Dream: The Commodification of Subjectivity in Twentieth-Century American Literature
  Lois Tyson

Understanding Narrative
  Edited by James Phelan and Peter J. Rabinowitz

Framing Anna Karenina: Tolstoy, the Woman Question, and the Victorian Novel
  Amy Mandelker

Gendered Interventions: Narrative Discourse in the Victorian Novel
  Robyn R. Warhol

Reading People, Reading Plots: Character, Progression, and the Interpretation of Narrative
  James Phelan

www.ingramcontent.com/pod-product-compliance
Lightning Source LLC
Chambersburg PA
CBHW030137240426
43672CB00005B/165